BASS LESSON GOLDMINE

AUDIO ACCESS INCLUDED

100 ROCK LESSONS

BY STEVE GORENBERG & MATT SCHARFGLASS

C000259618

To access audio visit:
www.halleonard.com/mylibrary

Enter Code
5019-1167-0688-6980

ISBN 978-1-4803-9843-6

HAL•LEONARD®
CORPORATION

7777 W. BLUEMOUND RD. P.O. BOX 13819 MILWAUKEE, WI 53213

In Australia Contact:
Hal Leonard Australia Pty. Ltd.
4 Lentara Court
Cheltenham, Victoria, 3192 Australia
Email: ausadmin@halleonard.com.au

Visit Hal Leonard Online at
www.halleonard.com

CONTENTS

Lessons 1–50 by Steve Gorenberg

Lessons 51–100 by Matt Scharfglass

An essential part of learning the bass guitar is memorizing where on the fretboard all the notes are located. A good place to start is with the notes in first position, which encompasses the first four frets. Start by memorizing the names of the open strings. The lowest-sounding string, also known as the fourth string, is E. The string above that in pitch is the third string, A. The next highest string is the second string, D, and the highest-sounding string is the first string, G.

EXAMPLE 1

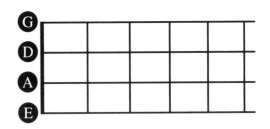

The fretted notes in first position should correspond to each of the four fingers of your fret hand. Fret the notes at the first fret with your index finger, the notes at the second fret with your middle finger, and so on. For now, let's focus on just the natural notes—the notes of the musical alphabet that contain no sharps or flats. The natural notes in first position on the fourth string are E, F, and G.

EXAMPLE 2

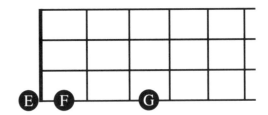

The natural notes on the third string are A, B, and C.

EXAMPLE 3

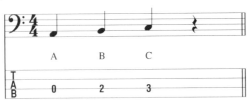
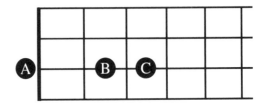

In the following exercise, we've combined the third- and fourth-string notes. The note names are indicated between staves. Saying the names of the notes aloud while playing through the exercise will help you memorize them.

EXAMPLE 4

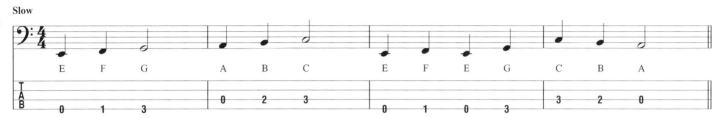

The notation, tab, and diagrams below show the natural notes on the second and first strings.

EXAMPLE 5

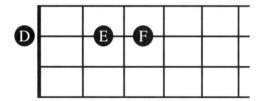

EXAMPLE 6

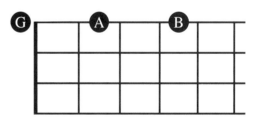

Here's an exercise that incorporates the first-position natural notes on the first and second strings. Be sure to use the correct fret-hand fingers to fret the notes and recite the note names as you play.

EXAMPLE 7

LESSON #2: FINGERSTYLE BASICS

Whether you play bass guitar with your fingers or a pick is a matter of personal preference. Many guitar players who switch over to bass will naturally begin by playing with a pick, but playing fingerstyle will enable you to be more versatile with your tone and gain more control over dynamics. Certain bass lines that incorporate octaves and other wide interval stretches are easier to execute with your fingers.

Start by resting your forearm on top of the bass, allowing your relaxed hand to drape down toward the strings. Pick a point above the strings to anchor your pluck-hand thumb. Most players will anchor their thumb on top of the pickup. If your bass has two pickups, anchor your thumb on the neck pickup (the one that's closer to the fretboard).

For basic fingerstyle playing, you should concentrate on using your first (index) and second (middle) fingers. Allow the fingers to hang down and touch the strings with the spongy part of their first joints. Your fingers should be relaxed and slightly curved, not stiff or tense.

Let's start by playing the open third string, A. Pluck the string by moving your first finger in towards the bass in a slightly upward motion so that your finger plucks the string near the pickup and comes to rest against the fourth string after plucking the note. Most of the motion should come from slightly bending your finger at the second joint, as if you're pinching your finger towards your anchored thumb.

Once you've got the plucking motion down, try the same thing with your second finger. If you're already a pick player, you might find playing with your bare fingers unnatural at first, but practice the motion until you get the hang of it and you can produce a clear, clean tone. Remember to keep your hand and fingers relaxed but anchored firmly in place by your thumb. The key is in the follow-through of the pluck, whereby your finger comes to rest against the string above the one played. With this motion, you can give the note a nice, strong attack and your finger has a natural stopping point that will keep it from flying off the bass. This technique also helps to mute any accidental noise from the adjacent string. Once you've gotten comfortable with the technique, you can move the placement of your thumb to achieve a different tone. Some players prefer a moveable thumb that they'll anchor on one of the lower strings, instead of the pickup. This is helpful when playing notes on the first or second strings because it reduces the amount of reach your fingers will need to pluck the string. You can also try placing your thumb closer to the bridge for a tighter, brighter tone or closer to the neck for a warmer, rounder sound.

For the most part, you should always try to alternate between the first and second fingers, similar to alternate picking. There are some instances when you'll break this rule because the specific bass line may require you to do so, but these are cases that you will gradually discover as you master the technique. The exercises that follow will help you get comfortable with alternating your fingers. The numbers below the tab staff represent which pluck-hand finger to use for each note.

EXAMPLE 1

Slow

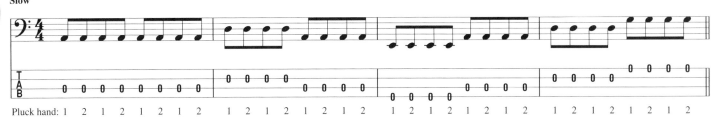

Pluck hand: 1 2 1 2 1 2 1 2 1 2 1 2 1 2 1 2 1 2 1 2 1 2 1 2 1 2 1 2 1 2 1 2

EXAMPLE 2

Slow

Pluck hand: 1 2 1 2 1 2 1 2 1 2 1 2 1 2 1 2 1 2 1 2 1 2 1 2

EXAMPLE 3

Slow

Pluck hand: 1 2 1 2 1 2 1 2 1 2 1 2

Some of the greatest bass players prefer to play with a pick. Chris Squire of Yes uses a pick exclusively. Paul McCartney, who was originally a guitar player, also uses a pick. Using a pick tends to produce a tighter, brighter sound on the bass, but you can experiment with tone settings and various picks and strings to achieve a warmer bass sound. There are different sizes and shapes of picks, but it's essential to use a heavy or extra-heavy pick when playing bass.

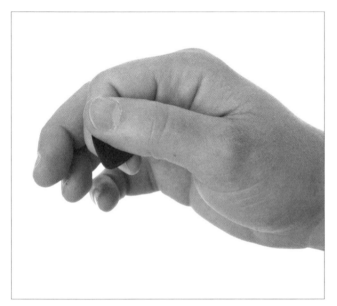

Hold the pick between the index finger and thumb of your pick hand, leaving just the tip of the pick pointing out perpendicular to your thumb. Grasp the pick firmly between your thumb and finger, but leave the rest of your fingers relaxed and open—don't make a fist.

Place your forearm on top of the bass, allowing your hand to drape down close to the strings, almost parallel to the bridge. You can experiment with the placement of your hand to figure out what you're most comfortable with. One method is to anchor the side of your hand against the bridge to give you better control. You can also gently rest the other fingers of your pick hand on the strings that aren't being played so they can serve as an anchor for your hand while muting unwanted noise from adjacent strings.

Notes can be picked in a downward or upward direction. The symbols below indicate downstrokes and upstrokes and will be used throughout the following exercises.

$$\sqcap = \text{Downstroke}$$

$$\vee = \text{Upstroke}$$

This first picking exercise is designed to get you started with alternate picking by playing eighth notes on the open strings. The picking motion should come exclusively from your wrist. Try using the fingers from your left and right hands to help mute the surrounding strings.

EXAMPLE 1

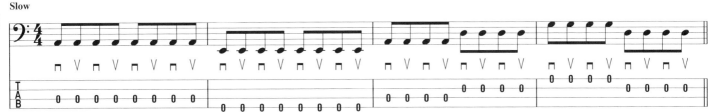

While alternate picking is essential for faster rhythms like 16th notes, you might want to use downstrokes exclusively when playing slower rhythms to get an even, heavier attack on each note.

EXAMPLE 2

Sometimes economy picking is preferable to strict alternate picking. If you are moving from one string to another while picking groups of three notes, it might make more sense to use consecutive downstrokes or upstrokes. Play through the minor scale below, using economy picking as indicated.

EXAMPLE 3

LESSON #4: WARMUP EXERCISES

In this lesson, we'll focus on some warmup exercises to strengthen your left- and right-hand coordination. It's good to have an exercise routine to run through to help stretch and loosen up your hands prior to a gig or session. Some of these exercises are based on finger patterns, rather than scales, and therefore are not necessarily musical. You can play them anytime, even without plugging in, but it's a good idea to practice them along with a metronome in a steady, even tempo, and gradually build up speed.

This first exercise focuses on stretching out your fret hand in first position. Keep your fingers aligned one finger per fret, instead of moving your hand back and forth to cover the stretch. Also try to keep your first finger planted firmly at the first fret while reaching for the other notes. For all of the following exercises, the fret-hand fingerings are indicated below the tab staff.

EXAMPLE 1

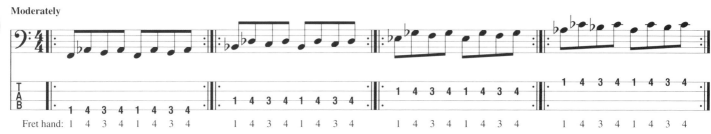

This next exercise uses all four fingers in the first position and is a slightly more complicated version of the previous example. Try to maintain consistent alternate picking or fingering with your pluck hand.

EXAMPLE 2

Here's another fret-hand exercise that focuses on a stretching pattern that travels up the fretboard and back down. It's shown here using the fourth and third strings. Once you've got the pattern down, transpose it up to the third and second strings and then to the second and first strings.

EXAMPLE 3

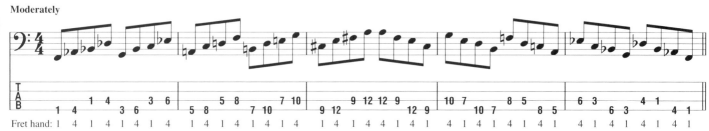

Now let's try a few pluck-hand exercises. The first is a minor pentatonic pattern that uses alternate fingering in the pluck hand, indicated below the tab staff.

EXAMPLE 4

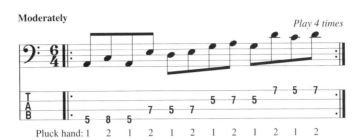

This next pluck-hand exercise follows a root–5th–octave pattern. We're still using a comfortable alternate fingering for this exercise. Lift your fret-hand fingers from each fretted note after playing it to keep the notes from ringing out over each other. This will build good coordination between both hands.

EXAMPLE 5

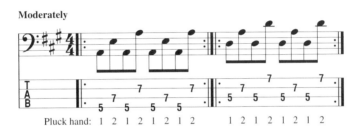

For this next exercise, we'll break the alternate-fingering rule to play the root, 5th, and octave in a different order. Follow the pluck-hand fingering under the tab staff and this time keep your fret-hand fingers in place to allow the notes to ring out. You'll notice that, in cases like this, it sometimes makes sense to make adjustments to the traditional alternate fingering.

EXAMPLE 6

These exercises are just a few examples that you can add to your warmup routine. You can create and add some of your own that target areas of your playing that you'd like to strengthen.

LESSON #5: ECONOMY OF MOTION: FINGERSTYLE

For most straightforward fingerstyle playing, alternating between the first and second fingers of the pluck hand is effective and can be used pretty consistently, but there are instances when it is preferable to break this rule. Hold your hand up outstretched with your fingers together and you'll notice that your middle finger is significantly longer than your first finger. If you translate that to your bass playing, you can see that your middle finger is able to reach for notes on the higher-pitched strings more quickly and efficiently. Sometimes this happens naturally when using alternate fingering, but sometimes you'll want to adjust the fingering slightly.

Take a look at the example below, where we've altered the fingering to better accommodate the reach up to the octave on the "and" of beat 2.

EXAMPLE 1

Sometimes when playing combinations of eighth notes and 16th notes, you may wish to alter the pluck-hand fingering so that you can lead with your first or second finger on the more prominent notes, depending on the context and what feels comfortable. You may find that you prefer to use your first finger for downbeats and your second finger for upbeats to stay consistent when playing repetitive patterns.

Below are a couple of simple rhythms shown first with a strict, alternate pluck-hand fingering and then with the fingering changed to something you might find a little less awkward.

EXAMPLE 2

EXAMPLE 3

Just as reaching up for higher strings is more comfortable with the middle finger, traveling from a higher string to a lower one can often be made smoother by using the index finger. Here are a few examples where this is useful.

EXAMPLE 4

EXAMPLE 5

EXAMPLE 6

You can see from the previous examples that, when you're playing the octave, 5th, and root in descending order, this can be achieved comfortably by basically dragging your first finger downward along the strings in time, plucking all three with the same finger. This occurs naturally because your finger will come to rest on the next lower string after plucking each note. As with most pluck-hand techniques, these are suggestions and you might subconsciously use the fingers that just feel most comfortable. A good rule to remember is that, if you're playing something and it just doesn't feel right, or there seems to be a little too much of a pause or awkwardness between the notes, break down the riff and play it slowly and work it out. Once you find a comfortable solution, practice it and build up speed gradually until you've got it mastered. Eventually, you won't have to think about the details—your fingers will instinctively handle most situations without you being aware of the exact mechanics.

LESSON #6: SLAPPING BASICS

Slapping is a percussive technique that's a useful part of any bass player's arsenal. Slapping continues to go in and out of fashion with changing rock styles, but there are famous players from all eras who have mastered the technique and become slap virtuosos. Bootsy Collins, Les Claypool, Mark King, and Flea have all demonstrated amazing slap-bass skills.

Basic slapping technique involves slapping a string with the pluck-hand thumb and popping the higher strings with a pluck-hand finger. Your hand should be relaxed and positioned near the neck so that your thumb is over or near the end of the fretboard.

Slap the string with the side of your thumb so that it smacks the string in a slightly downward motion, creating a percussive sound. Your hand should be relaxed and the motion should come entirely from rotating your forearm back and forth. Using this rotating motion, your thumb should bounce off the string. With this technique, control is essential and therefore you should use your fret hand to help mute the other strings.

To get a feel for the technique, practice slapping the notes on the fourth and third strings in the exercise below. Slapping is indicated with a "T" between the notation and tab staves.

EXAMPLE 1

Most slap-bass lines incorporate a lot of muted notes. In the exercise below, the muted notes are achieved by deadening the strings with your fret hand.

EXAMPLE 2

Now let's add some popping. The middle finger of your pluck hand should grab under and behind the string and pull outward, snapping it away from the fretboard to create a sharp, percussive popping sound. Popping is indicated with a "P" between the notation and tab staves.

EXAMPLE 3

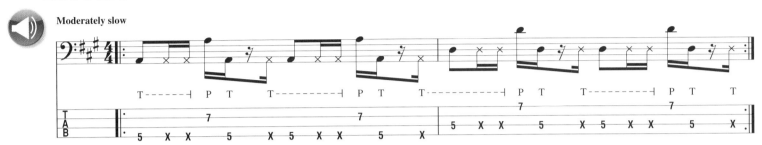

Hammer-ons are also used extensively with slapped notes, and pull-offs can be effective with the popped notes. The following examples incorporate some of these techniques and represent just a few simple ideas to get you started. Slapping is a rhythmic technique and needs to be played with precision, so practicing with a metronome or drum machine is essential. The key is to keep your hand relaxed and gradually build up speed, making sure your rhythm is solid.

EXAMPLE 4

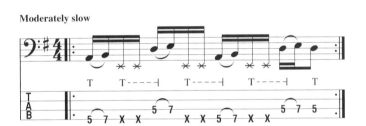

EXAMPLE 5

EXAMPLE 6

LESSON #7: MUTED NOTES

Adding muted notes to your playing will lend more character and energy to a groove. Fully muted notes are represented by X's in the notation and tab staves. The function of muted, percussive-sounding notes is to help emphasize the other notes in the groove, to accent the drum pattern, or to control the dynamics.

There are a few different techniques that you can use for muting, but let's start with the muting of regular fretted notes. The example below features steady eighth notes, then two variations containing muted notes. While plucking the muted notes, lift your fret-hand finger slightly so that it's no longer fretting the note, but instead resting lightly on the string to deaden it. Depending on where the fretted note is located on the neck, you may get some unwanted harmonic noise sneaking through. If this happens, you can use a few of your fret-hand fingers to mute the string when necessary.

EXAMPLE 1

Here are a couple of simple bass lines, shown first without mutes and then with some muted notes added. Notice that, instead of playing fully fretted notes with the kick drum, we've added muted notes. This keeps you locked in with the drummer's kick drum while still emphasizing the downbeats.

EXAMPLE 2

EXAMPLE 3

Muting open strings is actually a little more difficult. If you're playing an open-string rhythm, you'll have to use your fret hand to mute the string in time and then completely release your hand from the string to avoid affecting the open-string notes.

EXAMPLE 4

Moderately slow

The use of muting in syncopated rhythms is popular as well. Sometimes a simple riff that's used in the chorus of a song can also be played quieter with some strategic muted notes for the verse, giving it a very different quality. The more you jam with live drummers, the more opportunities you'll find where you can naturally throw in muted notes to accent the groove.

EXAMPLE 5

Moderately slow

If you're using a pick, you can employ the palm-muting technique that guitar players use. To get the palm-muting sound, gently rest the side of your hand on the strings, near the bridge, while you pick. You can get great results with palm muting, especially if you're playing through distortion or overdrive. The "P.M." symbols located between the notation and tab staves indicate palm muting.

EXAMPLE 6

Moderately slow

LESSON #8: FINGERSTYLE RAKES

Fast fingerstyle rakes can be used to play descending arpeggios or to add a series of muted notes to spice up a groove. Rakes are played by dragging a single pluck-hand finger down the strings in a descending motion, playing one note per string. You can perform rakes with any finger, depending on the context.

The first example below is a basic metal groove that adds octave–5th–root rakes to liven it up. In this example, it makes sense to rake with your second finger because it can comfortably reach up for the octaves that start the rakes. The suggested pluck-hand fingering is indicated under the tab staff.

EXAMPLE 1

Here's an example in open position. The first two bars are a standard metal bass line in A minor, which gets repeated in bars 3–4 with an added rake that moves from the first string to the third string. Notice how the simple addition of the rake makes it sounds like an entirely new riff. Either pluck-hand finger can be used to perform the rake, so see which finger feels more natural to you.

EXAMPLE 2

Rakes can also be used effectively in walking bass lines. The example below climbs up C#m7 chord tones and rakes down strings 1–3 in a triplet rhythm to land on the A chord.

EXAMPLE 3

Now let's add some muted rakes. The simple B minor rock groove below is played twice, the second time with a 16th-note triplet rake sprinkled in. Keep the first three strings muted with your fret hand to produce the effect.

EXAMPLE 4

Moderately

Muted rakes work very well with funk styles and swing feel. Check out the examples below for some ideas. The first is a funk bass groove with 32nd-note muted rakes. The second example is in swing feel and walks up a dominant seventh arpeggio, with a muted triplet rake at the end.

EXAMPLE 5

Moderately slow

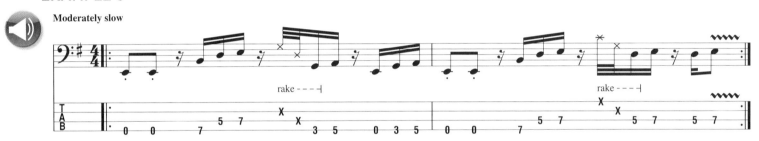

EXAMPLE 6

Fast

LESSON #9: FINGERSTYLE WITH THREE FINGERS

While most bass players will pluck the strings using just their index and middle fingers, some have perfected the technique of adding their ring finger to the mix. Three-finger technique can be used to play lightning-fast riffs and give you more speed and stamina when playing rhythms. Keep in mind that many of the world's greatest players do amazing stuff with two fingers (or sometimes just the index finger), and that having greater control using two fingers is often better than trying to play everything with three fingers. That said, let's explore how to incorporate the third finger and go through some exercises designed to strengthen this technique.

Most three-finger players will lead with their third (ring) finger because it feels more natural. If you place your hand on a table and drum your fingers in a row—the way you might do if you're impatient or fidgety—you'll notice that the natural order will be from your third finger to your first finger. The natural rhythm this produces is a galloping combination of two 16th notes and an eighth note, which translates easily to the bass. You'll often encounter this rhythm in metal bass lines, and this three-finger gallop technique is a simple device that you can use.

The first exercise below shows the basic gallop rhythm, with the pluck-hand fingering displayed under the tab staff. The second exercise shows how you can switch back and forth from the gallop to a regular two-finger technique where it makes sense.

EXAMPLE 1

EXAMPLE 2

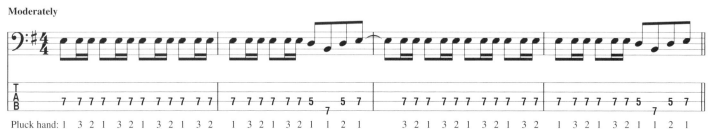

The next natural step is to play regular triplets, leading with the third finger on each downbeat. This will get you playing consistently, giving each note equal time. When you can play this fast enough, you'll be able to throw flurries of 16th-note triplets into your riffs.

EXAMPLE 3

The most difficult part of using the three-finger technique is learning to play even groupings of notes like eighths and 16ths. You'll need to start out slowly and use a metronome to gradually build speed while rewiring your brain to shift the downbeats from finger to finger. It's a slow process, but if you have the patience to master the technique, you'll be able to play rapid-fire rhythms with ease.

Start out by playing muted notes as shown below. The downbeats should be slightly accented so as to help you keep track of where they occur relative to each pluck-hand finger. The accented fingers are indicated in bold under the tab staff. Notice how the downbeat will fall on a different pluck-hand finger each time. This is why slow and steady practice with a metronome is essential to build up a consistent, accurate, and clean technique.

EXAMPLE 4

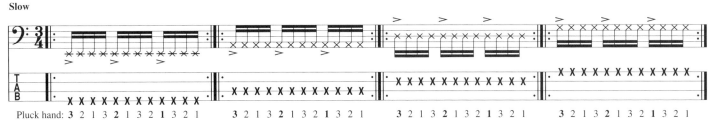

The 3–2–1 fingering can also be altered slightly to make passages more comfortable. Some players will play in a 1–2–3 order, or even a 3–2–1–2 order. Try playing different songs, riffs, and scales using three fingers and see what works best for you.

Take a look at the A minor scale below and notice how we've altered the pluck-hand fingering to make some of the switches between strings more comfortable.

EXAMPLE 5

If you've been playing fingerstyle with two fingers for a long time, adding a third finger can be a slow process. Compare your two- and three-finger techniques constantly to be sure that you're not exaggerating finger movements and your fingers aren't sweeping too far away from the strings. Remember: the goal of this technique is to attain more speed; therefore, if you're wasting too much motion with your pluck-hand fingers, then you're defeating the purpose.

LESSON #10: DROP D TUNING

Alternate tunings have grown in popularity in metal and modern rock, and drop D tuning is the easiest and most popular to learn. Some bands have made a career out of playing exclusively in drop D, which involves detuning the lowest string one whole step, from E to D. This gives you the extra low open D string to work with and is usually used to write songs and riffs in D major or D minor. Tuning the lowest string to D on guitar opens up a new world of chord voicings, and even five-string bass players will often detune their fourth string to match the guitar riffs and positions.

You can use a chromatic tuner to detune your fourth string to D, but it's also easy to do on the fly by matching the string to the pitch of the second string, D, which is one octave higher. You can do this by using the open strings or by using 12th- or fifth-fret harmonics (shown below). First, play the note on the second string and let it ring out. Then, strike the note on the fourth string and detune it until the notes blend together into a perfect octave.

EXAMPLES 1A–C

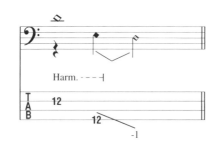
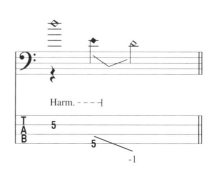

The first thing to notice is that the notes on the fourth string will now match the notes on the second string, albeit an octave lower. If you've got the fretboard memorized, it will make it easier for you to keep track of the detuned fourth string. You should also be aware that all of the pitches that you knew when the string was tuned to E will now be shifted up two frets higher. The more you play in drop D, the more familiar you'll be with the shifting of these pitches. Do your best to think ahead a little at first so you don't accidentally hit the wrong notes.

Play through the first-position notes shown below in drop D. We've adjusted the fret-hand fingering (shown under the tab staff) so that your first finger is positioned at the second fret in order to reach the G note at the fifth fret of the fourth string.

EXAMPLE 2

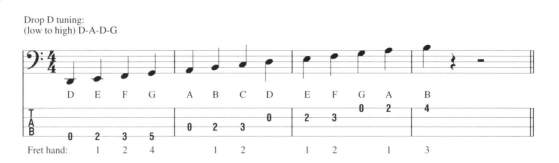

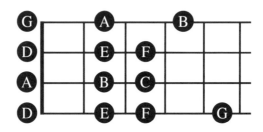

It will also help to memorize some key natural notes along the D-tuned fourth string. The easiest to mix up at first will be F, G, and A, which are now at the third, fifth and seventh frets, respectively.

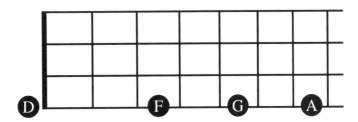

One of the benefits of drop D is that every note on the fourth string now has its 5th and octave stacked above it on the same fret. This is also true for harmonics, making harmonic chords simple to play.

Take a look at the riff below, which uses the roots and 5ths of a chord progression. In normal tuning, this would require much more fret-hand movement, but in drop D, it's easy to play the roots and 5ths by barring the two strings with a single finger.

EXAMPLE 3

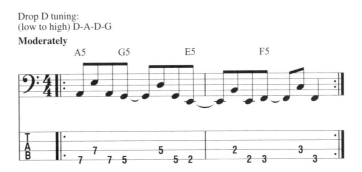

For most guitarists, playing octaves in standard tuning is a fairly simple task, but on bass, the string gauge and stretch involved makes this more cumbersome. When you're in drop D tuning, you can play octaves on the fourth and second strings very comfortably by fingering the lower note with your second finger and the octave with your third finger.

In the example below, keep your fret-hand fingers firmly planted on the notes, allowing them to ring out together, and slide them like a moveable double stop throughout.

EXAMPLE 4

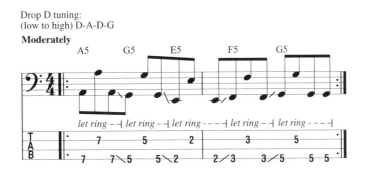

One of the greatest hardware inventions for the bass is the Hipshot Bass Xtender, a replacement machine head for the fourth string that has a lever and a moveable gear that will immediately shift the tuning of the fourth string to D if you've set it up properly and tuned in advance. I'll usually add this upgrade to any new bass purchase right away. Not only does it allow you to flip from E to D (and vice versa) in an instant between songs, but you can also get used to reaching for it in the middle of a song, too. Say the song's bridge modulates to D or is perfect for adding in some low Ds. Just flip the lever to drop D right before the bridge and then back to E when you're finished. Billy Sheehan has been known to use the Hipshot like this in the middle of songs.

The five-string bass has been gaining in popularity in all genres of music over the past few decades. Some rock and metal players use them exclusively, and if your metal band features seven-string guitar players, a five-string bass is probably essential to playing the songs. The five-string bass has an additional lower string, tuned to a low B. This allows you to play two-and-a-half steps below the standard low E of a four-string bass. If you started out playing four-string and already know the fretboard and some theory, learning the notes on a five-string isn't very difficult. Since the bass is tuned in equal intervals, all of your scale patterns and intervals remain the same.

Below are the notes in open position on the five-string bass.

EXAMPLE 1

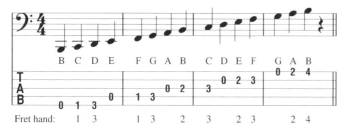
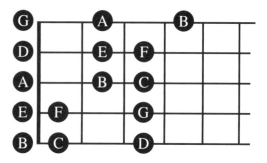

Contrary to popular belief, one of the greatest benefits of the low B string is not necessarily the availability of the lower notes, but the ability to play a greater range of notes anywhere on the neck within a short distance on the fretboard. Two-octave scales can be played practically within one position.

Below are examples of two-octave E minor and E minor pentatonic scales, starting in fifth position on a five-string.

EXAMPLE 2

EXAMPLE 3

Two-octave arpeggios are also very easy to play. The examples below show two-octave E major and E minor arpeggios, starting in fifth position.

EXAMPLES 4A–B

There are obvious pros to playing a five-string, but there are also some cons you should be aware of if you want to tame the five-string beast. The best way to become accustomed to the five-string is to start out by playing the upper four strings like you would a regular four-string bass and gradually and sparingly incorporate some of the fifth-string notes. Just because low Bs and Cs are available to you, doesn't mean you *have* to play them. Most players that get a new five-string will seize every opportunity to use these notes, and if a song is in the key of E or G and goes up to a B or C chord, they'll jump on those low notes right away. This usually isn't the best choice for most music because you'll be creating a wide frequency gap between the guitar player's range and the bass line. The low notes should be used economically, unless you're playing a death metal song that is built around a detuned or seven-string guitar riff in that range. Trust your ears and be honest with yourself about whether it sounds good or not. Be careful with notes that go below a low D, making sure they enhance the music, instead of sounding offensive.

The low B on a five-string has a frequency of 31Hz, and the human ear can only hear down to 20Hz. These low notes are bigger, longer waveforms that require larger speakers (10- and 12-inch speakers have a harder time reproducing them), compression, and time to fully resonate. Playing Bs or Cs in repetitive eighth- and 16th-note rhythms don't really allow these notes to breathe, and what you'll be hearing are more of the upper harmonics. Sustained low notes and occasional low notes used in a descending riff work much better.

Another issue you may encounter is that, since the low B string is a much thicker gauge, it's difficult to match its timbre with the other strings. This is something that can present a challenge when you're recording, so you may want to experiment with pickup height to even things out the best you can.

Finally, if you're a pick player, be aware that you'll have to work harder to make sure that the fifth string is muted when you're not playing it. The vibrations from the other strings may cause it to vibrate sympathetically and add a low rumble to your sound. Although playing a five-string is basically the same as a four-string with one extra string, because of the logistics and special circumstances present with these low frequencies, you'll need to slightly adjust your playing technique to keep your sound clean.

LESSON #12: BASS GUITAR MAINTENANCE

Many beginners are hesitant to make adjustments and alterations to their basses. This is probably a good thing; you wouldn't want to attack a new $1000 instrument with power tools until you really know what you're doing. But there are some very simple and harmless things that you can learn how to do on your own that can save you time and money, and just might help you out of a technical emergency at a gig. Most of the tips and tricks that you'll learn will come with time through trial and error. For example, the first time your bass drops to the floor, you'll realize that strap locks are the greatest invention since sliced bread. Or after the first time you accidentally step on your cord and yank it out of the bass in the middle of a song, you'll always loop the cord through your strap, instead of letting it hang freely.

In this lesson, we'll take a look at some of the basic things that you can do yourself—things that can't harm the instrument if you do them incorrectly the first few times. When you first start playing and you've got your first bass, you might want to bring it to a professional for basic setups and string changes. While a professional will do a great job and you'll love the way your bass feels after a thorough tune-up, this routine will get old fast. If you learn how to handle the basics yourself, you won't have to bother spending the money or parting with your bass while it's being worked on. The one thing that I would recommend letting a professional adjust for you is the truss rod. If you find that your neck is bowed and needs to be adjusted, you can harm the neck permanently by trying to mess with it without knowing what you're doing, particularly if it's a neck-through, and not a bolt-on.

Most new guitars will include a few simple tools, like the Allen wrenches that you need to make minor adjustments, but it's good to keep a small set of jeweler's screwdrivers and common Allen wrenches in your case, as well as a small set of wire cutters for cutting strings or fixing cords. Also, keep a roll of duct tape with your gear at all times—don't worry about what it's used for right now, just know that you will find a thousand uses for it and you'll always need it. And remember that, if you ever lend your roll of duct tape to the guitar player or singer, it will probably disappear forever.

KEEP IT CLEAN

One of the simplest things that you can do on your own right away is to learn how to clean and polish your instrument. The best ways to keep your bass clean is to keep it in the case when you're not playing it, and always wash your hands before you pick it up. You'll be amazed at how much more life you get from a set of strings if your hands are clean when you play. It's a good idea to drop by your local guitar store and pick up a small guitar-tech kit, which will include some cloths, guitar polish, lemon oil for the neck, and string cleaner. When spraying guitar polish, work in small sections and wipe them down right away, avoiding the strings as much as possible. Read the directions that come with whatever polishes and cleaners you buy, and don't just use cheap furniture polish instead. Another thing that comes in handy is a can of compressed air to spray dust and dirt out of the electronics and volume and tone pots. You can use it around the pickups, as well as in the little nooks and crannies of the bridge and tuners.

CHANGING THE STRINGS

Changing the strings yourself isn't difficult at all, once you get a feel for it. Remove and replace the strings one at a time, instead of removing the old set all at once. This will help keep the tension on the neck fairly consistent. Stick the end of the new string through the hole at the end of the bridge and up over the saddle. Next, pull the string all the way through until the ball end is pulled tight against the outside of the bridge. Inside the string posts on the headstock, there will be a hole that you need to stick the end of the string into before you begin winding.

You will almost certainly need to trim down the string length before you wind it onto the post. You don't want to leave the string too long, however, and have too much winding around the post, and if you cut it too short, you're totally out of luck. A good length to wind around the post is about six inches of excess string. On a Fender bass, six inches is the distance from the first post (fourth string) to the last post (first string). Pull the string tight to pick up the slack. Then, pinch it with your thumb and finger at the post that you're about to wind it around. Next, move that point back to the first post and measure out from there to the last post, snipping off the excess with a wire cutter (scissors won't work because the strings are too thick).

Once the string is cut, stick the end directly into the hole inside the string post until it stops and then bend it down in a 90-degree angle to the side through the groove in the post and hold it firmly in place while you begin winding the tuning peg. This will give the winding a clean start. Be sure that you're winding in the proper direction—the string should always come off the inner side of the post, whether it's on the top or bottom of the headstock. From there, you want to continue to wind the string under itself in a nice, neat coil. Once the coil is cleanly set in motion, I'll usually pull it taught from the post back to the nut and hold it in place there, pressed down firmly with my right-hand index finger while winding it with my left hand, gradually letting the slack slip under the right-hand finger until the string is tight and coiled neatly around the post. Once the string is on, tune it to the appropriate pitch and then massage the string by pinching it in small segments with the thumb and index finger a few inches apart from each other to slightly stretch out the string and break it in. Next, retune the string and massage it again. If you massage the strings a little bit before you start playing, you won't need to stop and retune every few minutes.

PICKUPS

You can adjust the height and angle of the pickup(s) by loosening or tightening the screws on the top and bottom, or the sides. If you have two pickups, the one that's closest to the bridge will have a crisper, more treble sound, usually to enhance the warmer, fuller neck pickup. Adjusting the height and angle of the pickups will affect the volume of the individual strings. You may not notice these subtle differences when you're practicing at home, but when you get into a louder band environment, the differences can be glaring. If the volume of the low E string is louder than the other strings, you can change the angle of the pickup slightly so that it's farther away from the low E.

If you have active pickups, your bass will require a battery (usually one 9-volt). In most cases, there is no on/off switch—when you plug a cable into the input jack, the circuit becomes active. A battery will usually last for months with regular playing, but not if you leave the guitar plugged in around the clock. Try to keep this in mind whenever you put the guitar down, because leaving it plugged in for a few days at a time will drain the battery fast.

A dying battery will make the signal sound weak and introduce noise, as if you're using a bad cable. The battery may or may not be easy to change, depending on where it's located. Sometimes the battery is tucked underneath the pick guard and isn't easily accessible. In cases like this, you'll have to remove a lot of screws (or even the strings), so go slow and be careful—you don't want to strip the screws or the wood, as this will cause you difficulties later on. It's not a good idea to take an electric screwdriver to these tiny, delicate screws; instead, they should be carefully removed with a human touch. If you do happen to strip the wood, a quick home remedy involves either some wood filler or taking a small piece of a wooden toothpick and shoving it into the stripped hole and then screwing the screw into it. This is a quick fix and usually works like a charm. If you find yourself removing those little Phillips-head screws a lot and the heads begin to strip, take one to a hardware store to find exact replacements and stock up on some spares.

THE BRIDGE

There are two adjustments you can make on the bridge: the action (string height) and the intonation (string length). You'll want to lower the action to a comfortable height; the lower you go, the easier it is to fret the strings, making it easier to play faster with less effort. If you go too low, you'll run the risk of introducing fret buzz and string noise, especially if you have an aggressive pluck-hand technique, so try to find a nice balance. Lower or raise the action by adjusting the tiny screws on the saddles (usually, there are two for each string). String height across all four strings should be fairly consistent and even, but a slight curve works well to accommodate the different string gauges. If you think your action is too high but you're still getting a lot of buzz, then the neck might need to be adjusted by a professional. Some older stock bridges have a problem with the third and fourth strings magically lowering themselves throughout the course of a gig. Older Fender stock bridges are notorious for this problem. What's happening is that the low vibrations are rattling and loosening the screws, causing the saddle to drop lower and lower. If you find that your bass is having this problem and you don't want to replace the bridge, you can use Loctite to seal the loose screw and keep it from moving while you're playing.

The intonation is adjusted for each string by using the screws at the end of the bridge and moving the individual saddles forward or backward. This will slightly lengthen or shorten the freely vibrating section of the string. If the intonation is off, your open strings will be in tune but your fretted notes will sound sharp or flat. Using an electronic tuner, first play an open string and tune it, then fret the note at the 12th fret and see if it is also in tune. If it's a little bit off, you'll need to adjust the intonation for that string. If the 12th fret note is sharp, then you should increase the length of the string slightly by tightening the intonation screw, which will move the saddle for that string back a little. If the note is flat, then you should loosen the screw to shorten the length of the string. Keep in mind that every time you make a slight adjustment, the open string will go out of tune a little, so you might need to check and retune the string each time you make an adjustment. Do this until both the open string and the 12th-fret note are perfectly in tune. Repeat the process for each string.

LESSON #13: FRETBOARD MEMORIZATION

An important step to mastering the bass is to learn and memorize the notes of the fretboard. You should make it your goal to be able to point to any note on the neck and instantly know its name. The key to understanding music theory and making it work for you is learning how to directly apply that information to the bass, and learning the fretboard is essential in that regard. You need to know the language of your own instrument in order to maximize your potential as a player. Memorizing all the notes is a gradual process—and it may seem overwhelming to you at first—but there are shortcuts and recognizable patterns that can give you an advantage and make the task much easier and less intimidating.

First, let's take a look at the half step/whole step formula for natural notes in the musical alphabet. A half step is the distance of one fret on the bass; a whole step is the distance of two frets. You should make it your goal to know where all the natural notes are located on the bass; from there, you'll just need to move a fret in either direction for the sharps and flats.

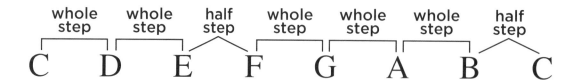

The first notes that all beginners learn on the bass are the names of the open strings. If you already know these notes, you automatically know the names of the notes at the 12th fret, which are exactly one octave higher than the open strings.

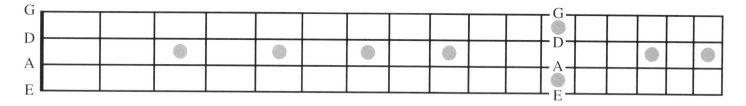

If you've ever tuned your bass using the fifth-fret tuning method, you would have noticed that each note at the fifth fret is the same note as the next higher open string. Let's also include the C note on the first string, which will give us all of the notes at the fifth fret.

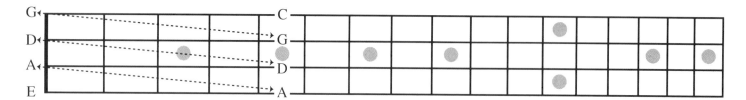

The next shortcut that you can easily recognize revolves around the notes at the seventh fret. These notes are one octave higher than the open strings below them. We can include the B note on the fourth string to complete this set of notes at the seventh fret.

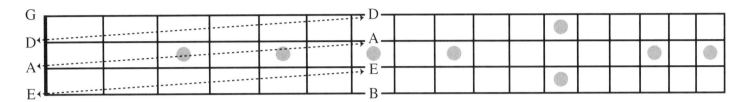

Most beginners start off by learning the natural notes in first position. If you already know these notes, then you automatically know the names of the notes one octave higher, in 12th position.

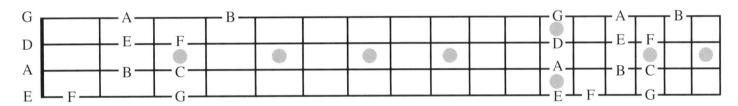

At this point, we've got most of the fretboard covered. The only gap left is the space between the seventh and 12th frets. This might be the most difficult area of the neck to learn, and it will come gradually, but a good way to approach it is to use the half step/whole step formula to count up from the seventh fret or count down from the 12th fret.

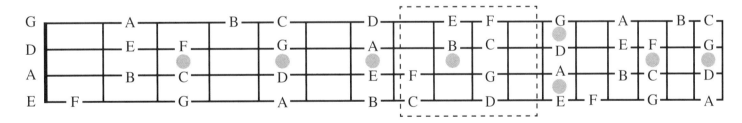

LESSON #14: THE MAJOR SCALE

The major scale forms the foundation of most other scales and chords in Western music. The notes of the major scale are famously showcased in the song "Do-Re-Mi" from *The Sound of Music*. The major scale has a relatively happy, light-hearted sound.

If you count up from C to C in the musical alphabet (C–D–E–F–G–A–B–C), you'll have the C major scale. The first note of the scale, C, is called the tonic—the note that gives the scale its letter name. C major is unique in that it contains all natural notes (no sharps or flats). The distance from the first C to the next higher or lower C in the musical alphabet is called an octave.

Below is one octave of the C major scale, starting at the third fret of the third string. The root notes, C, are indicated with white dots in the scale diagram.

EXAMPLE 1

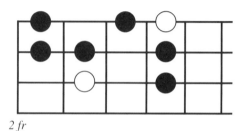

2 fr

The notes of the major scale are separated by two different types of intervals—half steps (H) and whole steps (W). Natural half steps occur in the musical alphabet between the notes B and C and E and F; all other intervals are whole steps. With this knowledge, we can take a look at the C major scale and see that the half steps occur between the third and fourth and seventh and eighth (octave) degrees of the scale. This information gives us the formula (W–W–H–W–W–W–H) for the major scale. All major scales, no matter the key, contain this same series of half steps and whole steps.

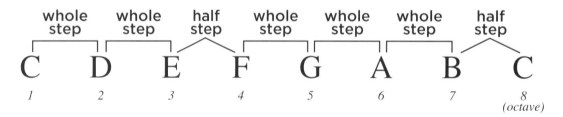

The one-octave C major scale above is a closed-position scale (it contains no open strings), therefore it is a moveable scale pattern. We can move the pattern to any position on the neck to start on any note and it will give us the major scale in that key. We can also use the half step/whole step formula to determine the notes in the scale.

Below is the D major scale. If we take the letter names in the musical alphabet from D to D, we can manipulate the intervals by adding sharps to some notes in order to raise their pitches by a half step, giving us the formula we need for the major scale. By raising the F to F♯, we now have the correct whole step between E and F♯, as well as the necessary half step between F♯ and G. The same thing happens if we raise the C to C♯, the correct pitch for the seventh step of the scale.

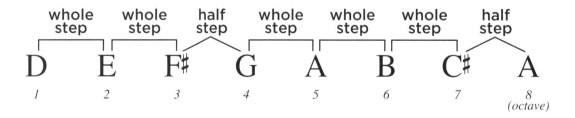

EXAMPLE 2

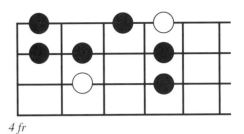

4 fr

We can cover the entire fretboard by using five basic scale patterns. All of these scale patterns are closed-position, so they can be moved up or down an octave on the neck or transposed to any other key. Memorize each of the scale patterns and keep track of where the root notes are located in each position.

Here are the five major scale patterns, with the root notes indicated by white dots in the scale diagrams.

EXAMPLE 3

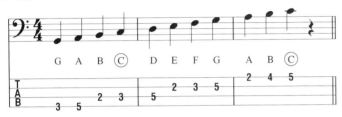

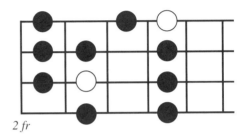

2 fr

EXAMPLE 4

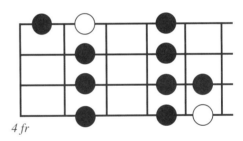

4 fr

EXAMPLE 5

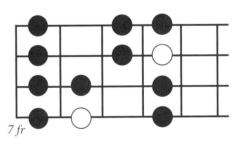

7 fr

EXAMPLE 6

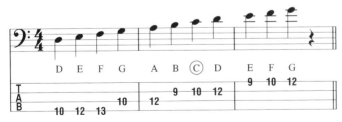

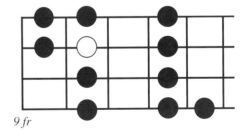

9 fr

EXAMPLE 7

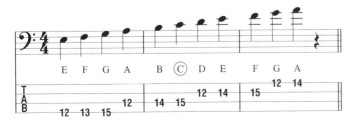

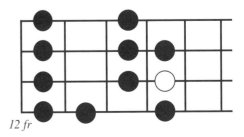

12 fr

LESSON #15: THE MINOR SCALE

One of the most widely used scales in rock and metal is the minor scale. Minor keys have a dark or melancholy characteristic. Western music has incorporated a few altered versions of the minor scale, but for this lesson, we will learn the original—and most popular—version, natural minor (also referred to as simply the "minor scale").

The basic tonal characteristic of the scale comes from the lowered (flatted) 3rd. In minor keys, the 3rd is one-and-a-half steps above the tonic (root), whereas in major keys, the 3rd is two whole steps above the tonic. The ♭3rd is what gives the minor scale its dark and sad tonality.

If you count up from A to A in the musical alphabet (A–B–C–D–E–F–G–A), you'll have the A minor scale. The A minor scale is unique because it's the only minor scale that contains no sharps or flats.

Below is one octave of the A minor scale, starting at the fifth fret of the fourth string. The root notes, A, are indicated with white dots in the scale diagram.

EXAMPLE 1

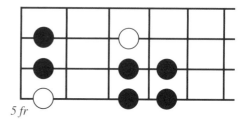

The natural half steps in the minor scale occur between the second and third and fifth and sixth degrees of the scale. All of the other intervals in the scale are whole steps. This information gives us the formula (W–H–W–W–H–W–W) for the minor scale. All natural minor scales, no matter what key, contain this same series of half steps (H) and whole steps (W).

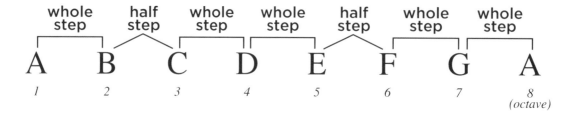

The root-position A minor scale above is a moveable scale pattern, making it easy to transpose the scale to any position on the neck. We can also use the half step/whole step formula to determine the notes of any other natural minor scale.

Below is the D minor scale. If we take the letter names in the musical alphabet from D to D, we simply need to add a flat to the B note in order to come up with the correct sequence of half steps and whole steps.

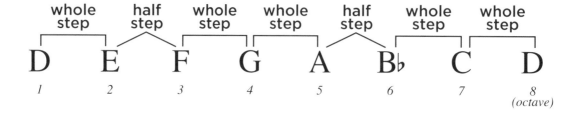

EXAMPLE 2

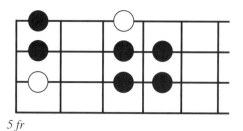

There are five basic scale patterns that enable us to cover the entire fretboard. These scale patterns can be moved up or down an octave on the neck or transposed to any other key. Here are the five natural minor scale patterns in the key of A minor, with the root notes indicated by white dots in the scale diagrams.

EXAMPLE 3

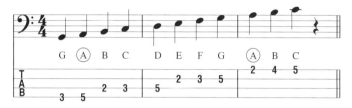
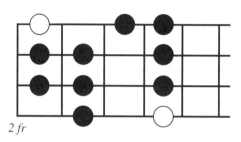

EXAMPLE 4

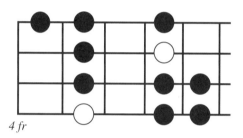

EXAMPLE 5

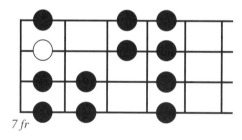

EXAMPLE 6

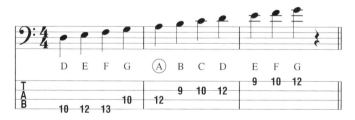
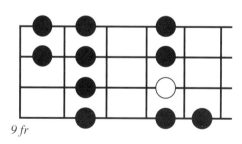

EXAMPLE 7

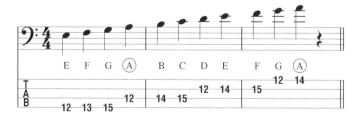
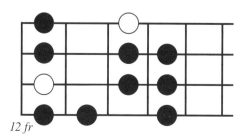

LESSON #16: MAJOR PENTATONIC SCALE

Pentatonic scales are used extensively in rock and popular music for playing riffs and improvising. The major pentatonic scale is a five-note scale that's an abbreviated version of the regular, seven-note major scale. Major pentatonic is comprised of the first, second, third, fifth, and sixth steps of the regular major scale, leaving out the fourth and seventh steps.

Here's one octave of the G major pentatonic scale in root position, starting at the third fret of the fourth string. The root notes are indicated by white dots in the scale diagram.

EXAMPLE 1

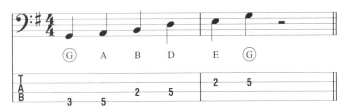
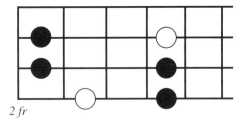

Since the pentatonic scales are the scales that you'll use the most, it's imperative that you learn and memorize them in every position on the fretboard. There are five distinct positions that will cover the entire fretboard, and these can be moved up or down one octave or transposed to any other key.

Here are the five scale positions in the key of G major:

EXAMPLE 2

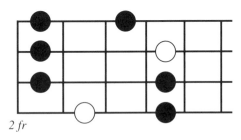

EXAMPLE 3

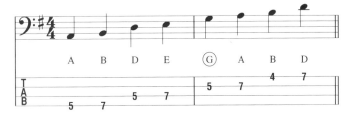
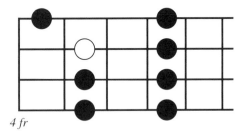

EXAMPLE 4

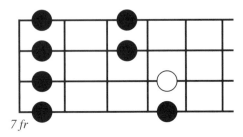

EXAMPLE 5

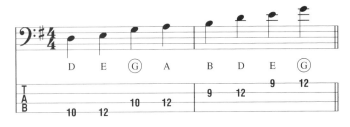
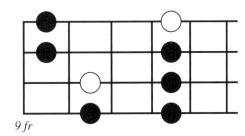

EXAMPLE 6

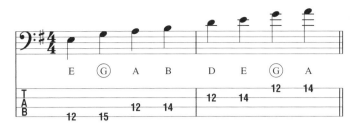
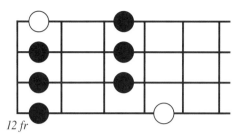

Since all of these scale patterns contain two notes per string, they are fairly easy to play and memorize. A good way to visualize them is to remember that they all overlap each other, so the notes on the right side of one pattern are the same as the notes on the left side of the next pattern. The scale diagram below shows the first two positions, with a box around the notes that the two positions have in common.

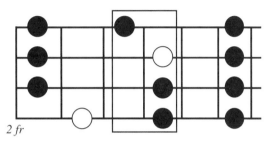

A very popular and simple way to utilize the major pentatonic scale is to connect a few positions with slides, enabling you to use your first and third fingers exclusively, avoiding the four-finger stretches.

The following examples illustrate how you can overlap patterns by using just the first and third fingers.

EXAMPLES 7A–C

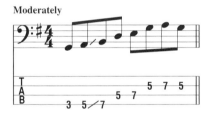

Here are some common applications of the major pentatonic scale in bass lines and bass fills. Many popular bass lines are built from fragments of the pentatonic scale.

EXAMPLE 8

EXAMPLE 9

MINOR PENTATONIC SCALE

The minor pentatonic scale is the most commonly used scale and the foundation for the vast majority of rock music. It appears in the main riffs of countless songs, from Aerosmith's "Toys in the Attic" to Michael Jackson's "Billie Jean." The minor pentatonic scale is a five-note scale that's an abbreviated version of the seven-note natural minor scale. Minor pentatonic utilizes the first, third, fourth, fifth, and seventh steps of the natural minor scale, omitting the second and sixth steps.

Let's take a look at one octave of the E minor pentatonic scale, starting at the seventh fret of the third string. The root notes are indicated by white dots in the scale diagram.

EXAMPLE 1

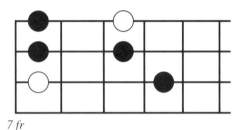

7 fr

We can play the notes of the minor pentatonic scale anywhere on the neck by using five different patterns that can be moved up or down an octave or transposed to other keys. The first of these scale patterns can be referred to as the "first position" of the scale because it's the one that begins on the root note, E. This scale pattern can either be played at the 12th fret or in open position (an octave lower). We've included both versions here.

EXAMPLE 2

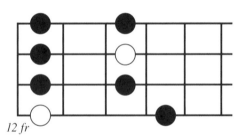

12 fr

EXAMPLE 3

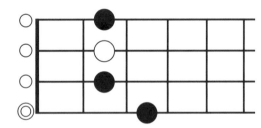

EXAMPLE 4

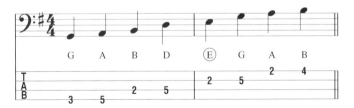
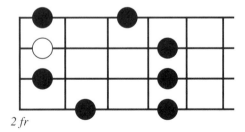

2 fr

EXAMPLE 5

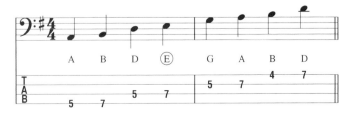
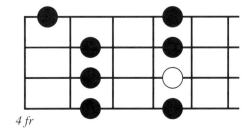

4 fr

EXAMPLE 6

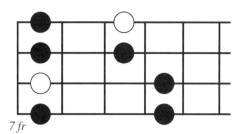

7 fr

EXAMPLE 7

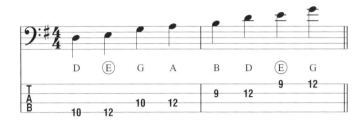

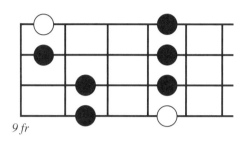

9 fr

A good way to memorize the patterns is to recognize that they overlap each other. Each scale pattern contains only two notes per string, and the notes on the right side of one pattern are the same as the notes on the left side of the next pattern. The adjacent scale diagram shows the fifth and first position patterns, with a box around the notes that they have in common.

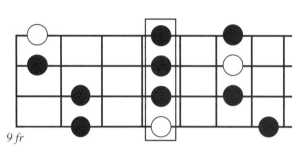

9 fr

By combining neighboring scale patterns, you can play minor pentatonic riffs using just the first and third fingers, avoiding the more difficult four-finger stretches. Here are a couple of examples that combine neighboring patterns by using a few simple slides.

EXAMPLES 8A–B

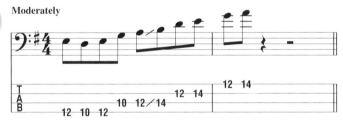

Here are some cool bass lines that use the E minor pentatonic scale. Try transposing them to other keys and then work on coming up with some of your own.

EXAMPLE 9

EXAMPLE 10

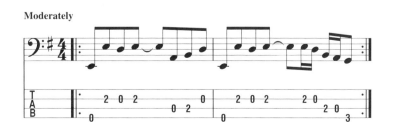

LESSON #18: THE BLUES SCALE

The blues scale is very common in rock and blues and can be heard extensively in the catalogs of bands such as Led Zeppelin, Aerosmith, and Guns N' Roses. The scale consists of six notes: the same five notes as the minor pentatonic scale (1–♭3–4–5–♭7), plus the flatted 5th, called the blues tritone. This note can function like a chromatic passing tone between the 4th and 5th or like a half-step neighbor tone to those two notes. The tonal characteristic of the blues scale is similar to that of the minor pentatonic scale, but a little sexier and with more personality.

Here's one octave of the E blues scale, starting at the seventh fret of the third string. The root notes are indicated by white dots in the scale diagram.

EXAMPLE 1

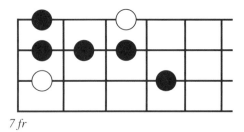

Now let's transpose this scale down an octave and play it in open position, ascending and descending.

EXAMPLE 2

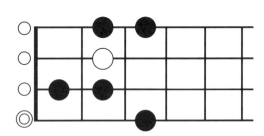

Below are a couple of bass lines that use the E blues scale. Experiment with the scale, transpose it, and come up with a few of your own licks.

EXAMPLE 3

EXAMPLE 4

Bass players won't often bend strings like guitar players because the gauges of the strings are too thick to do more than a half-step bend. By using the blues tritone, you can incorporate this fun technique on the bass, too. Here's an example:

EXAMPLE 5

There's also a major version of the blues scale, which contains the same scale steps of the major pentatonic scale (1–2–3–5–6), plus an additional chromatic passing tone between the 2nd and 3rd. If you're familiar with the terms "relative major" and "relative minor" (scales that have different roots but share the same notes), then you'll notice that E minor and G major are relative scales. Therefore, the minor-based E blues scale has a relative major-based blues scale—the G major blues scale.

Below are a couple of ways that you can play the G major blues scale, followed by an example of how major blues scales can be used in a bass groove over a I–IV chord change in a major key.

EXAMPLES 6A–B

EXAMPLE 7

TWO-OCTAVE MAJOR AND MINOR SCALES

The purpose of learning and practicing two-octave scales is to help you break the mindset of being locked into one position and to help you visualize a scale across the entire fretboard. Playing a scale in one place, from root note to octave and back down, is good to start with, but it's not as useful in practical applications.

The two-octave major and minor scales in this lesson can be added to your practice and warmup routines. While they'll help you gain speed and accuracy for moving around the neck, when you're improvising, you'll probably just play sections of these scales and do something more creative and musical with them. The scale diagrams and fingerings here are suggestions to get you started, but you might discover different fingerings that are more comfortable for you personally, so be encouraged to experiment and alter them.

Let's start out with a two-octave C major scale. The notation and tab below show the scale ascending and descending, with the fret-hand fingerings displayed below the tab staff. You'll notice that, for consistency, we've suggested sliding up with the third finger and sliding down with the first finger. There are also scale diagrams for both the ascending and the descending versions of the scale.

EXAMPLE 1

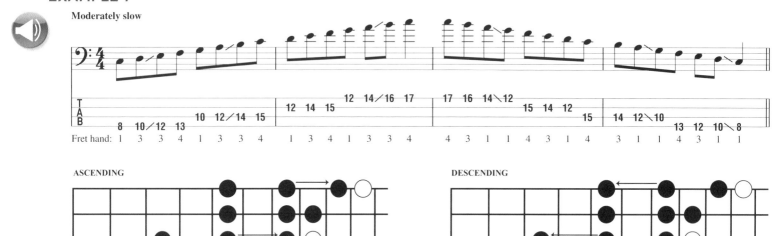

Now let's transpose the scale into a few popular keys. The first is G major, which follows the same pattern as the C major scale above. The next is E major, which utilizes the open E string, giving you one less slide to perform in the pattern.

EXAMPLE 2

EXAMPLE 3

The minor scale is a little more difficult to map out as a two-octave pattern because of the order of the intervals. The first minor scale below is A minor, starting at the fifth fret of the fourth string. In the ascending version, we are using the fourth finger to slide up and shift positions. In the descending version, most of the downward slides are executed with the first finger, with the exception of the slide on the first string. Here we've chosen to slide downward with the fourth finger so we can avoid an otherwise uncomfortable stretch. Those wide, five-fret stretches don't present much of a problem for guitar players, but there's a risk of hitting a clam on the bass because of the much wider fret spacing. If you have giant hands and you're comfortable with those wide reaches, go ahead and give it a shot.

EXAMPLE 4

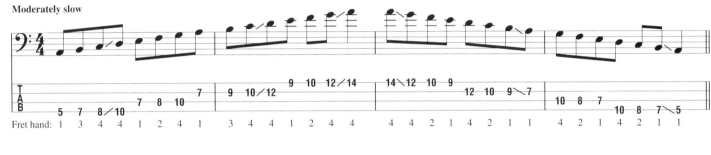

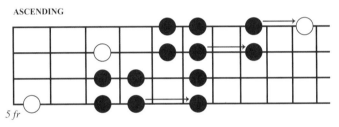

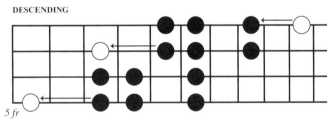

Finally, let's transpose the two-octave minor scale to some other keys. First up is B minor, so all you need to do is move the previous pattern up two frets and you've got it. Lastly, let's utilize the open low-E string again, this time for a two-octave E minor scale.

EXAMPLE 5

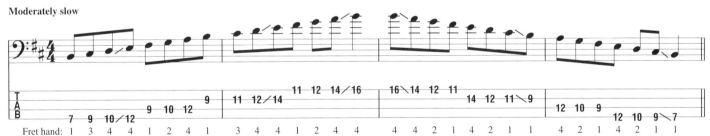

EXAMPLE 6

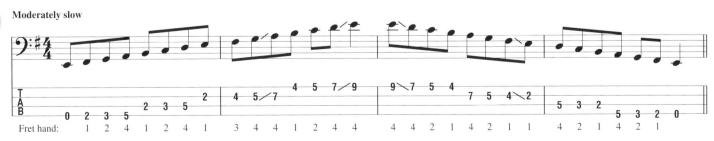

LESSON #20: TWO-OCTAVE PENTATONIC SCALES

The major and minor pentatonic scales are the most used scales in rock, and knowing your way around them in all positions on the neck is essential. In this lesson, we'll take a look at some different ways that you can play two full octaves of these scales. Since the pentatonic scale is comprised of wider intervals, sometimes it will work best to connect the patterns in chunks, rather than attempting to create seamless slides on each string that will only give you one or two notes per position. Using partial positions of the scales can be very effective, rather than strictly playing up to the octave and back down to the root note. Keep in mind that, just because the root note is theoretically the first step of the scale, doesn't imply that it should be the lowest note that you're playing; it simply implies that the root note is *home*, the note where you should land and where the scale resolves. In most musical applications, you'll likely be playing *around* the root note, keeping it grounded as the anchor and tonal center and improvising with notes in the scale that are both above it and below it.

First, let's take a look at a two-octave G major pentatonic scale. The suggested fret-hand fingerings are indicated under the tab staff. Notice how the highest G note (12th fret) is pretty far out of the range of the rest of the notes, but if we ignore that high G, we can come up with some pretty tasty riffs by using the rest of the notes, which are right within our reach.

EXAMPLE 1

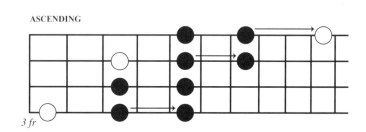

The closed-position minor pentatonic scale presents more of a challenge when trying to find ways to play it across two full octaves while keeping most of the comfortable 1–3–1–3 fret-hand fingering intact. This is where it's helpful to break it up into sections and jump with your whole hand to a different position, rather than trying to use slides.

Here are three ways of doing this with the A minor pentatonic scale. Each one jumps directly from the scale's first position to its third position, but on a different string.

EXAMPLE 2

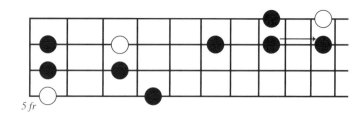

EXAMPLE 3

Moderately slow

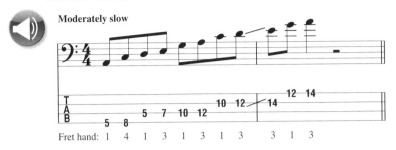

Fret hand: 1 4 1 3 1 3 1 3   3 1 3

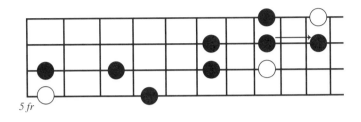

5 fr

EXAMPLE 4

Moderately slow

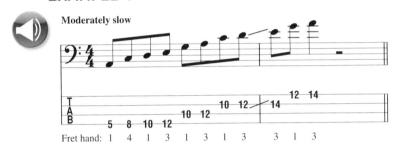

Fret hand: 1 4 1 3 1 3 1 3   3 1 3

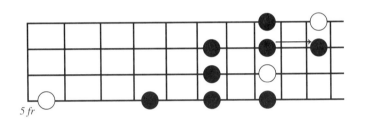

5 fr

Now let's try a two-octave E minor pentatonic scale. Since we are using the open low-E string, this is a very easy pattern to maneuver around in.

EXAMPLE 5

Moderately slow

Fret hand: 1 3 3 1 3 1 3   3 1 3

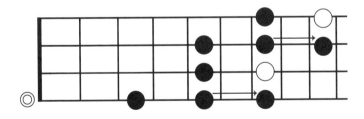

At this point, you're probably recognizing a lot of these scale patterns and positions from songs and riffs that you may have played in the past. The more familiar you become with pentatonic scales and how to maneuver from position to position, the easier it will be for you to learn new songs or improvise your own distinct riffs. Remember to experiment with the scale fingerings and figure out what works best for you. As long as you're playing the right notes, there are no concrete rules with regard to fingerings.

LESSON #21: 5THS AND OCTAVES

The most commonly used intervals in bass lines are 5ths and octaves. The finger patterns for these are consistent anywhere on the bass, making them easily accessible in any playing context. You can bring to life many simple one-note bass lines by adding a few strategic 5ths or octaves.

An octave can be played above any note on the fourth or third strings without changing position on the bass. The octave is located two frets and two strings higher from any given root note. This pattern remains the same anywhere on the bass.

EXAMPLE 1

  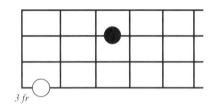 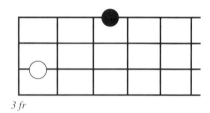

Octaves can typically be used to accent snare-drum hits, either in a regular beat or in a basic drum fill.

EXAMPLE 2

Octaves can also be used in the creation of bass lines. The first example below shows a simple bass line that alternates between root notes and octaves for each beat. The second example shows a walking bass figure that uses octaves, reminiscent of a disco bass line.

EXAMPLE 3

The term "5th" refers to the fifth note of the scale from any given root note. Most chords contain a 5th, and the interval is the same in both major and minor chords. A 5th above any root note is played two frets and one string higher. A 5th below the root note is played at the same fret, one string lower.

EXAMPLE 4

 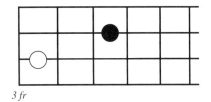 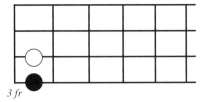

There are numerous ways that 5ths can be incorporated with great effect into a simple bass line. Below is a simple two-chord groove, shown first with just the root notes, followed by a series of examples that incorporate 5ths both above and below the root notes.

EXAMPLE 5

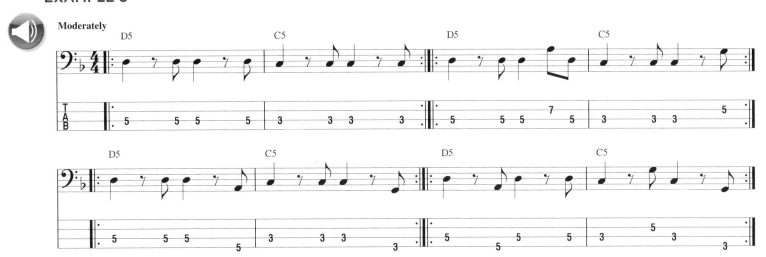

Here are two more examples of how you can use 5ths and octaves to accent the drums in a syncopated bass line.

EXAMPLE 6

EXAMPLE 7

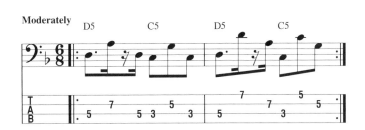

Once you're comfortable with 5ths and octaves, you can use them just about anywhere in your playing. If you pay close attention to the beat and work with the drummer, you can incorporate these notes very effectively.

LESSON #22: ARPEGGIOS

An arpeggio is defined as the individual notes of a chord played separately. In this lesson, we'll focus on major and minor arpeggios and the different fingerings used to play them. You can use arpeggios to build your bass lines around the major and minor chords played by the guitar or keyboard. Arpeggios are comprised of the root, 3rd, and 5th. If you start with a root note and play every other note of the scale, you will outline the notes in the arpeggio.

Let's begin with the A major arpeggio. The root note, of course, will be A, the 3rd will be C♯, and the 5th will be E. We can also add the octave A on top. There are three basic ways to play the arpeggio on the fretboard, beginning with either the first, second, or fourth finger. All three patterns are shown below. The fret-hand fingering for each is indicated under the tab staff. You'll probably favor one of the fingerings over the others, but it's important to memorize all of them so you'll have the notes readily available to you, no matter what finger is playing the root note.

Practice the arpeggios in both ascending and descending order and in time, as shown in the exercises. The arpeggios have been presented with the accidentals shown in the notation (i.e., no key signature) to make it easier to compare the major and minor arpeggios in this lesson.

EXAMPLES 1A–C

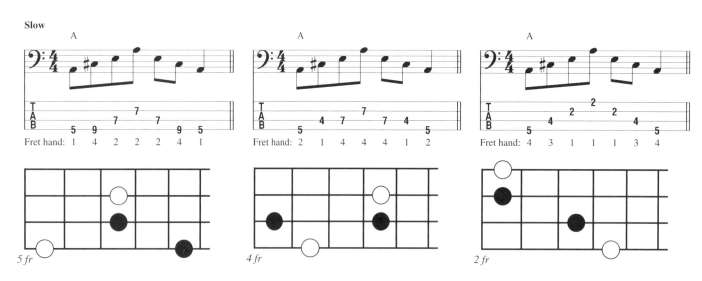

The minor arpeggios are similar to the major ones. The 5th will be the same interval in both major and minor; however, the minor arpeggio contains a *minor* 3rd, which is one fret lower than the major 3rd. The notes of the A minor arpeggio are: A, C, and E.

Here are three versions of the A minor arpeggio:

EXAMPLES 2A–C

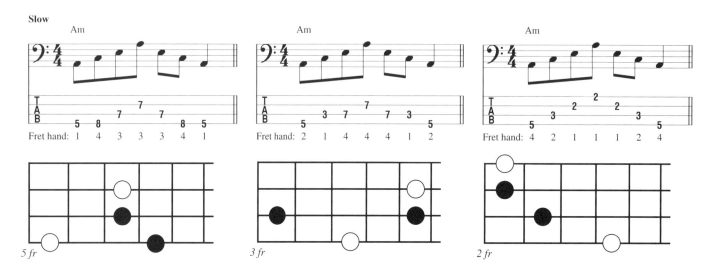

Here's an example of a simple two-chord progression that uses the arpeggios in their most basic form:

EXAMPLE 3

Arpeggios are frequently used in walking patterns, too. Here's a familiar I–IV–V progression that is outlined with arpeggios and throws in the 6th as a melodic neighbor tone:

EXAMPLE 4

It's also common to come across a chord progression that cycles in 5ths. When this happens, you'll have chord tones in common from one chord to the next; that is, the 5th of the first chord will be the same as the root note of the next chord. You can create a bass line like the one below, which basically enhances the arpeggios with chromatic passing tones from the 3rd to the 5th of each chord.

EXAMPLE 5

Here are a couple of examples of two-octave major and minor arpeggios. There are two versions for each, with the fret-hand fingering indicated under the tab staff. The first version of each utilizes some stretches but stays in one position. The second version is played by pivoting your hand slightly while ascending and descending.

EXAMPLES 6A-B

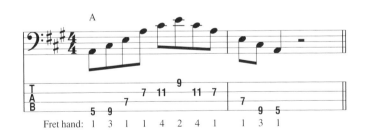

EXAMPLES 7A-B

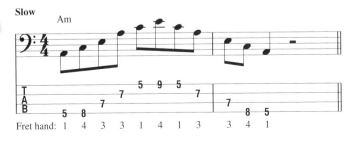

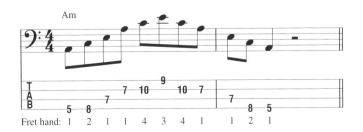

LESSON #23: SEVENTH CHORDS

There are four different types of seventh chords that occur in major keys: major seventh, minor seventh, dominant seventh, and minor seventh flat-five. The notes of each chord can be played individually on the bass to create the seventh-chord arpeggios. These arpeggios are essential to playing walking bass lines and creating melodic bass lines over complex chord changes. All of the finger patterns for the seventh-chord arpeggios are moveable and are consistent anywhere on the bass, so once you've got them down, you can transpose them to any key. Each of the arpeggios is presented with A as the root note so you can easily compare the differences between them.

The major seventh arpeggio consists of the root, major 3rd, 5th, and major 7th. Major seventh chords have a light and airy tonal quality.

EXAMPLE 1

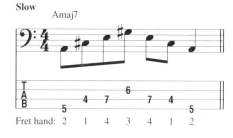
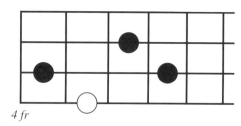

The minor seventh arpeggio contains a root, minor 3rd, 5th, and minor 7th. Minor seventh chords have a slightly darker quality than a regular minor triad. You might encounter minor seventh chords in brooding metal ballads that use arpeggiated guitar figures.

EXAMPLE 2

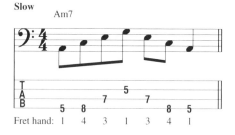
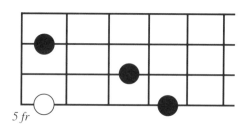

The dominant seventh chord contains a root, major 3rd, 5th, and minor 7th. These chords are used often in blues. They retain a major sound because of the major third, but the minor 7th adds a slightly melancholy quality to them.

EXAMPLE 3

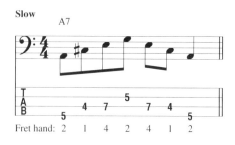
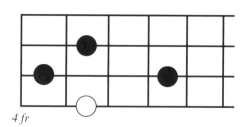

The minor seventh flat-five chord is the most dissonant of the seventh chords in this series. It contains a root, minor 3rd, diminished 5th, and minor seventh.

EXAMPLE 4

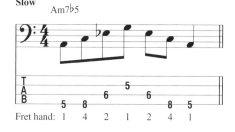
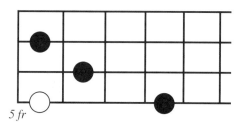

Let's take a look at a few ways the seventh-chord arpeggios might be used in simple bass lines. The dominant seventh arpeggios are very common in blues music, and oftentimes a typical I–IV–V chord change will be altered to make them all dominant seventh chords. The simple, familiar walking bass line below, played here in the key of A, demonstrates this by outlining the chords exclusively with dominant seventh arpeggios (the 6th is used as a passing tone).

EXAMPLE 5

You may notice that the minor seventh arpeggio is actually very similar to a minor pentatonic scale. The minor seventh arpeggio contains four notes, while the minor pentatonic is a five-note scale that contains all of the notes of the arpeggio, plus the 4th. Here's an example of a bass line that outlines the minor i–iv–v progression exclusively with minor seventh arpeggios:

EXAMPLE 6

In a major key, we can build a seventh chord on each step of the scale. If we don't alter the notes of the scale at all (i.e., keep them diatonic), we'll come up with the seventh chords that naturally occur on each step. This formula is consistent in all keys.

EXAMPLE 7

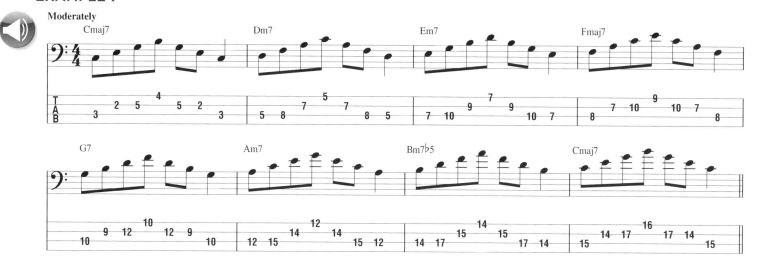

LESSON #24: DOUBLE STOPS

Double stops are two-note chords on the bass. They can be incorporated into bass fills or used to build bass lines and riffs. The most common double-stops use 3rds, 4ths, or 5ths, but you can create a double stop with any interval that fits the chord progression or key.

Double stops sound much better on the bass in the higher register, using the higher strings. Lower double stops and chords sound muddy because of the thick string gauges and low frequency of the notes, whose longer wave forms and overtones tend to clash. The only exception are octave double stops, whose overtones blend nicely. Since the bass is tuned consistently in 4ths, the finger pattern for double-stop intervals is the same anywhere on the fretboard, making them easy to memorize, move, and transpose to other keys.

Let's start out with the double stops that you can play on adjacent strings. If you're playing fingerstyle, you can pluck both strings simultaneously by using an individual finger for each note (use your index finger for the lower string and your middle finger for the higher string). Another popular way of striking double stops and chords is to reverse-rake the notes with the back of your fingers (fingernails) in a downward motion. Curl your pluck-hand fingers up into a fist and, in a quick, spring-like motion, spread your fingers out and downward, striking the strings with the fingernail portions of your fingers. This will give you a sharp, multi-finger attack.

Using the C note at the 10th fret of the second string as the lower note, the double stops below cover most possibilities.

EXAMPLE 1

You'll notice that the minor 3rd and minor 6th double stops sound a bit muddier, making them less useful. Again, this is due to the clash in overtones. The higher up in the register you play double stops, the cleaner they'll sound, and many of these intervals will only sound pleasant way up on the fretboard. Also take note that the C note might not be the root; determining which note is the root depends on the context. For example, the 4ths double stop in the previous example could actually be considered an inverted fifth (power) chord, making the root F, not C.

The diminished 5th double stop may not sound useful either, but on the contrary, it's one of the more popular ones. This is because the notes are the major 3rd and the minor 7th of a dominant seventh chord. For example, if you were to add a G note below the double stop, it becomes the root of a G7 chord.

Here's an example of how this diminished 5th double stop can be used in context over an A7 chord:

EXAMPLE 2

There are endless uses for double stops. Here's a cool, little bass line using 4ths in the key of A minor. For the pluck-hand technique, you can play the lower notes with your index finger and still reach up to strike the double stop. This might be a little more difficult at a fast tempo, so many bass players adopt a fingerstyle technique borrowed from the guitar. This involves using your thumb to downstroke the lower notes and playing the double stops with your first and second fingers. If you're not used to incorporating your thumb to pluck notes, this technique will take some practice, but it can be very useful once you've got it.

EXAMPLE 3

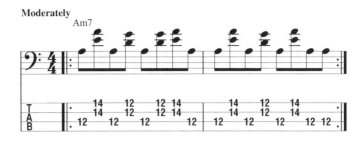

Now let's take a look at some wider-interval double stops.

EXAMPLE 4

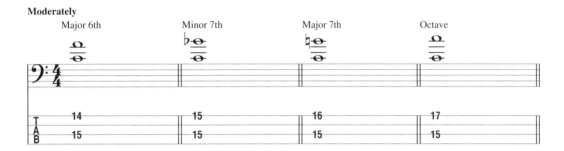

You can pluck these wide intervals with the two-finger technique, employing a bit of a wider spread in the pluck hand, or you can use the thumb and first finger to pluck them simultaneously with a pinching motion. You can also pluck these notes individually in succession, keeping both notes fretted with the fret hand and allowing them to ring out over each other.

Lastly, here are double stops that use just the outer strings, with the notes separated by more than an octave. While the intervals are 10ths, they are actually 3rds that have been transposed up an octave. These wide intervals are exceptions that actually work quite well in the lower register due to the distance between the two notes, which allows their overtones to blend well.

EXAMPLE 5

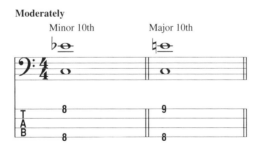

The above double stops really need to be played with the pluck-hand thumb/first finger pinch method if you're playing the notes simultaneously. However, you can create some cool bass lines by playing the notes individually and allowing them to ring over each other, as shown below.

EXAMPLE 6

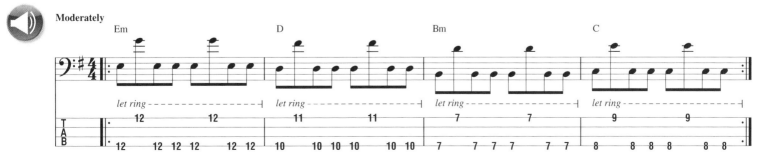

LESSON #25: HAMMER-ONS

The hammer-on is a widely used technique for playing fast runs or creating colorful effects with grace notes. Hammer-ons are represented in notation and tab by slurs that connect the notes. If the second note in a slurred phrase is higher than the first note, this indicates a hammer-on. To play a hammer-on, pick or pluck the first note and then push down on the subsequent note with your fret-hand finger (without picking it).

In the first example below, we'll begin with a simple series of pentatonic scale hammer-ons that utilize the open strings. Practice getting the hammer-ons to sound smooth and in time. Once you've got the technique down, move on to the next example, which contains closed-position pentatonic hammer-ons.

EXAMPLE 1

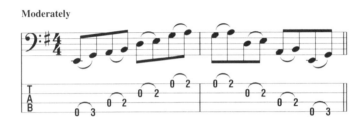

EXAMPLE 2

This next example applies the hammer-on technique to the notes of the major scale, slurring three consecutive notes. Pluck just the first note on each string, hammering onto the second and third notes in time.

EXAMPLE 3

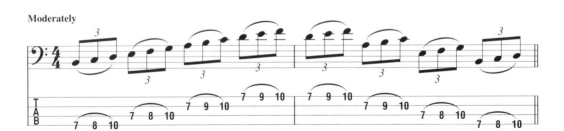

Now let's apply the hammer-on technique to grace notes. The grace notes in the following example are the smaller noteheads, which are slurred into the regular noteheads. Pluck the grace notes for just an instant, immediately hammering onto the main notes.

EXAMPLE 4

Now that we've explored some applications of the hammer-on technique, here are some exercises and riff-based examples where they can be applied:

EXAMPLE 5

EXAMPLE 6

EXAMPLE 7

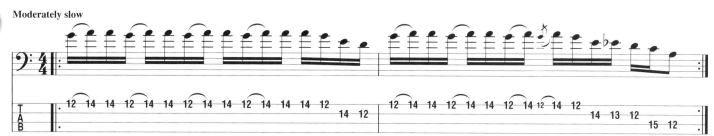

LESSON #26: PULL-OFFS

A pull-off is a technique that can be used to slur from a plucked note to a lower-pitched note on the same string. To execute a pull-off, pick or pluck the first note and then pull or snap your finger in a downward dragging motion from the string in order to sound the second note. Your fret-hand finger should already be in place (fretting the second note) before pulling off from the first note. Pull-offs are represented by slurs in notation and tab.

The examples below contain a series of pull-offs that use pentatonic scales in open and closed positions.

EXAMPLE 1

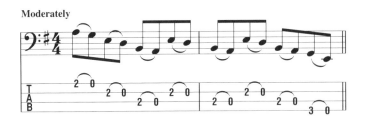

EXAMPLE 2

Here are some examples of how the pull-off technique can be used to play riffs and bass fills:

EXAMPLE 3

EXAMPLE 4

EXAMPLE 5

Now let's take a look at a couple of examples that combine multiple pull-offs. Practice these examples slowly at first, making sure that your timing is accurate and the pull-offs are clean. Remember: you can't simply lift your finger from the first note to get the pull-off note to sound; it's more of a downward dragging motion, so that you're simultaneously pulling off and plucking the string slightly with your fret-hand finger. Once you're comfortable with this technique, it can be used to play lightning-fast riffs and runs.

EXAMPLE 6

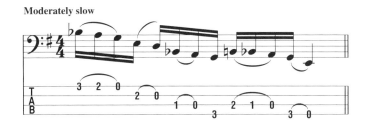

EXAMPLE 7

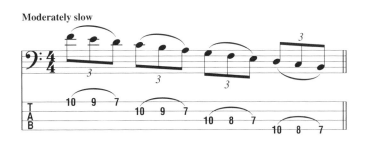

LESSON #27: SLIDES

There are many different ways to slide notes to give your bass lines and fills more personality. Slides are represented in notation and tab by diagonal lines that depict upward or downward motion (i.e., slides to and from notes). To slide a note, keep your fretting finger pressed down on the note and move your hand up or down the neck in the indicated direction.

The most common and basic slides are slides from a note or into a note. These slides end or begin at an indiscriminate, arbitrary place on the fretboard; they're often used for emphasis, or to accent a floor-tom hit or a cymbal crash on the drums. When sliding from a note, pluck the note on the beat and immediately slide the note down the fretboard. Oftentimes, these accented power slides will slide down from the 12th fret or from the octave of the key that you're playing in, but the pitch itself is hardly sustained and is less important than the slide effect itself. When sliding into a note, pluck the string slightly before the beat and then quickly and immediately slide up into the indicated note.

EXAMPLE 1

The following slides connect one note to another. These are regular slides and the note at the end of the slide should also be plucked.

EXAMPLE 2

Oftentimes, slides are indicated in the notation and tab as a way of hinting at the fingering, telling you that you should use the same fret-hand finger to fret both notes. The following example is a basic A minor pentatonic riff with an ascending slide between the fifth and seventh frets on the third string and a descending slide between the fifth and third frets. You can see that the fret-hand fingering is a simple 1–3–1–3 pattern. The ascending slide should be executed with your third finger, moving your hand position up two frets, and the descending slide should be played with your first finger, moving from fifth to third position.

EXAMPLE 3

Slides are also time sensitive, and there is a difference between the two examples below. The first example shows half notes joined by a slide. You should arrive on beat 3 in time, but since the slide begins on beat 1, it should last the duration of two full beats. If we want to sustain the first note before sliding it, we would notate it the way it's shown in the second example. Here, the first note is a dotted quarter that is tied to an eighth note, which slides up to beat 3. Notice in the tab, beat 2.5 is shown in parentheses, indicating the note is not to be struck, but instead is the point where the upward slide should begin.

EXAMPLES 4A–B

Legato slides are indicated with slurs, indicating that you should only strike the first note and then slide up or down to the second note (without re-striking).

EXAMPLE 5

Legato slides can also encompass more than one slide. Start the riff below with your third finger. When you reach the highest notes on the first string, an up and down legato slide is performed with your third finger.

EXAMPLE 6

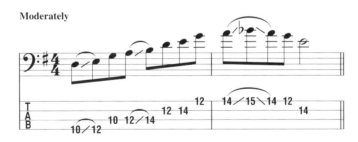

Grace-note slides are also common. Play the grace note slightly before the beat and immediately slide into the regular note on the beat. These are similar to the "slides from nowhere" at the beginning of this lesson, except that the grace note gives a definitive starting point for the slide.

EXAMPLE 7

BASIC ROCK RHYTHMS

The bass player's most important role in a rock band is to work with the drummer and lay down a solid groove. Rhythmic contribution is just as important as playing the right notes or adding melody to your bass lines. It's essential that bass players are familiar with the drum beat and in sync with what the kick and snare drum are playing. You may not always be playing the exact same beats as the kick drum, but it's usually a good place to start and will ensure that you're locked in with the drummer.

Let's start off with some basic counting. In most rock and blues, the music is divided into measures of four beats, known as 4/4 time. When a band counts off, "One, two, three, four" at the beginning of a song, it represents one complete measure of music. Different types of notes are held for different durations within a measure. For example, a quarter note gets one beat because a quarter note is held for one quarter of the measure. Quarter notes are counted as "one, two, three, four." If we divide those notes in half, we get eighth notes. Eighths can be counted as "one-and, two-and, three-and, four-and." We can further divide eighth notes in half to create 16th notes, which are counted "one-ee-and-uh, two-ee-and-uh," etc.

The example below shows the notation for quarter notes, eighth notes, and 16th notes, with counting prompts displayed between the notation and tab staves.

EXAMPLE 1

Now let's mix some quarters, eighths, and 16ths together within measures to create some typical patterns. Listen closely to the drums to familiarize yourself with each beat and what the kick drum and snare are doing.

EXAMPLE 2

One of the most popular ways to lay down a rock-solid groove is to play exclusively on the kick drum and rest on the snare drum hits on beats 2 and 4. This is the most basic way to give life to the groove and let it breathe.

The example below shows four different variations of a simple kick-drum pattern. Practice locking in with the kick drum while keeping your foot tapping in steady quarter notes—"one, two, three, four"—and you'll begin to feel the groove as it takes shape.

EXAMPLE 3

Now let's practice that same basic idea, but this time, hold and sustain the notes through the snare hits, instead of cutting them short. The pattern in the second measure contains a struck note on beat 4, demonstrating that you don't need to avoid playing on the snare-drum hits entirely. On the contrary, this is a very popular rhythm pattern that you'll encounter often.

EXAMPLE 4

The use of 6/8 time has steadily grown in popularity and is probably the second most popular time signature to play in. This meter is characterized by its six eighth notes per measure, with the emphasis on the first and fourth eighth notes, essentially dividing the measure in half (two groups of three eighth notes per measure). For this very reason, 6/8 time is not the same as 3/4 time. In 6/8, you are more or less counting in triplet groups: "*one*-two-three, *four*-five-six."

The following example shows some of the most common 6/8 rhythmic patterns.

EXAMPLE 5

LESSON #29: SYNCOPATED RHYTHMS

A syncopated rhythm is a rhythm that stresses the off-beats, instead of the typical downbeats. Beats 1 and 3 are generally the accented downbeats in rock music. Beats 2 and 4 are also downbeats, but they are known as the "backbeat" and are typically where the snare-drum hits occur in basic rock music. Syncopation occurs when we place the emphasis on the upbeats, instead of the downbeats.

The following examples contain the most basic types of syncopation. The first example moves the downbeat of the second measure back to the "and" of beat 4 of the first measure. This is a very common device that you'll encounter often. The second example contains a phrase that repeats in groups of three, placing the accents on some of the upbeats.

EXAMPLE 1

EXAMPLE 2

Here's another example of simple syncopation. In the first version, notes are played on all of the upbeats, starting on the "and" of beat 1 and resolving on beat 3 of the second measure. The second version is exactly the same, except we've halved the note values and created a syncopated 16th-note rhythm.

EXAMPLES 3A–B

Let's check out a few more complex versions of syncopation. The first four examples involve some degree of 16th-note syncopation. The last example shows some syncopation in 6/8 time.

EXAMPLE 4

EXAMPLE 5

EXAMPLE 6

EXAMPLE 7

EXAMPLE 8

LESSON #30: SHUFFLE FEEL

Shuffle feel is a rhythmic device made popular by its use in blues and swing, but it's used extensively in all genres of music. The most basic version of shuffle feel is an uneven eighth-note rhythm in which the second eighth note of each beat lags a little, making the rhythm swing. The first eighth note of each beat actually gets 2/3 of the beat, while the second eighth note gets 1/3 of the beat.

The chart below compares a regular, straight eighth-note rhythm with the shuffle rhythm notated in triplets.

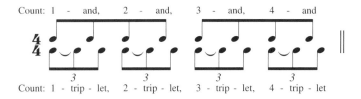

The shuffle rhythm is a much easier concept to understand by hearing it. The example below is initially played as straight eighth notes, then as triplets that are grouped to depict the shuffle rhythm.

EXAMPLES 1A–B

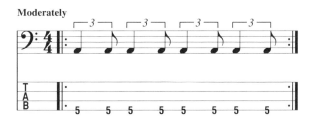

In the example above, we've used triplets to show the shuffle rhythm written in exact time (rhythmic) measurement; however, the term shuffle is actually used to describe a rhythmic feel that should be applied to regular eighth notes. When you encounter the shuffle feel in written music, it will be indicated at the beginning of a song (or section of a song) using the rhythmic equivalency shown below, indicating that you should apply the shuffle, or swing, feel to the entire song or section. This makes it easier to read and write the music.

Here's an example of a shuffle-rhythm bass line written out using the equivalency indicator.

EXAMPLE 2

Oftentimes, you'll encounter a bass line that's played in quarter notes, possibly a walking bass line, but the overall feel of the music is a shuffle feel. You might not have written music or a chart to tell you that it's a shuffle feel either. In these cases, it's essential to listen to the drums or guitar, as they will let you know if the music is using the shuffle swing. Some of the clues to listen for are the hi-hat rhythm, or maybe the guitarist is playing chords on all of the upbeats, à la reggae. You might even get a clue from listening to the vocal line. Even if the bass is playing mostly quarters, it's still important for you to know that it's a shuffle and to have a grasp on the groove of the song, as there may be some eighths thrown into the bass line, or you may want to add a few fills or ghost notes, and these should all lock in to the shuffle feel.

Here are a few more shuffle examples using quarter notes and eighth notes:

EXAMPLE 3

EXAMPLE 4

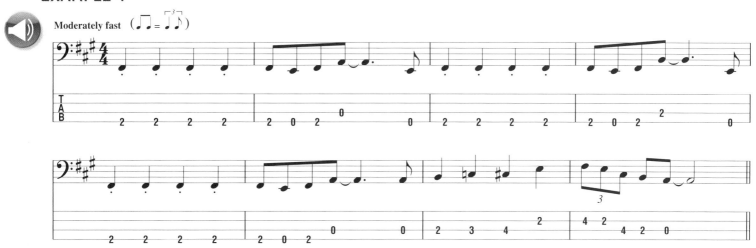

In addition to the blues, you'll encounter the shuffle feel in many different styles of rock, pop, or even metal. The tempos will vary dramatically, and it's not unusual to encounter very fast shuffle rhythms. Shuffle feel may not come naturally to you at first, especially at faster tempos, but it's used so commonly that it's essential for you to get it down until it becomes second nature. To help you recognize shuffle rhythms, take a listen to some of the common examples throughout the years. Some famous classic rock examples of the shuffle feel are "Tush" by ZZ Top, "Don't Stop" by Fleetwood Mac, and "Pride and Joy" by Stevie Ray Vaughan. Pop hits like Toto's "Rosanna" use a shuffle, and Cheap Trick's "I Want You to Want Me" is a good example of an up-tempo shuffle. You'll even encounter shuffles in modern rock songs, like Green Day's "Longview," and No Doubt's "Different People" has a very fast shuffle feel. The shuffle feel is also used in some metal classics, like Van Halen's "Bottoms Up!" and "I'm the One" and Black Sabbath's "Fairies Wear Boots." Other classic rock shuffles include "My Generation" by the Who, "Same Old Song and Dance" by Aerosmith, and "Tie Your Mother Down" by Queen.

LESSON #31: 12/8 TIME

Many slow blues songs are played in 12/8 time, which consists of 12 eighth notes per measure. Typically, 12/8 time is grouped into four equal groups of three eighth notes, placing the downbeats in such a way that it sounds like four triplets per measure in 4/4 time.

The examples below show 12/8 time initially counted as 12 eighth notes, with the perceived downbeats in bold type, and then as four groups of triplets, as you should probably count it.

EXAMPLES 1A–B

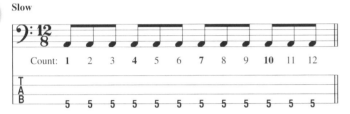

In 12/8 time, you may also see a series of quarter note/eighth note combinations for each beat, as shown below. This is the same rhythm as using bracketed triplet figures or shuffled eighth notes, indicated by the shuffle prompt, in 4/4 time.

EXAMPLES 2A–C

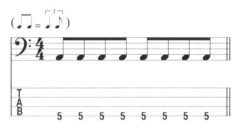

In the cases above, notating the music in 12/8 can be subjective but it's usually done for ease of reading. It's much easier to read and count the 12/8 version than to be inundated with tons of triplets and triplet brackets in 4/4 time. This becomes obvious when you begin to introduce 16th notes, which will be especially common at a slow tempo. Here's an example:

EXAMPLE 3

Now let's take a look at a slow 12/8 example with some syncopated rhythms and ties involved.

EXAMPLE 4

Blues progressions (I–IV–V) often feature 12/8 meter. Some examples of slow blues in 12/8 are "Since I've Been Loving You" by Led Zeppelin and "Red House" by Jimi Hendrix.

Here's an example of a slow blues progression in the key of A minor:

EXAMPLE 5

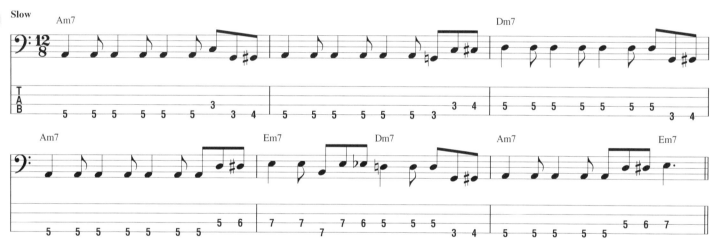

It's not uncommon for metal or progressive metal songs to be written in 12/8, as well. This is useful when you've got a distinct triplet rhythm going throughout a song or part of a song. Many metal songs may have the bulk written out in 4/4 and then switch to a 12/8 section for a bridge or solo section. Some famous examples of metal songs in 12/8 are "The Four Horsemen" and "For Whom the Bell Tolls" by Metallica.

Here's an example of a fast 12/8 metal riff:

EXAMPLE 6

LESSON #32: COMPLEX TIME SIGNATURES

Complex time signatures are used a lot in heavy metal and progressive rock. There are many combinations of note values and ways to group them into measures, and we'll take a look at some of the more common ones here.

Usually, you won't see too many time signatures in which the upper value is more than double the lower value—for example, 9/4 time—because this can actually be subdivided into a repeating pattern of two measures that are easier to count, like 4/4 plus 5/4. When you're first learning a song in an odd time signature, it may be helpful to break the measures down into smaller sections and compare them to more common times signatures like 4/4 or 6/8.

A meter like 5/4 can be thought of as measures of 4/4 with an extra beat added to the end of each measure, as indicated with brackets in the following example.

EXAMPLE 1

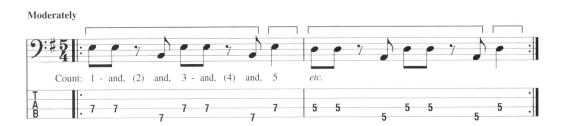

Depending on the bass line and what the drums are playing, 5/4 might also be felt in groups of 3+2 or groups of 2+3. Again, it all depends on the context.

In the example below, it might help to count it out in groups of 2+3, as indicated between the notation and tab staves.

EXAMPLE 2

If the song is in a true grouping of six beats per measure, 6/4 time can be used. If most of the song is in 4/4 and there happens to be a single bar of 6/4 somewhere, it probably should be written out as 4/4 plus an extra bar of 2/4.

Here's an example of a true 6/4 riff, where each measure should feel like one-and-a-half measures of 4/4. The straight drum beat is what classifies this as 6/4 time. Changing the drum beat could easily make this example feel like 12/8 or 6/8.

EXAMPLE 3

You can think of 7/4 time in a few different ways. You might feel it as straight 4/4 with the last beat of every other measure cut off. Divide 7/4 time into either 3+4 or 4+3, as shown below.

EXAMPLE 4

Usually, 5/8 time will be grouped to feel like an eighth note short of 6/8. You can count it as "one, two, three, four, five," but the emphasis will normally be on beats 1 and 4, just like in 6/8. As with the other odd time signatures, this is subjective and it depends on the context.

EXAMPLE 5

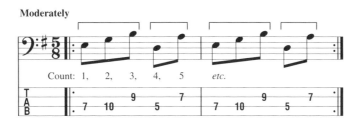

Typically, 7/8 time will feel like an eighth note short of 4/4. If you group the eighth notes as 4+3, the downbeats will be placed in the same location as in 4/4 time, on beats 1 and 3. This can be counted so that the first part of the measure feels like half a bar of 4/4, and the remaining three eighth notes will feel like half a bar of 6/8.

EXAMPLE 6

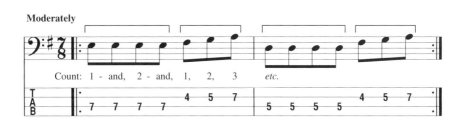

LESSON #33: DORIAN MODE

One of the most popular modal scales is Dorian, the second mode of the major scale. If we were to play one octave of the major scale, starting on the second step of the scale, it would give us that major key's relative Dorian mode. For example, in the chart below, which uses the notes from the C major scale (all natural notes), you can see that the D Dorian mode has its own unique series of whole steps and half steps.

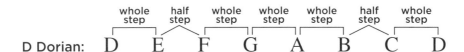

Let's take a look at the A Dorian mode, a more commonly used key. We can use two different methods to figure out what the notes of the scale should be: by starting on the note A and using the half step/whole step formula or by determining what the relative major key is to A Dorian in order to get the key signature. Since Dorian starts on the second step of the major scale, and A is the second step of G major, then the key signature for A Dorian will be the same as the key signature for G major—one sharp, F♯.

Your goal should be to learn to play the Dorian mode in every position on the fretboard, allowing you to improvise or create bass parts in Dorian anywhere on the neck. The following six scale patterns cover the fretboard from open position to 12th position. The root notes are indicated in the scale diagrams by white dots.

EXAMPLE 1

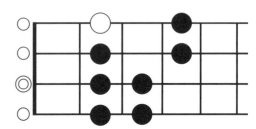

EXAMPLE 2

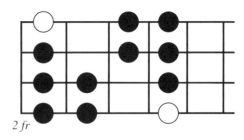

EXAMPLE 3

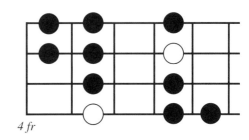

EXAMPLE 4

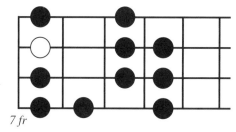

7 fr

EXAMPLE 5

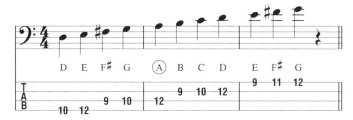
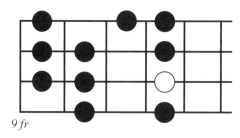

9 fr

EXAMPLE 6

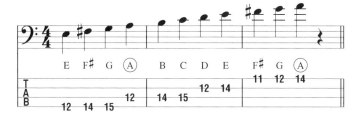
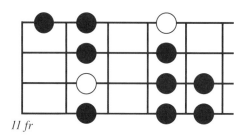

11 fr

Since the Dorian mode contains a minor 3rd, it is considered a minor-sounding scale and can sometimes be used in minor keys, depending on the chord progression. The Dorian mode is very closely related to the minor scale; the only note that's different is the sixth step, which is a half step higher than the sixth step of the minor scale.

The chart below compares the A minor scale with the A Dorian mode.

	1	2	♭3	4	5	♭6	♭7	8 (1)
A Minor:	A	B	C	D	E	F	G	A

	1	2	♭3	4	5	6	♭7	8 (1)
A Dorian:	A	B	C	D	E	F♯	G	A

You'll almost never encounter modal key signatures in rock music. Instead, a minor key signature will be used to indicate a basic minor tonality. When Dorian is being used, there will be accidentals present in the notation, showing that the scale is being altered to Dorian. In the case of A Dorian, it will be written in the key of A minor (no sharps or flats) and F♯s will be present in the music, indicating that the sixth step has been raised a half step. This tells you that the song (or that part of the song) is in A Dorian.

Here are a few bass parts in A Dorian that have been notated in the standard A minor key signature:

EXAMPLE 7

EXAMPLE 8

LESSON #34: MIXOLYDIAN MODE

Mixolydian is the fifth mode of the major scale. If we play one octave of the major scale, starting on the fifth step of the scale, it gives us that major key's relative Mixolydian scale. For example, in the chart below, which uses the notes of the C major scale (no sharps or flats), you can see that the G Mixolydian mode has its own unique series of whole steps and half steps.

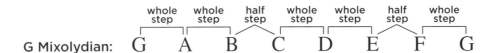

Let's take a look at the Mixolydian mode in A. We can use two different methods to figure out what the notes of the scale should be: by starting on the note A and using the half step/whole step formula or by determining what A Mixolydian's relative major key is in order to get the key signature. Since Mixolydian starts on the fifth step of the major scale, and A is the fifth step of D major, then the key signature for A Mixolydian will be the same as the key signature for D major—two sharps, F♯ and C♯.

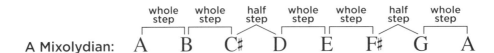

The following six scale patterns enable you to play the A Mixolydian mode anywhere on the fretboard from open position to 12th position. The root notes are indicated in the scale diagrams by white dots.

EXAMPLE 1

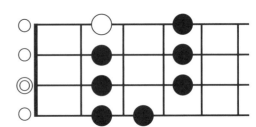

EXAMPLE 2

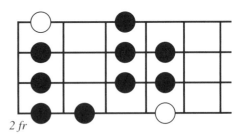

2 fr

EXAMPLE 3

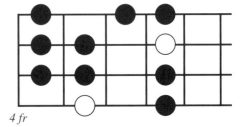

4 fr

EXAMPLE 4

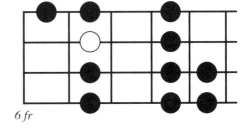

6 fr

EXAMPLE 5

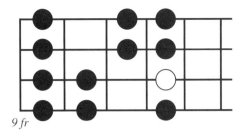

EXAMPLE 6

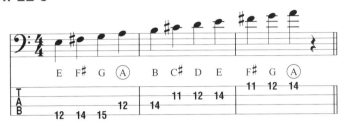
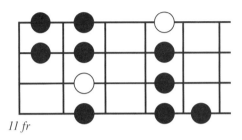

Since the Mixolydian mode contains a major 3rd, it is considered a major-sounding scale and can be sometimes used in major keys. The only difference between the Mixolydian mode and the major scale is that the Mixolydian mode contains a ♭7th, which makes it ideal to play in most major blues songs and against dominant seventh chords.

The chart below compares the A major scale with the A Mixolydian mode.

	1	2	3	4	5	6	7	8 (1)
A Major:	A	B	C♯	D	E	F♯	G♯	A
	1	2	3	4	5	6	♭7	8 (1)
A Mixolydian:	A	B	C♯	D	E	F♯	G	A

If the Mixolydian mode is being used in a rock song, a major key signature will probably be used, with accidentals added in the notation to lower the 7th, indicating that the scale is being altered to Mixolydian. In the case of A Mixolydian, it will be written in the key of A major (three sharps) and G naturals will be present in the music, indicating that the seventh step has been lowered a half step. This tells you that the song (or that part of the song) is in A Mixolydian.

The examples below, written in the key of A major and with the 7ths lowered a half step in the notation, showcase some bass lines that use A Mixolydian.

EXAMPLE 7

EXAMPLE 8

LESSON #35: LOCRIAN MODE

The Locrian mode is the darkest and most sinister mode. It didn't get much play until the darker heavy metal bands from the '80s, like Metallica and Slayer, popularized it. The Locrian mode has become very popular in heavy metal and is mostly used for riff-based music. Locrian is the seventh mode of the major scale. If we were to play one octave of the major scale, starting on the seventh step of the scale, it would give us that major key's relative Locrian mode. For example, in the chart below, which uses the notes of the C major scale (all natural notes), you can see that the B Locrian mode has its own unique series of whole steps and half steps.

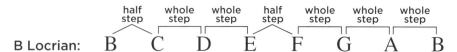

Let's take a look at the Locrian mode in E, the most commonly used key. We can use two different methods to figure out what the notes of the scale should be: by starting on the note E and using the half step/whole step formula above or by determining what the relative major key is to E Locrian in order to get the key signature. Since Locrian starts on the seventh step of the major scale, and E is the seventh step of F major, then the key signature for E Locrian will be the same as the key signature for F major—one flat, B♭.

By learning how to play the E Locrian mode in every position on the fretboard, you'll be able to create bass parts and riffs in Locrian anywhere on the neck. The following six scale patterns cover the fretboard from open position to 12th position. The root notes are indicated in the scale diagrams by white dots.

EXAMPLE 1

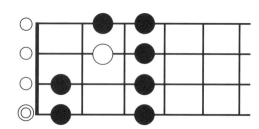

EXAMPLE 2

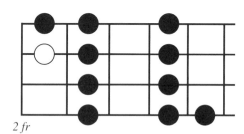

2 fr

EXAMPLE 3

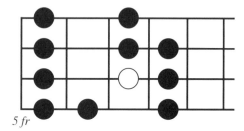

5 fr

EXAMPLE 4

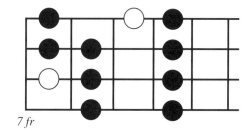

7 fr

EXAMPLE 5

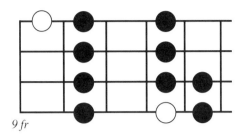

EXAMPLE 6

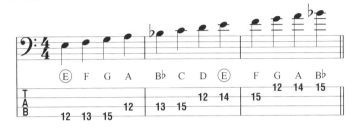
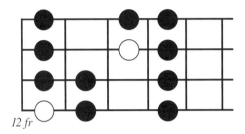

Since the Locrian mode contains a minor 3rd, it is considered a minor-sounding scale. The Locrian mode is somewhat closely related to the minor scale because it contains the minor 3rd, but what gives the Locrian its distinct tonality are the lowered 2nd and 5th.

The chart below compares the E minor scale with the E Locrian mode.

	1	*2*	*♭3*	*4*	*5*	*♭6*	*♭7*	*8 (1)*
E Minor:	E	F♯	G	A	B	C	D	E

	1	*♭2*	*♭3*	*4*	*♭5*	*♭6*	*♭7*	*8 (1)*
E Locrian:	E	F	G	A	B♭	C	D	E

You'll almost never encounter songs notated in a Locrian key signature. Instead, a minor key signature will be used to indicate a basic minor tonality. When Locrian is being used, accidentals will be present in the notation, indicating that the scale is being altered to Locrian. In the case of E Locrian, the mode will be written in the key of E minor (one sharp, F♯), but F naturals and B♭s will be present in the music, indicating that the second and fifth steps have been lowered a half step. This tells you that the song (or that part of the song) is in E Locrian.

Here are a couple of riffs in E Locrian that have been notated in the standard E minor key signature:

EXAMPLE 7

Moderately
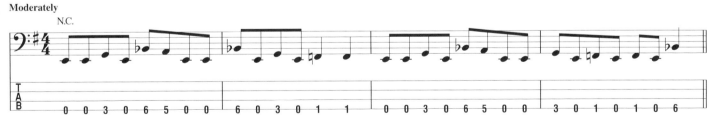

EXAMPLE 8

Moderately slow

LESSON #36: COMMON ROCK PROGRESSIONS

The majority of rock songs are comprised of a series of chords placed in a specific order called a chord progression. First, let's take a look at some basic chord theory so that you'll be able to recognize and apply in any key the following popular chord progressions.

The basic chords in a musical key are created by starting with any specific note in the scale and then stacking every other note of the scale on top of it. For example, using the first note of the C major scale (C), we can add the third note (E) and the fifth note (G) of the scale. This will give us the notes of a C major triad: C–E–G (R–3–5). In this fashion, we can build a chord on every step of the scale. Some chords will be major and some will be minor, depending on which step of the scale the chord is built on. This is true for every major key.

In order to figure out the order of the chords for each key, we use Roman numerals. Uppercase Roman numerals refer to major chords, while lowercase Roman numerals refer to minor chords. The 3rd of each chord determines whether it's major or minor. If we use triads (three-note chords) exclusively, all of the chords will be major or minor in quality, with the only exception being the seventh chord, which is a diminished chord because it contains a diminished 5th.

I	ii	iii	IV	V	vi	vii°
C	Dm	Em	F	G	Am	B°
major	minor	minor	major	major	minor	diminished

Now let's transpose these chords to another key, A major. As you can see, the order of the major and minor chords is exactly the same.

I	ii	iii	IV	V	vi	vii°
A	B	C$\sharp$	D	E	F$\sharp$	G$\sharp$°
major	minor	minor	major	major	minor	diminished

You can also build chords in minor keys by harmonizing the minor scale.

i	ii°	III	iv	v	VI	VII
Am	B°	C	Dm	Em	F	G
minor	diminished	major	minor	minor	major	major

Here is the order of the chords in major and minor keys, shown with only Roman numerals:

Major Keys

major	minor	minor	major	major	minor	diminished
I	ii	iii	IV	V	vi	vii°

Minor Keys

minor	diminished	major	minor	minor	major	major
i	ii°	III	iv	v	VI	VII

Now let's take a look at some of the most popular chord progressions used in rock music. The I–IV–V progression is a classic that's been used since the early days of rock music, and it's still used in many songs today. Most blues songs are based on a I–IV–V progression. It's also not unusual to switch up the progression a little, both rhythmically and with the order and duration of the chords. Classic songs like "Louie Louie" and Joan Jett's "I Love Rock and Roll" are based on I–IV–V progressions.

Here are a couple of ways that the I–IV–V progression can be used:

EXAMPLE 1

EXAMPLE 2

Another popular progression is the I–V–vi–IV, which forms the basis of thousands of pop songs.

EXAMPLE 3

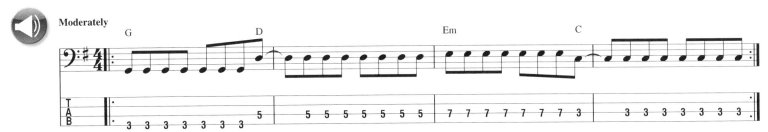

EXAMPLE 4

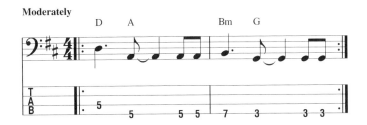

Here's another popular three-chord progression that's often used in major keys: I–♭VII–IV. By lowering the seventh chord one half step, it becomes a major chord.

EXAMPLE 5

Now let's take a look at one of the most popular minor progressions: i–VI–VII–i. This progression is used in many rock songs, but especially in heavy metal songs by bands like Iron Maiden.

EXAMPLE 6

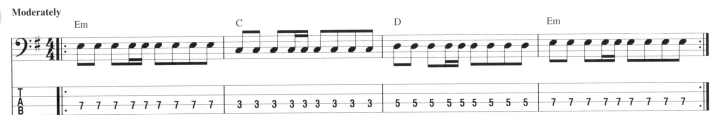

Lastly, here's a variation of the previous chord progression in which the minor v chord is added to the mix. Notice that we've also switched up the order of the chords a bit here, giving us a i–VII–VI–v progression.

EXAMPLE 7

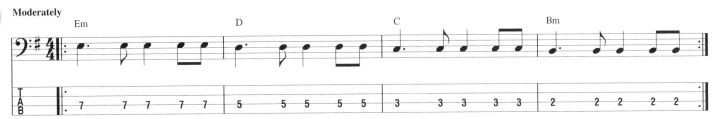

LESSON #37: MELODIC BASS LINES

Adding melody to your bass parts can really compliment the song, the progression, and the flow of the music. In order to accomplish this effectively, you should know your scales and the chord progressions that you're working with, whether they're major or minor chords, and the Roman-numeral analysis that makes up the chord progressions. It isn't too difficult to add a few melodic notes on the fly to connect the chord changes, but you can also spend plenty of time writing intricate bass parts that contain excellent melodic passages.

Let's start with a basic I–IV–V progression in C major so that it's obvious what the scale tones are, since there should be no sharps or flats.

EXAMPLE 1

Chord progressions like the one above are often altered so they're not evenly divided into one-chord-per-measure arrangements. You might also encounter progressions that give you less time to fit in some scale passages, like the one below.

EXAMPLE 2

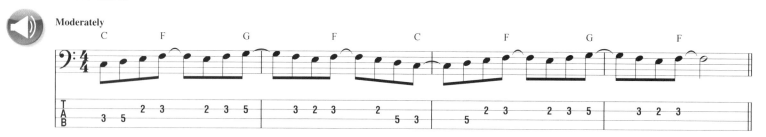

Here are a couple of examples of bass melody added to a simple I–V–vi–IV chord progression:

EXAMPLE 3

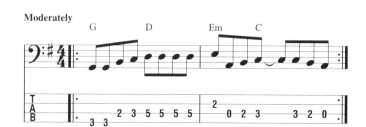

EXAMPLE 4

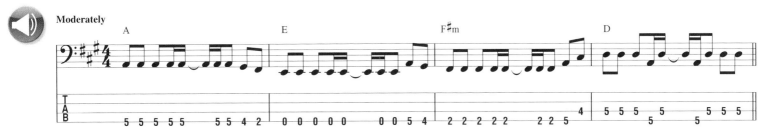

Now let's try some simple ideas with a I–♭VII–IV progression in the key of A. In this example, it's preferable to use some accidentals to help the melody adhere better to each of the major chords, instead of getting some out-of-place major 7ths (G♯). This, in addition to C naturals being used against the G and D chords, actually places the progression into more of an A Dorian key. That said, we can use C♯s on the A chord to keep it sounding major.

EXAMPLE 5

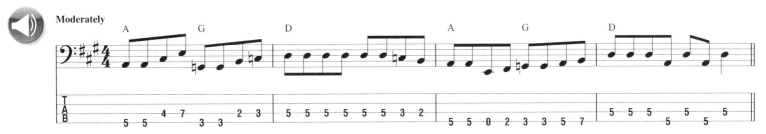

Finally, here are some simple ways to beef up the standard minor i–VI–VII progression in the key of Em by using the notes of the E minor and E minor pentatonic scales.

EXAMPLE 6

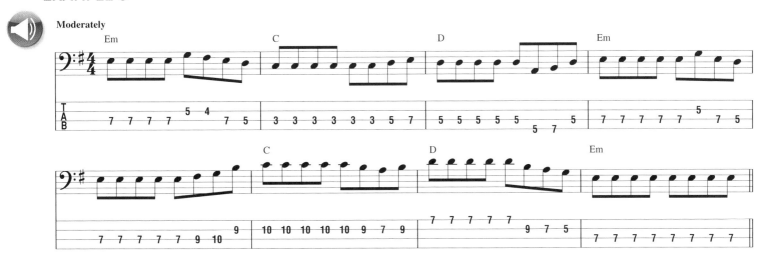

LESSON #38: CHROMATIC PASSING TONES

The use of chromatic notes to connect from chord to chord is very common in bass lines of all styles. Chromatic passing tones can also be used to connect the notes within arpeggios and scales. The most popular chromatic passing tone is the addition of the ♭5th to the minor pentatonic scale, which turns it into the blues scale.

EXAMPLE 1

The example below shows another simple use of chromatic passing tones in an A minor chord progression. The open E acts as both the 5th of the Am chord and as a chromatic note leading into the F chord. There are also short chromatic passages that lead into the G chord and the final Am chord.

EXAMPLE 2

Here's a bass fill that adds a slight variation to the A minor blues scale. In addition to the usual ♭5th passing tone, there's a chromatic passing tone between the octave A and the ♭7th (G).

EXAMPLE 3

Chromatic passing tones work well in combination with arpeggios, too. The following I–V progression is outlined with A major and E major arpeggios, with some additional chromatic passing tones thrown in. In the first measure, the bass line climbs up the A major arpeggio to the 5th, E, which becomes the root of the next chord.

EXAMPLE 4

The same idea can be applied to a I–IV progression, as well. On the D chord, we drop down to the 3rd of the chord (F♯) and then climb chromatically up to the 5th, A, which is the root of the next chord.

EXAMPLE 5

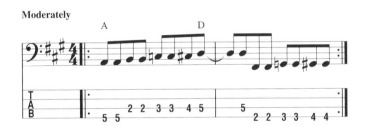

Here's another example using the I–IV progression:

EXAMPLE 6

Here's one more example using the I–V progression. Notice that the root notes are placed in a couple of different octaves.

EXAMPLE 7

LESSON #39: HARMONICS

There are several different techniques that you can use to create harmonics on the bass. The most common is the natural harmonic, which is played by lightly resting a fret-hand finger on the string at a specific point (without actually pressing down and fretting the note) and then plucking the string with the pluck hand. If you place your fret-hand finger in exactly the right spot, it will ring out as a chime-like, higher-pitched note. Once you pluck the string and the harmonic is vibrating, it will sustain even when you take your fret hand away.

Every note on an instrument produces what are called overtones. Overtones are a series of harmonics that naturally exist above any fundamental note that is played. When you play a natural harmonic, the vibrating string gets divided into exact fractions of the full length of the string, which subtracts out the fundamental note of the open string and produces the isolated harmonic overtones. For example, the lowest harmonic is the 12th-fret harmonic, which is an octave higher than the pitch of the open string. The 12th fret is exactly half the distance from the nut to the bridge. When you play a 12th-fret harmonic, instead of the entire length of the string vibrating, a dead spot is created at the 12th fret—called a node—and the string vibrates in two equal sections.

For useful applications, the lower part of the overtone series is made up of the notes of a dominant seventh chord, spread out over several octaves. Once you know the overtone series for each of the four open strings, you'll know all of the useful harmonics that can be played in standard tuning on the bass.

Here is the harmonic overtone series for each of the four open strings. Harmonics are indicated by diamond-shaped noteheads.

EXAMPLE 1

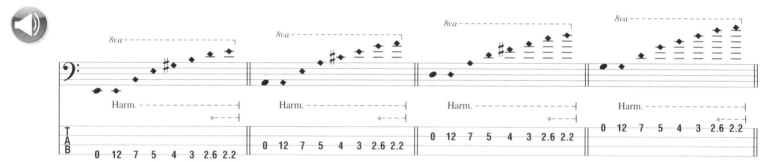

*Harmonics located between 2nd & 3rd frets.

Here's a fretboard diagram of the first seven frets of the bass that shows the most commonly used harmonics (the 12th-fret harmonics are simply one octave higher than the open strings). Although not shown here, there are multiple places on the neck to play some of these harmonics, but with some experimentation, you may come across a few more harmonic hotspots that you'll want to use. Notice that the exact locations of the harmonics are shown. For the harmonics right on the fret lines, place your finger directly above the fret wire, rather than behind it.

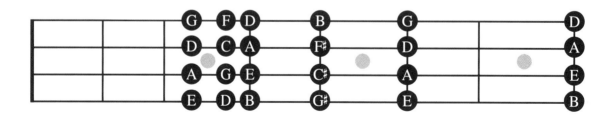

Once you know where the harmonics are located, you can also use them to play chords or scales. Here's an example of a B minor scale using only harmonics.

EXAMPLE 2

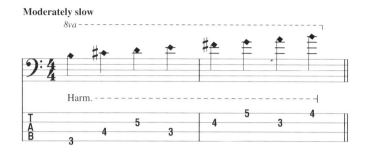

It takes a grasp of some basic music theory to build your own chords from natural harmonics, and you are somewhat limited to the notes in the previous chart, but there are plenty of possibilities.

The example below contains a few chords to get you started. If you're mixing regular notes and harmonics together, it will be difficult to strike them at the same time and get a proper attack. Instead, fret and hold the normal note first, letting it ring while adding the harmonics above it.

EXAMPLE 3

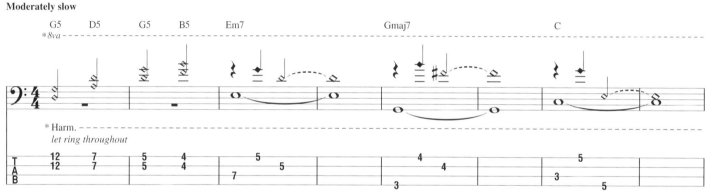

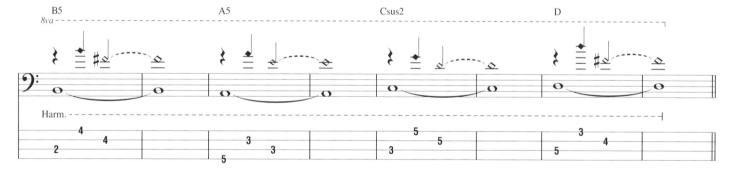

Playing strong, audible harmonics in a live band setting can prove challenging for a bass player. The higher the harmonics are in pitch, the fewer overtones are available above them, making them increasingly softer. Distortion really brings out harmonics well, but if you normally play with a very clean tone, you'll need to use a compressor to hear the higher harmonics. Also, once you change the tuning of the bass, all of the natural harmonics change as well. For example, if you're in drop D tuning, the harmonics on the fourth string will be the notes of a D7 chord.

You can also play artificial or tapped harmonics, enabling you to play harmonics above fretted notes, instead of just using the open strings. These harmonics will definitely be softer and more challenging to execute, but with the proper gear and effects, anything is possible.

To play a tapped harmonic, simply fret any note and tap the string hard with a pluck-hand finger exactly 12 frets higher than the fretted note. To play an artificial (or pinch) harmonic, you can use your pluck-hand thumb to produce an artificial node exactly 12 frets above the fretted note. Rest the very tip of your thumb in place on the string, plucking the string with your index finger with intensity. Artificial harmonics are not limited to just 12 frets above the fretted note—or on the fretboard, for that matter. You can create an artificial harmonic node at any point on the string that's in the harmonic series above the fretted note.

LESSON #40: PAUL McCARTNEY STYLE

Bass players from all styles of rock will cite Paul McCartney as one of their influences, not only for his playing, but for his perfect melodic songwriting instincts, which he also applied when constructing his bass lines.

Like the Beatles' music, Sir Paul's bass playing evolved throughout the '60s and continued to do so throughout his years with Wings and his solo career. McCartney is one of the most famous pick players (he started out playing guitar and switched to bass in the very early years of the Beatles out of necessity). Still, he's never played bass like a guitar player, as many guitarists turned bassists do. His bass lines are filled with melody, walking, and groove, all surrounded in a warm, round, thumping tone and a brilliant back beat inspired by the original rock and R&B greats. McCartney's bass of choice is the violin-shaped, hollowbodied Hofner bass that he made famous. The Hofner is often referred to as the "Beatle bass."

As a songwriter, McCartney is a master of melody, and this translates to his bass lines, too. He's constantly using scale passages to seamlessly connect the chords in a progression, and will often use inversions, playing the 3rds or 5ths in the bass to achieve a linear, melodic line. McCartney also makes great rhythmic choices to distinguish different sections of songs, to emphasize certain chords within a progression, and to keep the rhythm in between lyrics and vocal phrases flowing and interesting.

This first example illustrates McCartney's great walking instincts and is typical of his playing on the Beatles' early works. It starts off with a continuous scale that descends seamlessly through the first two chords of the progression. From there, it alternates from outlining the arpeggios to simple root–5th patterns.

EXAMPLE 1

In this next example, Paul plays a pumping, arpeggiated eighth-note line, but keeps it interesting by shifting the downbeat back a half beat in the bass, to the "and" of beat 4, even though the guitar, drums, and vocals all remain anchored to beat 1.

EXAMPLE 2

During the *Rubber Soul* and *Revolver* era, Paul often would come up with a pentatonic riff and transpose it for each chord of the progression. This idea can be heard in "Day Tripper," "Drive My Car," and "Taxman."

EXAMPLE 3

McCartney was also a master of writing great bass parts that would end up becoming the hook of the song. Below is a riff reminiscent of the famous bass part in "Come Together."

EXAMPLE 4

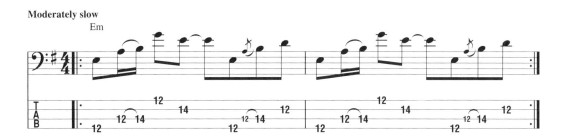

The next example showcases Paul's excellent melodic and rhythmic instincts. In the first measure, he plays the 5th of the Bm chord, F♯, in lieu of the root note in order to create a descending melody in the bass. In this example, the vocals would sing for six beats and then rest for two. You can see that McCartney slides in some subtle syncopation between the vocal phrases, at the end of the second and fourth measures.

EXAMPLE 5

Lastly, here's an interesting example in which the pedaled low D is placed directly on the backbeats (beats 2 and 4) and the bass notes of the chords are played as a melody in the upper octave. This is often the opposite of what most bass players would do in similar situations.

EXAMPLE 6

LESSON #41: JOHN PAUL JONES STYLE

The great, unsung hero of the mighty Led Zeppelin was John Paul Jones, the man who received the least attention for often doing the most work. Besides being one of rock's most influential bass players, Jones is also a keyboardist, producer, and master arranger who plays a host of other versatile instruments. He spent most of the '60s as a session player and arranger, and his string arrangements can be heard on famous tracks such as "She's a Rainbow" by the Rolling Stones and "Sunshine Superman" by Donovan. Much of Led Zeppelin's groove in the early days can be attributed to Jones' and drummer John Bonham's appreciation for Motown and James Brown. When performing live with Led Zeppelin, Jones would split his time between playing incredibly complex bass lines and playing the keyboards with bass pedals—a move that undoubtedly inspired future keyboard/bass players like Geddy Lee.

Jones generally favored the Fender Jazz bass for most of his time in Led Zeppelin, eventually switching to Alembic basses. He is a master of improvisation who didn't relegate himself to duplicating the recorded bass lines in concert, and it's been said that some of the great bass lines on the Zeppelin albums were done in one take.

This first example is inspired by the chorus section of "Communication Breakdown." Oftentimes, Jones doubles the guitar riff and plays simple root notes throughout the verses, but when the chorus hits, he takes off running. Check out this fast walking line that alternates between arpeggios with passing tones and pentatonic riffs.

EXAMPLE 1

John Paul Jones was adept at coming up with great melodic bass hooks that breathe life into mellow verses. This passage is similar to the verses in "Ramble On."

EXAMPLE 2

This next example is a classic metal-style Zeppelin riff that the guitar and bass might play together.

EXAMPLE 3

Here's another arpeggiated blues figure with some riffs thrown in to make it more interesting. In cases like this, Jones would usually set up a basic motif and use it as a starting point, then alter it and liven it up throughout the song.

EXAMPLE 4

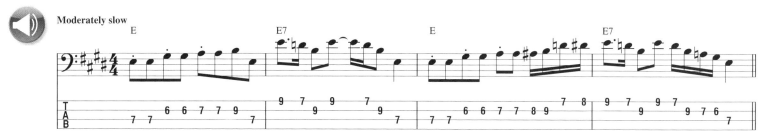

Sometimes, Zeppelin could get pretty funky with their metal-style riffs. Here is a fast and challenging pattern reminiscent of the bass lines found on their later albums *Physical Graffiti* and *Presence*:

EXAMPLE 5

Led Zeppelin was also known for their ripping heavy metal rhythms that helped to serve as a showcase for drummer John Bonham. These gallop-style rhythms no doubt influenced future bands like Iron Maiden and Metallica.

EXAMPLE 6

LESSON #42: JOHN ENTWISTLE STYLE

Nicknamed "The Ox," the Who's John Entwistle is considered by many to be one of the greatest rock bass players of all time. His bright treble tone and active fingerstyle technique gave his playing one of the most unique and recognizable bass sounds ever recorded. Entwistle used all four fingers of his pluck hand to rake the strings and deliver lightning-fast runs and riffs. From the early days of the Who, Entwistle cemented his place in bass history with the famous solo section in "My Generation," which showcased his style and monstrous distorted sound. His busy, syncopated playing style clashed considerably with drummer Keith Moon's over-the-top theatrical style, yet somehow they came together to create a brilliant and creative rhythm section. It's been jokingly stated that Entwistle didn't play in the pocket; he played the whole pair of pants. For most bass players, this approach could easily cause a train wreck, but Entwistle's melodic choices and early musical training gave him the ability to take risks and achieve great results that always fit perfectly with the song and the rhythm section.

This first example shows how Entwistle used the pluck-hand raking technique to beef up a simple I–IV–V progression. At first listen, it might come across a little sloppy, but the rhythmic choices, 16th notes and 16th-note triplets, are intentional and compliment Keith Moon's busy drumming style.

EXAMPLE 1

Here's a melodic example in the key of A, played over a simple IV–I chord change. By using the A major pentatonic scale in a descending melody, the 3rd of the D chord (F♯) is featured at the beginning of each phrase.

EXAMPLE 2

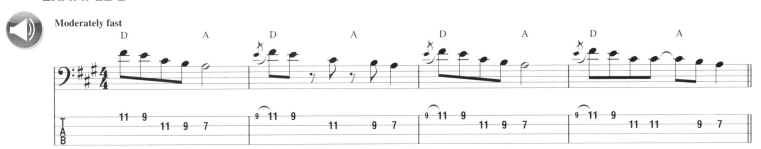

Here's something similar to the unique rhythm played during a solo section of "Won't Get Fooled Again." The bass is able to keep the groove moving by simply outlining the chords with roots and 5ths.

EXAMPLE 3

This next example is in the style of the bass line to "Pinball Wizard," on which Entwistle plays a repeated pattern based on the pentatonic scale, and then transposes it to follow the descending chord progression.

EXAMPLE 4

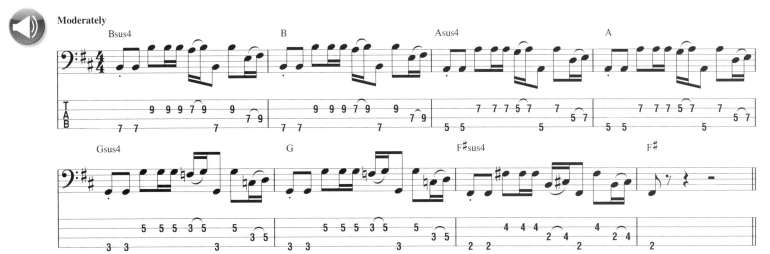

One of Entwistle's greatest bass showcases is the song "The Real Me," from the album *Quadrophenia*. Entwistle plays fills throughout the song, in between the vocal lines, and the intro and middle sections have minor pentatonic and blues scale solos that span the entire range of the instrument.

Below is just a taste of minor pentatonic soloing in this style.

EXAMPLE 5

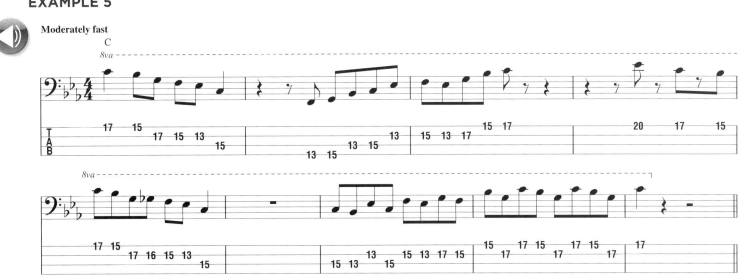

LESSON #43: GEDDY LEE STYLE

Throughout his four-decade career with Rush, Geddy Lee has attained recognition as arguably the greatest rock bass player of all time. Geddy's sound and playing style have evolved dramatically over the course of the band's discography. Rush will always be considered by many to be a progressive rock band, but there are many elements of hard rock, funk, ska, and heavy metal in their music as well.

Geddy's style can be generally broken down into three distinct eras that coincide with the band's evolution, and these periods overlap to a great extent. The first era is characterized by epic progressive rock pieces, odd time signatures, long instrumentals, and concept albums like *2112*. This period ends and the next one begins around the time of one of their greatest achievements, the release of their landmark album *Moving Pictures* (1981), which saw the band focused on writing shorter, more commercially accessible songs. Their first commercial hit, "The Spirit of Radio," from the previous album, *Permanent Waves*, foreshadowed this direction. In the first period of the band's evolution, Geddy largely played a Rickenbacker bass and went for a bright, crisp, midrange sound with a nice low-end growl. Beginning with *Moving Pictures*, Geddy started to use a Fender Jazz bass as well. He was also using a standard two-finger plucking technique.

Here's an example of a progressive rock riff that the bass and guitar might play in unison, written in one of the bands favorite odd time signatures, 7/8. This riff is in B Phrygian, as Geddy favored modal scales over pentatonics.

EXAMPLE 1

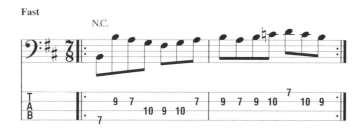

One signature element of Geddy's playing is the use of strategic, quick 16th-note jabs sprinkled within regular eighth-note bass fills, whereby he'll double down on a note in the scale and give it that extra kick. Here's an example of it in a D Mixolydian bass fill:

EXAMPLE 2

Around the time of *Moving Pictures*, guitarist Alex Lifeson began incorporating more and more sus2 chords into the progressions. Geddy addressed these by substituting his octaves with 9ths, and it became one of his great melodic signatures at the time. Bass lines that use this device can be heard in "YYZ" and "The Camera Eye."

EXAMPLE 3

Rush followed *Moving Pictures* with the 1982 album *Signals*, which ushered the band into a new era that would last for about a decade. This coincided with the beginning of the MTV era, when new wave and ska bands like the Police were ruling the charts. Most progressive rock bands had begun churning out commercial hits in lieu of 10-minute opuses. It was also the beginning of a technological revolution in regard to synthesizers, keyboards, and sequencers. At this time, Geddy's keyboard playing, which had been used sporadically as an enhancement, began to take center stage. Since the band believed they should arrange the songs in the studio for live performance, Geddy would often play keyboards throughout most of a song while relegating the bass to foot pedals and then split his time between keyboard and bass playing, depending on the section of the song. If there were only a few bass parts in a song, Geddy would make sure to put in some aggressive fills when it came time. This is apparent in songs like "Subdivisions." Geddy also abandoned the Rickenbacker bass and switched to a Steinberger (mostly due to its compact size, since he was playing behind keyboards a lot) and then to a Wal bass.

Here's an example of a ska-style bass line reminiscent of the song "Digital Man."

EXAMPLE 4

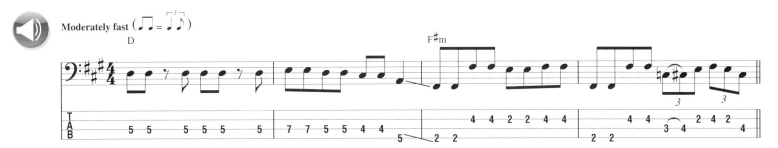

During the '80s, Geddy also began incorporating more chords and double stops, adding the thumb for downstrokes while using a fingerstyle technique. In the following example, the low As on the third string should be playing with the thumb, and the double stops above should be plucked with the index and middle fingers.

EXAMPLE 5

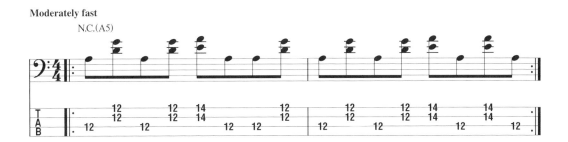

In 1993, Rush took another dramatic step forward by reclaiming their hard rock and power-trio roots with the album *Counterparts*. This began a new era for the band in which Geddy went back to primarily playing the bass and relegating most of the keyboards to sequencers and programmable foot pedals. He also switched back to using the Fender Jazz bass and has played it ever since. His pluck-hand technique also evolved to a newer, unique flamenco style. Using just one finger (or two fingers together), he would pluck the string in both directions; he would pluck the string normally and then flick it again on the back stroke with his fingernail. This enabled him to use his fingers more like a pick, attaining great speed and a unique tone. Although Geddy claims that he just began to play this way naturally and never looked back, it is a difficult technique for most people to get the hang of at first. It's best achieved by using a floating thumb technique, moving the thumb so that it always rests on the string above the one being plucked. Since Geddy plays this way exclusively now, listening to newer live renditions of the older classics on which he's updated the bass lines by applying this technique is great fun.

EXAMPLE 6

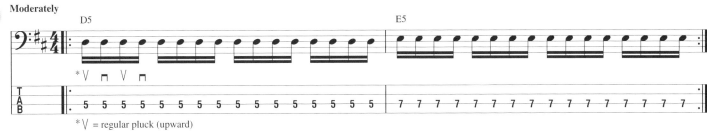

*∨ = regular pluck (upward)

⊓ = reverse pluck (downward)

LESSON #44: CHRIS SQUIRE STYLE

Yes's Chris Squire is one of the quintessential progressive rock bass players. Squire plays exclusively with a pick and favored the trebly Rickenbacker sound throughout the '70s. His bass tone has a specific growl to it due to his picking style, whereby he uses the edge of his thumb to slightly mute the string while striking it with the pick, giving it a bright yet warm tone. Squire is a master at melody and syncopation, weaving his bass lines seamlessly in and out of odd time signatures. He is also a founding member, songwriter, and principle background vocalist in the band, often singing and playing with ease parts that are rhythmically unrelated. Squire has a few great bass showcases on Yes albums, particularly *Fragile*'s "The Fish (Schindleria Praematurus)," which is played exclusively with overdubbed basses, and "Ritual," from *Tales from Topographic Oceans*.

Here's an example of how Squire might use melody and syncopation to connect a chord progression that moves through a few tonal centers.

EXAMPLE 1

This next example is in the style of the walking bass in "Yours Is No Disgrace," which showcases Squire's melodic instincts. The rest of the band drops out and the bass is playing solo but is still able to successfully outline the chord progression on its own.

EXAMPLE 2

Here's an aggressive, hard-driving rock bass line in E minor. This showcases Squire's growling bass tone and picking speed.

EXAMPLE 3

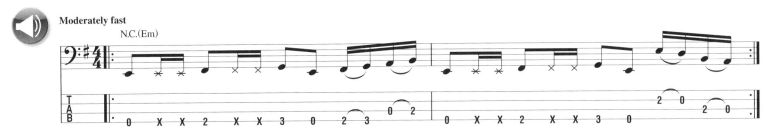

Here's another fast picking technique that Squire has used in numerous songs. He climbs up the neck and outlines the arpeggio, playing steady 16th notes and syncopating the line by periodically reaching up for the higher notes in each phrase.

EXAMPLE 4

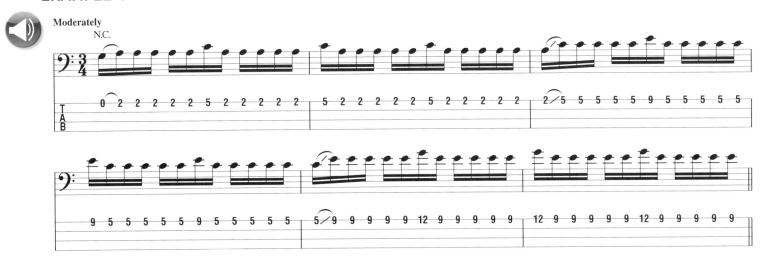

Finally, here's a harmonic bass line in the style of "The Fish." Squire sets up the underlying rhythm of the track by using a repeated harmonic line and then overdubs numerous basses on top of it to complete the track.

EXAMPLE 5

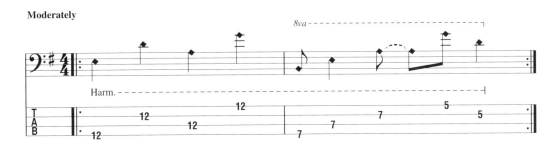

LESSON #45: GEEZER BUTLER STYLE

Black Sabbath's Geezer Butler is basically the godfather of heavy metal bass. His deep, grungy bass tone is the perfect complement to the Sabbath sound and has influenced metal bassists for decades (Metallica's Cliff Burton used distortion and wah-wah in much the same way that Geezer did). Geezer often uses more than two pluck-hand fingers for his fingerstyle technique, which helps him to achieve great speed and stamina. Songs like "Children of the Grave" and "Heaven and Hell" have relentless rhythms that Geezer pulls off with ease. He's a master of the pentatonic and blues scales and is featured in songs like "N.I.B." using wah-wah, pentatonics, and string bending. The original intro to "N.I.B." is a bass solo titled "Bassically," which was featured on Sabbath's debut album and introduced Butler's signature playing to the world.

This first example is a typical slow, sludgy metal riff in E minor. Black Sabbath invented and perfected this riff-based heavy metal style that's been in fashion ever since.

EXAMPLE 1

This next example is in the style of "N.I.B.," on which Geezer plays through distortion and wah and incorporates the classic bend up to the ♭5th.

EXAMPLE 2

Here's an example in the style of the mellow chorus section of "N.I.B.," on which Geezer plays a melodic pentatonic riff and transposes it repeatedly with the descending chord progression.

EXAMPLE 3

This next example is similar to the type of bass line played in "The Wizard." Geezer follows the chord changes and beefs up the bass part by selectively playing a root–5th–octave pattern.

EXAMPLE 4

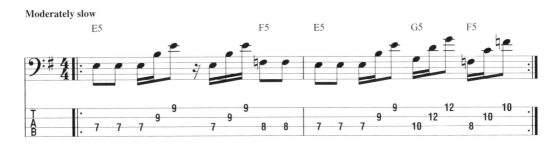

Despite their dark metal sound, Sabbath was influenced by R&B, too. It's not unusual for riffs and songs to be played with a heavy shuffle feel. Here is a bass line similar to part of "Fairies Wear Boots," on which Geezer improvises minor pentatonic and blues scale riffs under the guitar solo.

EXAMPLE 5

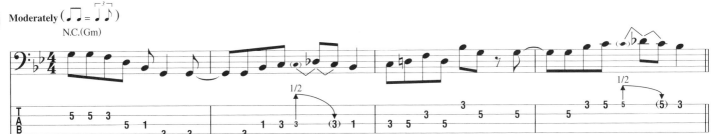

Geezer didn't always double the guitar riffs note for note. In this example, reminiscent of the bass line in the verse of "Into the Void," Geezer plays a driving rhythmic line behind the guitar riff, using lots of hammer-ons and grace-note hammer-ons.

EXAMPLE 6

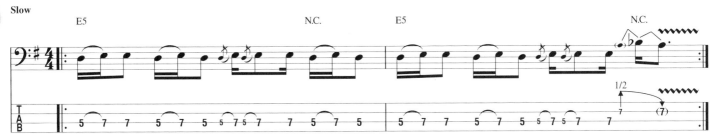

LESSON #46: STEVE HARRIS STYLE

The early '80s, pre-Metallica era of heavy metal was ripe with fresh talent like Ozzy Osbourne, Judas Priest, and AC/DC when Iron Maiden exploded onto the scene. Led by bass hero and principle songwriter Steve Harris, Iron Maiden quickly built a following and catapulted to the top with their third album, *Number of the Beast*. Steve Harris is known for his incredibly fast, strong fingerstyle technique. His signature gallop rhythm has often been imitated, but not duplicated. The biggest misconception is that Harris uses a three-finger technique when, in fact, he has always played with two fingers exclusively. Harris also uses flat-wound strings to glide easily around the neck and give him that recognizable tone. Although his style may sound like it hasn't evolved much over the years, and he's got his stock moves that he uses repeatedly, the one thing that's obvious throughout the Maiden catalog is that he continuously gets faster and faster, leaving most other fingerstyle metal players in the dust. In concert, Harris is nothing but consistent and precise.

Here's an example of Harris' signature gallop rhythm played against a i–VI–VII–i progression. You'll hear this in different keys and at different tempos throughout the Iron Maiden catalog.

EXAMPLE 1

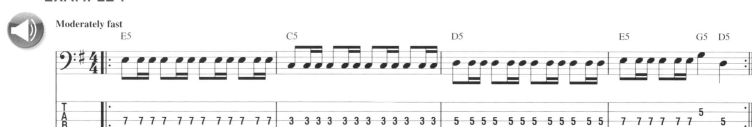

This example of a melodic bass line that moves with the chord changes showcases what can be referred to as the "Steve Harris arpeggio." Instead of using major and minor 3rds, Harris instead opts for the 4th, making the arpeggiated pattern uniform throughout the progression.

EXAMPLE 2

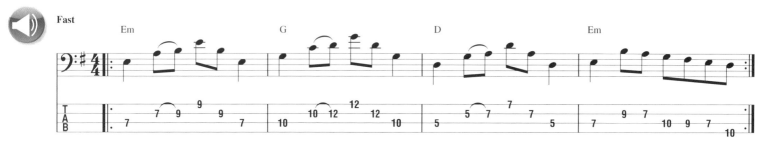

Similar to the 4th substitution above, Harris would sometimes use 2nds instead of minor 3rds in his minor pentatonic bass riffs. This keeps the entire riff in a uniform, 1–3–1–3 finger pattern. Similar riffs can be found in songs like "Two Minutes to Midnight."

EXAMPLE 3

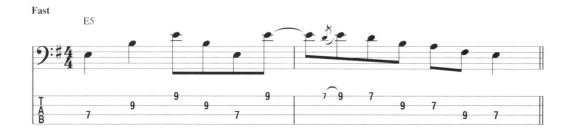

This next riff is in the style of "Aces High" and is a minor scale pattern played at an extremely fast tempo.

EXAMPLE 4

Here's another technique that Harris is fond of using during quieter instrumental sections or the bridge of a song. This riff outlines the D minor scale by pivoting around the open D string and alternately playing the descending scale tones above it (first string) in a syncopated fashion.

EXAMPLE 5

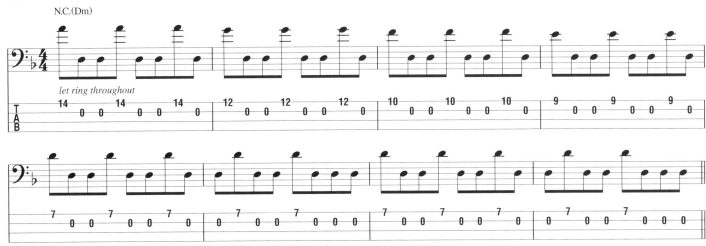

Along the same lines as the previous example, Harris will sometimes incorporate a fingerstyle guitar technique to play a figure similar to the one below. The notes on the second string should be downstroked with the thumb and the notes on the first string should be alternately plucked with the index finger.

EXAMPLE 6

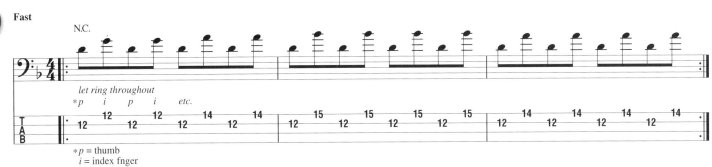

LESSON #47: CLIFF BURTON STYLE

Cliff Burton was one of heavy metal's biggest bass influences of the '80s. Burton died in a tragic accident at age 24, after the release of Metallica's landmark album *Master of Puppets*, but his contribution on just three albums was enough to cement his place in heavy metal history. Burton's stamp on the Metallica sound can still be heard today. He was responsible for convincing the band to abandon the over-saturated Los Angeles glam scene and set up camp in the San Francisco Bay area, enabling them to build their following and evolve in a fresh environment. James Hetfield also credits Burton for teaching him much of what he knows about music theory and harmony, greatly influencing Hetfield's songwriting and arranging. Since much of Metallica's material for their first album was written before Burton joined the band, his influence on the Metallica sound can really be detected all over their second release, *Ride the Lightning*, in the form of harmony leads, instrumental masterpieces, odd time signatures, and slower, dark ballads like "Fade to Black."

Cliff Burton had a monstrous three-finger pluck-hand technique, allowing him to play Metallica's lightning-fast signature riffs with ease. He was also known to use distortion and wah-wah while playing soaring bass riffs and solos in songs like "For Whom the Bell Tolls," "Orion," and his bass showcase masterpiece, "Anesthesia (Pulling Teeth)."

Here's an E Locrian riff that showcases Cliff's rapid three-finger gallop technique. This is a popular Metallica-style figure, reminiscent of the verses in the song "Battery."

EXAMPLE 1

In this next E minor example, the closely related Dorian mode makes an appearance at the end for a tasty bass fill that sets up the accented C#5–B5 power chord punches. It was fairly common for Metallica and Cliff Burton to mix modal scales in this way.

EXAMPLE 2

This next example is inspired by the slow, melodic middle section of the song "Master of Puppets." There are a few interesting things happening here. The 4/4 time signature is bracketed with bars of 2/4, which are dictated by the chord progression. Also notice the B/D♯ chord, which acts as a leading tone to the Em tonic and creates the harmonic minor tonality. The bass is playing root–5th–octave patterns to compliment and coincide with an arpeggiated guitar figure. As the progression repeats, Burton would often improvise different variations of the pattern using arpeggios while accenting any rhythmic variations played by the drums.

EXAMPLE 3

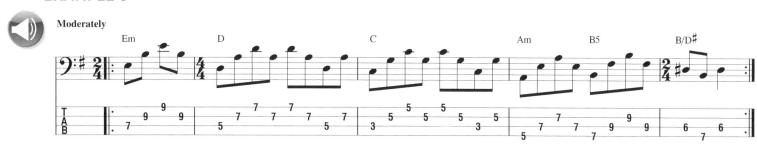

In his bass solos, Cliff Burton often would play arpeggio patterns high up on the fretboard and through distortion and some wah-wah. In "Orion," there's a sweet harmony bass solo that many have mistaken for multiple guitar tracks. These are some of Burton's signature moments, and the band was more than happy to showcase this unique sound in songs like "For Whom the Bell Tolls" and "The Call of Ktulu."

Here's a distortion-fueled arpeggio riff similar to the beginning of Burton's "Anesthesia (Pulling Teeth)":

EXAMPLE 4

LESSON #48: BILLY SHEEHAN STYLE

Billy Sheehan is one of the most unique and impressive rock bassists. Billy cut his teeth with his band Talas, from the Buffalo, New York area, and spent the '70s building a name for himself, often being billed as the "Best Bass Player in the World." Talas was eventually picked to open for Van Halen, and after David Lee Roth left VH to go solo, he enlisted Billy Sheehan to play alongside Steve Vai in a two-man technical assault that was one of the showcase gems of the '80s era of shredders. Before that, anyone lucky enough to have stumbled across Sheehan playing the clubs in those early days was treated to a shocking surprise—lightning-fast bass runs, incredible playing technique, two-handed tapping that had only been seen on guitar up till that point, screaming harmonics, and a perfect in-the-pocket groove, all wrapped up in a face-melting killer bass tone.

Much of Billy's bass "pyrotechniques" were made possible by his custom homemade basses and rigs. He would use two output jacks on his basses, giving an individual output to each of the pickups. Much more efficient than traditional bi-amping with a crossover, the dual output enabled him to run each pickup to an independent amp and effects line, giving him complete control over every aspect of his tone. It produced a sweet chorus effect, and with the use of tons of high-end compression, he could run the bridge pickup to a (primarily) treble channel and add some distortion to bring out all of the overtones, harmonics, and two-handed tapping. The neck pickup could then be run independently to a full bass tone without distortion, keeping the overall sound punchy and bright, with a clean bottom end.

Sheehan would often cap off a bass fill with a wailing high harmonic and add some vibrato or a bend by pushing on the back of the neck. After striking the harmonic, grab the top cutaway with your pluck hand for stability and then push on the back of the neck with your fret hand.

EXAMPLE 1

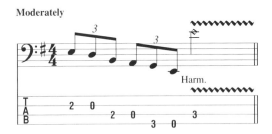

Here's a simple two-handed tapping run based on the E minor scale. In order to get these runs to work sonically in a band, you'll need to exhibit much more pluck-hand force than a guitar player, and a good compressor is essential.

EXAMPLE 2

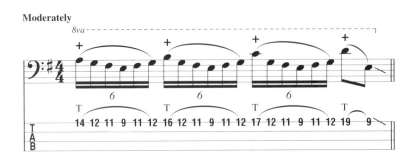

Here's another tapping trick that Billy used to play blindingly fast trills. By alternating between hammering on with the third finger and tapping with the pluck hand, trills can be played twice as fast, for an impressive effect.

EXAMPLE 3

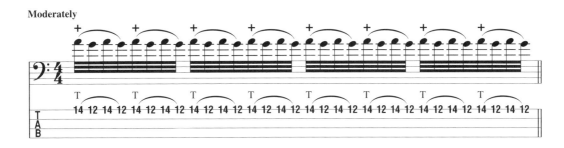

Sheehan is also adept at playing artificial harmonic runs by tapping the strings one octave above the fretted notes. Using your middle finger to perform tapping harmonics will give you more control and a firmer attack.

EXAMPLE 4

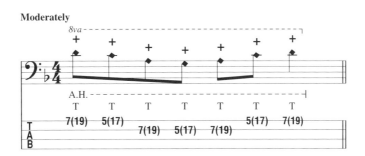

Sheehan's command of scales and scale patterns is apparent in his phrasing. Instead of playing simple up-and-down scale patterns or typical ascending and descending groups of three or four notes, he will often jump around the scale patterns in box-like groupings, coming up with very unique-sounding fills.

EXAMPLE 5

LESSON #49: TOM HAMILTON STYLE

One of the great unsung bass heroes of classic rock is Aerosmith's Tom Hamilton. Rock bass players since the '70s have claimed Hamilton as a big influence due to his excellent instincts, rock-solid groove, and pocket playing. He manages to blend in perfectly with the Aerosmith sound and always contributes to the song without overplaying or underplaying. Hamilton also co-wrote some of Aerosmith's greatest songs, including "Sweet Emotion," "Sick as a Dog," and "Janie's Got a Gun."

Hamilton learned a bit of guitar at a very early age but quickly picked up the bass by age 14 because the band that he wanted to join needed a bass player. He doesn't consider himself a guitar player turned bass player, but his early exposure to the guitar helped to shape the way he approached playing the bass. Since he didn't spend much time learning classic bass lines, note for note, his ear tends to gravitate towards the song and the arrangement, rather than to the bass parts. Because of this, he was able to create his bass lines without much conscious influence from specific bass players that preceded him. Nevertheless, Hamilton is a master at creating heavy groove bass lines from the major and minor pentatonic scales, blues scale, and arpeggiated walking bass lines. He is also one of the few bass players that will switch between fingerstyle and using a pick and is equally comfortable with both, enabling him to get a great R&B tone with his fingers or to play bright and steady 16th notes with a pick.

Aerosmith started out as a blues-based band, and blues jams and rhythm styles are prevalent throughout their early career. The following example is played with a blues shuffle feel at a steady tempo. The last measure is a great example of how Hamilton might sneak in a great bass fill.

EXAMPLE 1

The following example, played with a pick, is a steady, pumping 16th-note pedal like the one featured in "Lord of the Thighs." Hamilton has used this idea over steady drum beats in many different songs, often for a long intro or solo section. Keeping the groove in the pocket throughout requires some stamina.

EXAMPLE 2

This next bass fill begins with a tasteful pentatonic phrase and then shoots up the neck to play some pumping 16th notes at the octave, accented with grace-note hammer-ons. Fills like this have undoubtedly influenced many of Hamilton's contemporaries. Duff McKagan uses the exact same phrasing for the intro to the Guns N' Roses song "It's So Easy."

EXAMPLE 3

Aerosmith was also great at fast heavy metal tracks. This next riff, similar to "Toys in the Attic," is played at a very fast tempo and takes some steady pluck-hand coordination and strength to pull it off. Practice this slowly and with a metronome.

EXAMPLE 4

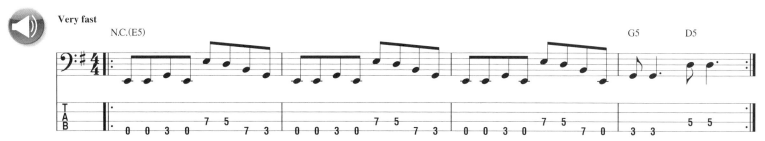

Hamilton created some great bass hooks, including quite possibly the most famous one of all time, the intro to "Sweet Emotion," the stylistic template for this next riff. The similar tone and vibe may have been inspired by Paul McCartney's great bass line in "Come Together."

EXAMPLE 5

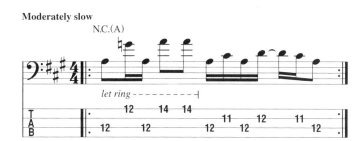

This last example is a funky rhythm in the style of the bass line to "Walk This Way." In the last measure, the bass slides up the neck to inject a tasty blues-scale riff.

EXAMPLE 6

LESSON #50: FLEA STYLE

One of the last great bass heroes of the 20th century is Flea from the Red Hot Chili Peppers. An expert at combining rock and punk influences with '70s funk, Flea earned a reputation as an energetic rock slapper, but his playing style has evolved and he has all but abandoned slapping on their later releases. Flea's playing is now defined by a rich, warm, melodic improvisational style, a perfect complement to the Chili Peppers' redefinition of the California rock sound.

Many musicians have been influenced by Flea's playing, most notably the bands out of the '90s Southern California beach scene, like No Doubt and Sublime. Growing up, Flea first played trumpet and was influenced by all of the jazz greats, and this background can be heard everywhere in his approach to the bass. Although Flea has constructed some great melodic bass lines and hooks, and will duplicate these live, when he's improvising over the changes, he tends to lay back quite a bit in the studio and go for a firm pocket with a "less is more" attitude. However, when you see him live, it's on! Rarely does he duplicate much of the bass fills from the recordings; instead, he improvises flawlessly and holds nothing back. He's also apt to cut loose and get a little busier when he's sitting in on other artists' recordings or laying down the bass for a one-off Chili Peppers track for a film soundtrack, like on Alanis Morissette's "You Oughta Know" or the Chili Peppers' "Soul to Squeeze."

This first example is a standard slapping figure in E minor with a shuffle feel. The triplet riff at the end of each measure uses two different techniques, one with a hammer-on and the other with a slide and pop at the end.

EXAMPLE 1

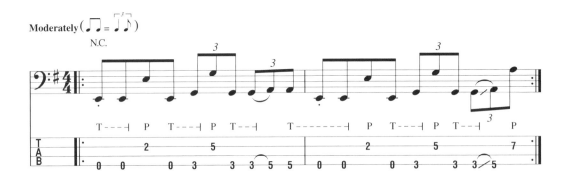

Around the time of the *Californication* album, Flea began to write more melodic bass lines that work as a repeated hook during verses or choruses. This next example is in the style of the title track to that album.

EXAMPLE 2

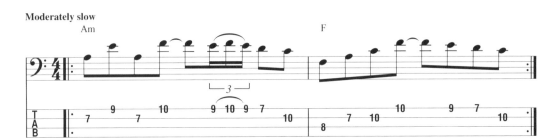

Even though Flea stopped using slap technique, he still played with an extremely funky style reminiscent of '70s funk players like Bootsy Collins. This next example jumps up and down the neck dramatically, playing riffs pulled from the G Dorian mode.

EXAMPLE 3

Here's another funky example using a fast 16th-note rhythm. This is a rhythm that Flea might establish as a hook and play repeatedly throughout the verses of a song.

EXAMPLE 4

This next example is in the style of "Dani California" and shows how Flea would play over a simple minor progression and added some tasty melodic runs using the minor pentatonic scale.

EXAMPLE 5

Around the time of the *Stadium Arcadium* album, Flea began using major and minor 10th intervals to bring out some nice melody in the bass. The 10ths are just major and minor 3rds played an octave higher. Whereas most bass players would typically play simple octaves, Flea opts for the more melodic wider intervals.

EXAMPLE 6

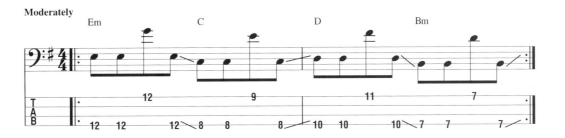

LESSON #51: 3RDS AND 10THS

The 3rd is arguably the most commonly utilized interval for harmonizing, and 10ths are simply 3rds played an octave higher. In this lesson, we'll learn how both intervals can be used either to add harmony to a single-note bass line or to function as building blocks for riffs.

First, let's play through a couple of exercises to get acquainted with how 3rds fall along the fretboard. The example below shows the C major scale harmonized in 3rds.

EXAMPLE 1

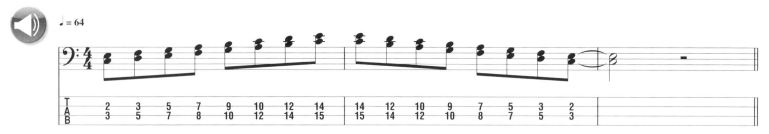

Now let's plug our knowledge of 3rds into some bass licks. In the following example, we're going to build a metal riff by moving minor 3rd intervals up and down the D and A strings, setting them against the open E string to create a single linear bass line.

EXAMPLE 2

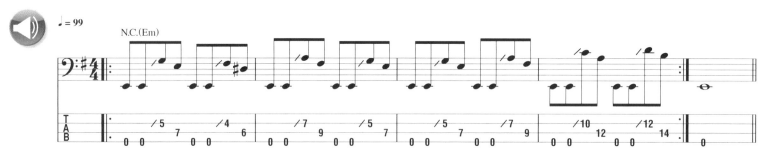

Similarly, this next line, inspired by Pearl Jam's Jeff Ament and Rush's Geddy Lee, moves a combination of major and minor 3rd intervals around the fretboard while sustaining the open A string.

EXAMPLE 3

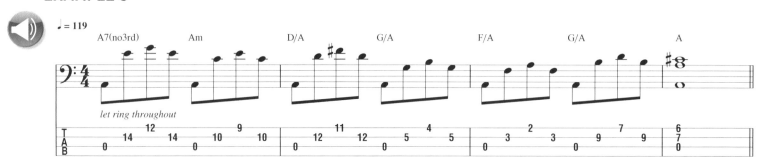

This fast metal line, inspired by Megadeth's Dave Ellefson, features major and minor 3rd dyads (two-note chords) as accents and played against the open E string. For the sake of speed, tone, and efficiency, this riff is best played with a pick.

EXAMPLE 4

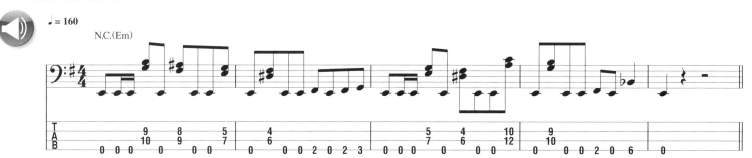

You may have noticed that, in the lower register of the bass, 3rds begin to sound somewhat muddy. For this reason, some bassists, especially where instrumentation is sparse, choose to fill the sonic spaces with 10ths, which are simply 3rds played an octave higher. The example below shows the B♭ major scale harmonized in 10ths.

EXAMPLE 5

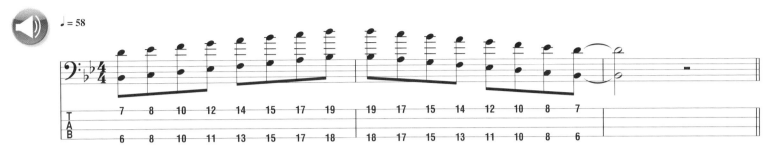

This old-school funk lick shows an A7 chord resolving to a D minor chord, using sustained, ascending 10ths to complete the resolution.

EXAMPLE 6

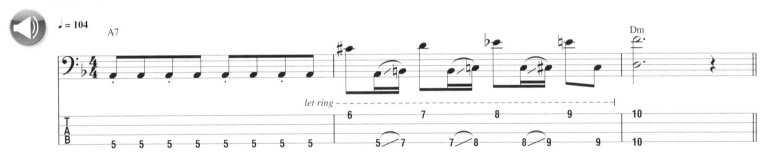

Here's a melodic 10ths line inspired by the Red Hot Chili Peppers' Flea:

EXAMPLE 7

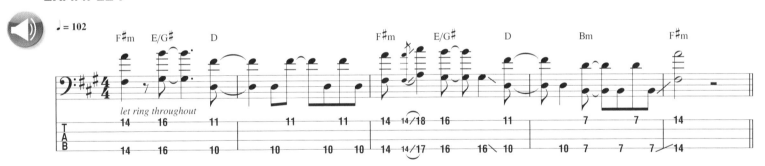

We'll close out this lesson with another soulful bass line, this time using 10ths as accents. To find what's most comfortable for your picking hand, experiment by plucking conventionally with two fingers, as well as using your thumb to sound the bottom notes and your index finger for the top notes. But most importantly, keep all the notes short and funky!

EXAMPLE 8

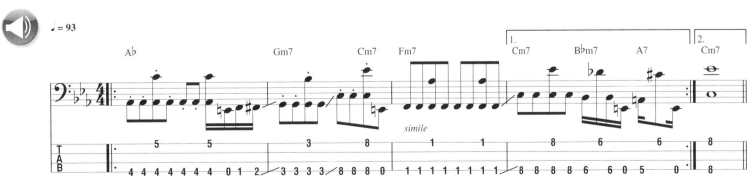

A 6th is the distance between a note and the sixth scale degree from that note. For example, if you're playing a C, its 6th would be A. In this lesson, we'll take a look at how 6ths relate to your own playing.

First, let's get acquainted with the sound of 6ths via a bit of ear training. Below, we'll ascend the C major scale in 6th intervals. Each note of the actual scale will be played on the A string, while its corresponding 6th is fretted on the G string.

EXAMPLE 1

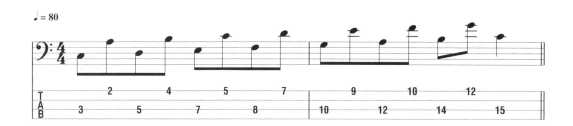

To get yourself accustomed to how 6ths lay on the fretboard in relation to each other, practice going up and down the same C major-plus-6th scale above, only in an alternating root–6th/6th–root pattern, utilizing finger slides to get from one group of 6ths to the next.

EXAMPLE 2

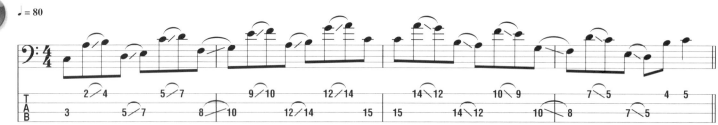

Now let's see how this interval works in a musical context. Legendary Motown great James Jamerson often employed major 6th intervals to make his bass lines bounce, as heard in Marvin Gaye's "What's Going On," Stevie Wonder's "For Once in My Life," and countless other R&B classics. Here's a lick in his style:

EXAMPLE 3

Jamerson disciple Jaco Pastorius also used major 6ths to fuel his own rapid-fire funk lines.

EXAMPLE 4

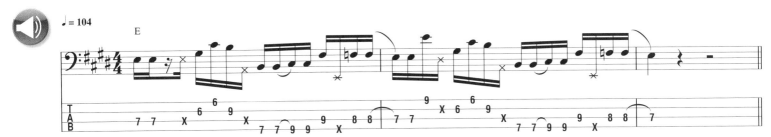

The 6th interval can also be used very effectively outside the R&B and funk idioms. In the following riff, we'll apply major and minor 6ths to a classical-tinged bass figure.

EXAMPLE 5

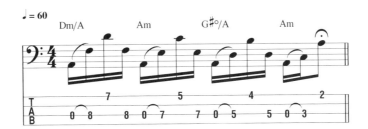

Up to this point, we've seen 6ths fretted two strings apart; now we'll explore a couple of musical examples containing 6ths played on adjacent strings. The following bluesy lick features chromatically ascending minor and major 6ths set against the open A string, which is sustained.

EXAMPLE 6

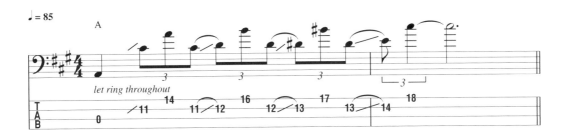

Finally, here's an old-school R&B-type bass figure in the style of Stax legend Duck Dunn, later appropriated by John Paul Jones, perhaps most famously in Led Zeppelin's classic "Ramble On." This lick, like the one preceding it, is also fretted on adjacent strings. To get from the root to the 6th smoothly, and without having to stretch the fretting hand excessively, we'll utilize finger slides, resulting in a slinkier sound.

EXAMPLE 7

LESSON #53: BASS CHORDS

Many bass purists cringe at the idea that I'm about to put forth but, at the end of the day, a bass guitar is still a guitar, and in this bassist's opinion, sometimes it's just plain fun to embrace the guitaristic aspects of the electric bass. We're not limited to single notes; on the contrary, we have at least four strings and 20 frets, so we too can play multi-timbral chords, just like our six-stringed brethren. In this lesson, we'll explore ways to apply full chords to bass lines.

First, let's take a look at some basic fretboard shapes for you to memorize and get under your fingers. These are provided for reference and as a starting point for you to discover and explore other shapes on the fretboard—for example, try moving any note in any of these shapes up or down one fret and see what happens.

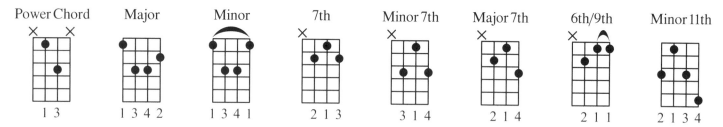

It should be noted that the fingerings shown under each diagram are only suggestions; everyone's hands are different. If you find that it's more comfortable to fret a chord in a different way than what's shown here, then by all means, go for it!

Now let's get into some bass lines, starting with this straightforward power-chord progression:

EXAMPLE 1

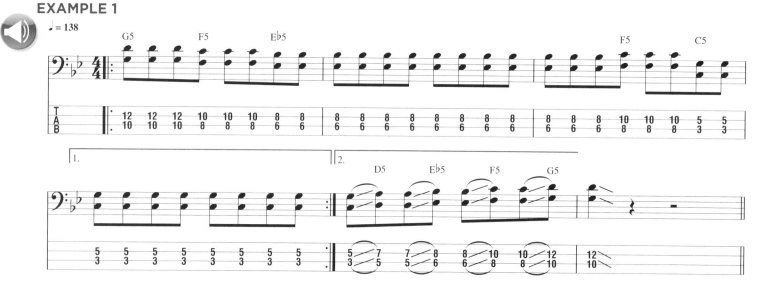

This next example also consists entirely of strummed chords, making ample use of minor 7th, major, and suspended 4th chord shapes.

EXAMPLE 2

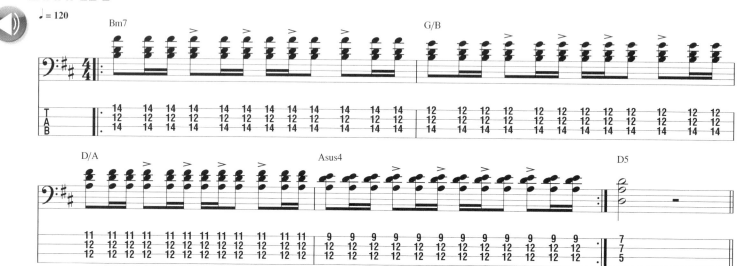

Now we'll bring the intensity down a bit with a stand-alone fingerpicked lick that uses a basic major fretboard shape, which is slid up and down the neck.

EXAMPLE 3

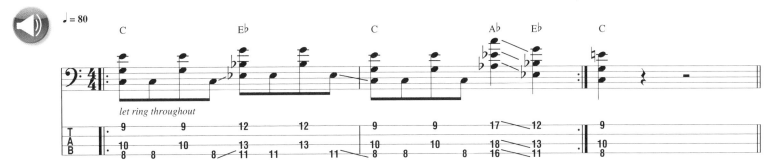

In the next three examples, we'll move away from strict chord-based bass lines and into grooves that integrate chords into single-note phrases to create one cohesive line.

Example 4 is fingerpicked and makes use of practically the full range of the bass. You'll need both thumbs for this lick—the Bm7/E chord in the first measure is strummed with the thumb, and the root of the D7sus4 chord in the third measure is fretted with the thumb on the E string. Be sure to let all notes ring out!

EXAMPLE 4

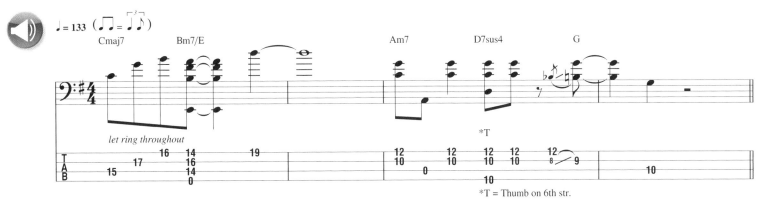

In the fourth measure of the old-school funk groove below, note how the 6th chord shape becomes a 9th (sans the 3rd) when slid down two frets and juxtaposed against the measure's overall (A) harmony.

EXAMPLE 5

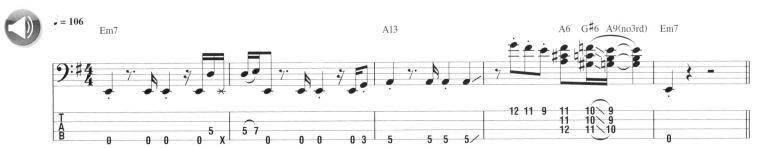

We'll conclude this lesson with another funk lick, this one inspired by Victor Wooten. We begin with a moderately fast but soulful solo line, resolving to a D7#9 chord, sharply strummed by raking the index finger across the strings in an upward motion, in the last measure.

EXAMPLE 6

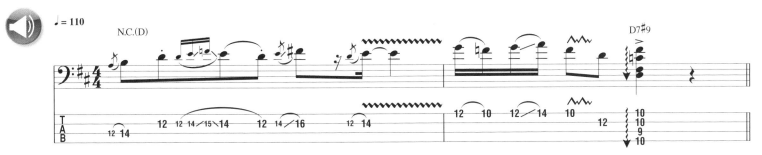

LESSON #54: MAJOR AND MINOR TRIADS

Constructing a bass line can often be as straightforward as going back to the basics—major and minor triads. In this lesson, we'll explore just how much can be done with a root, a 3rd, and a 5th. Bask in the simplicity!

The adjacent diagram depicts the easiest way to fret a major triad.

Using this fingering, let's jump right in and play this fast pop-punk groove spanning D, A, C, and G major triads.

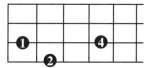

EXAMPLE 1

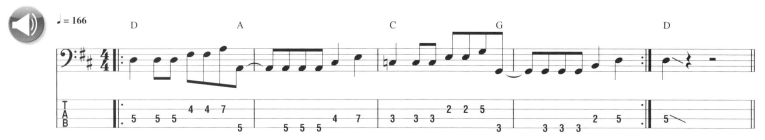

And now for something completely different: here's a blissed-out reggae groove using the same fretboard shape but, instead of playing fingerstyle or with a pick, we'll be palm-muting with the thumb and playing syncopated rhythms.

EXAMPLE 2

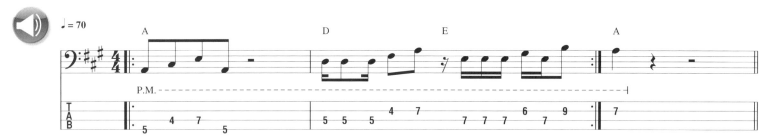

In this next example, we'll play a series of major triads while moving them up the fretboard.

EXAMPLE 3

Alternatively, you can fret a major triad like this:

This fingering works well for older rock 'n' roll styles, as you'll hear in the following '50s-flavored groove. Note the slide leading into the 3rd of the triad, which helps us avoid an uncomfortable fret-hand stretch from the third to the seventh fret.

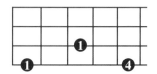

EXAMPLE 4

Paul McCartney frequently took advantage of this fretboard shape throughout his tenure in the Beatles. The following bass line takes a cue from his style.

EXAMPLE 5

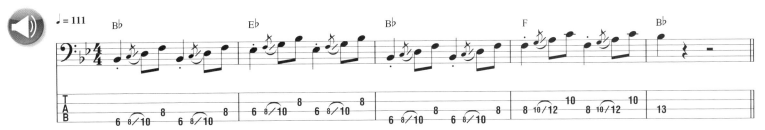

This diagram illustrates the easiest way to fret a minor triad:

Minor triads are often heard in ska music; check out this simple but very effective i–iv groove.

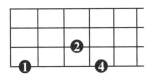

EXAMPLE 6

In this two-bar phrase, we'll step slightly outside the key signature to place two minor triads next to each other, resulting in a jazzy, modal sound.

EXAMPLE 7

LESSON #55: CHORD INVERSIONS

"Let's eat grandpa!"

"Let's eat, grandpa!"

An inversion is when a chord tone other than the root is placed at the bottom of a chord. Just as a single comma can save grandpa's life, changing a single note can carry major implications (of the harmonic variety).

Quick theory lesson: chords, at their most basic, are referred to as triads—groups of three notes, usually a root (the first note of a scale), a 3rd (the third note of the same scale), and a 5th (the fifth note of the scale), as shown in the G major chord below.

Because the root is at the bottom of the previous chord, we refer to it as root position. But if we take the 3rd, B, and put it at the bottom of the chord, we now have what is called first inversion. Same chord, different sound.

Now let's put the 5th (D) on the bottom. This is called second inversion. Fret the chord below and then go back to the root-position and first-inversion G chords and compare the sounds.

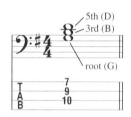

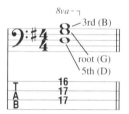

So how does this translate to your journey as a bass player? It opens up options for voice leading and adds color to your tonal palette. In this lesson, we'll play through a series of before-and-after musical phrases in which we take common chord progressions in root position and alter their inversions simply by moving a bass note here and there.

For our first example, we'll take a two-bar chord progression that's originally played entirely in root position and substitute the first chord with a first-inversion C chord. Listen to how the color of the entire phrase is changed just by this one move.

EXAMPLE 1

Now we'll switch out the root-position chord for the first inversion again, but this time on the third chord of the phrase.

EXAMPLE 2

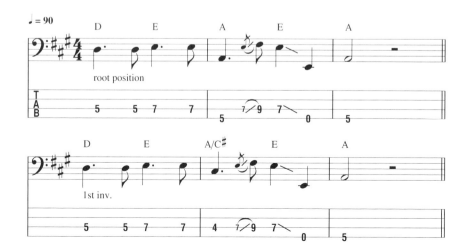

In this next example, listen to how the voice leading becomes more fluid when we put in the first-inversion chords after the double bar (the second repetition).

EXAMPLE 3

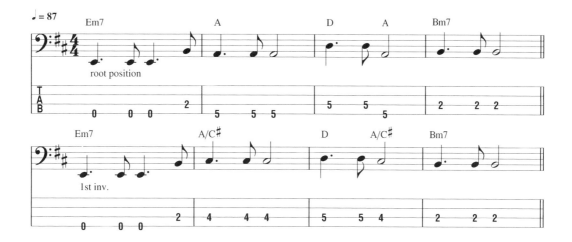

In the following musical passage, the second-inversion substitutions in the third measure are a nod to the Who's John Entwistle.

EXAMPLE 4

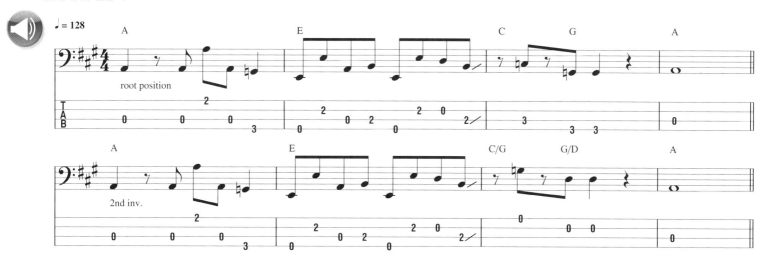

This next one is a trippy loop where we're going to change all the chords to second inversions the second time around!

EXAMPLE 5

For this last phrase, we'll replace the second chord with its first-inversion counterpart and the third chord with its second inversion. Not only does this change the overall color, it also smooths out the voice leading in the bass part.

EXAMPLE 6

LESSON #56: SUS2 AND ADD2 CHORD SHAPES

A suspended 2nd chord, which is spelled out as "sus2" in music notation, can be thought of as a power chord (root–5th) with a 2nd in place of where a 3rd would normally go. Its relative, the added 2nd chord—spelled "add2" in music notation—also contains a root, 5th, and 2nd, *plus* a major or minor 3rd. It's common to get these two chord types confused, so just keep in mind that a sus2 chord has no major or minor tonality, whereas an add2 chord does. In this lesson, we'll examine how these harmonies can be effective melodic devices in your bass toolkit.

SUS2 FRETBOARD SHAPE

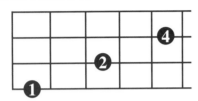

Sus2 chords have no major or minor 3rd and the resultant lack of resolution creates tension, which can be useful when you want to convey emotion or add another tonal color beyond the root and 5th, without necessarily committing to a light (major) or dark (minor) mood. This concept is illustrated in the following phrase.

EXAMPLE 1

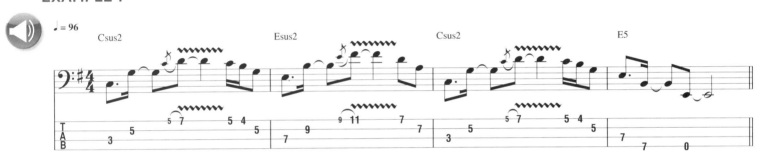

Arguably, one of the most highly visible uses of the sus2 fretboard shape in modern music can be found in Andy Summers' guitar part in the Police's "Message in a Bottle," whose signature riff is essentially a series of arpeggiated sus2 chords. The idea of building a harmonic template from the sus2 chord shape is further depicted in this next example.

EXAMPLE 2

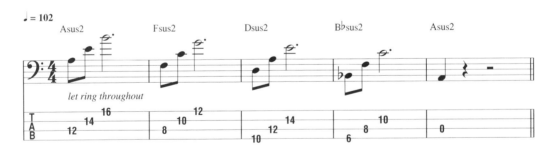

ADD2 FRETBOARD SHAPES

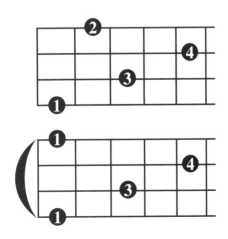
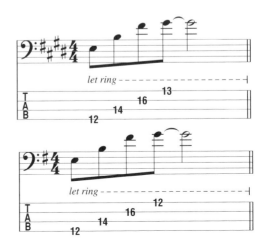

While these shapes are good for chording, they can be pretty demanding on the fretting hand due to the wide stretches. For playing lines using these harmonies, you may opt to use the fretboard shapes below and simply slide up to the high note when necessary.

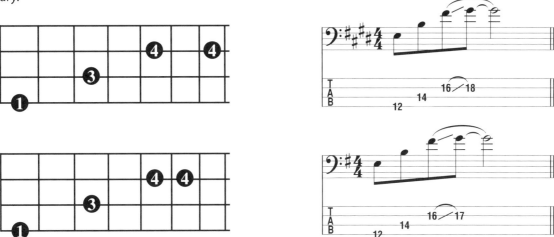

Let's take a look at the add2 shape in practice. This first example shows the bass playing arpeggiated, sustained minor and major add2 chords in a ballad setting. For the Eadd2, we can take advantage of the key signature (E major) and cheat a little with the fretting (and the stretch that goes with it) by putting the open E string on the bottom of the chord, instead of fretting the root at the 12th fret. Feel free to play this passage either with a pick or with your thumb and fingers, and be sure to let all the notes ring out so that both chords shimmer.

EXAMPLE 3

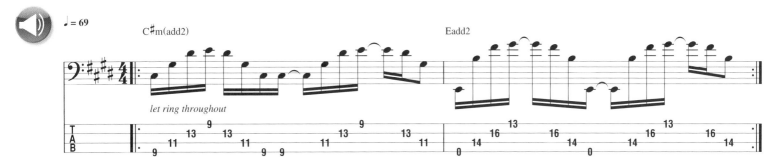

Here's an example of how add2 fretboard patterns can be inserted into a pop bass line:

EXAMPLE 4

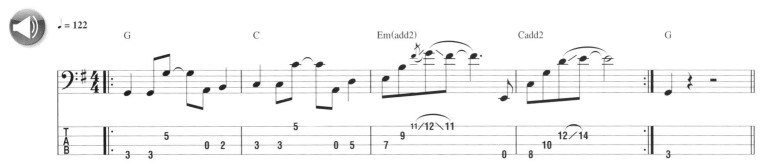

Last but not least, here's a funky, two-bar Latin vamp that makes ample use of the minor add2 pattern:

EXAMPLE 5

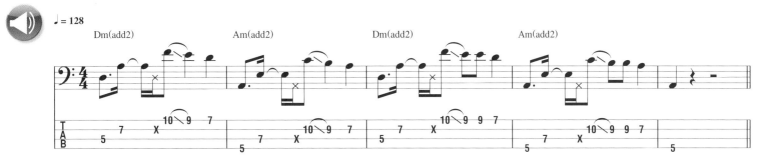

LESSON #57: BE YOUR OWN METRONOME

Funk master Larry Graham, who is most often credited with inventing slap bass, came upon the technique as a matter of necessity. As a teen, he accompanied his pianist mother on duo gigs. Since they lacked a drummer, Graham compensated by percussively thumping the low strings of his bass with his thumb on beats 1 and 3 to emulate a kick drum while snapping (or popping) the higher strings with his index or middle finger on the backbeats (beats 2 and 4) to imply a snare drum. And ultimately, by doing so he learned to become his own timekeeper. In this lesson, we'll focus on that most essential quality of solid rhythm-section playing: time.

Most people think of the drummer as the timekeeper of the group. I've been lucky to play with some great drummers but, every now and then, I've been unlucky enough to learn that they're not all great, and when that happens, someone has to keep the tempo steady. Jazz sax great Joe Lovano once told me during my college days, "That bass is also a drum kit," meaning we, as bass players, are as much a rhythm instrument as we are a harmonic one—the pocket depends on us—so it's imperative that we learn how to be our own metronomes. And if you indeed happen to be playing with a great drummer, your ability to keep solid time will be greatly appreciated because you'll make his or her job easier.

One way that I like to work on sharpening my time is by playing simple grooves with dead-note backbeats. The percussiveness lulls you into a tight tempo and the physical act of ceasing to pluck the strings in order to literally hit them on beats 2 and 4 helps to prevent rushing the non-percussive parts on beats 1 and 3.

The following musical exercises show various rhythms in differing tempos and musical styles punctuated by percussive thumps on the backbeats. The grooves start out simple and become progressively more complex. Focus on keeping the time steady, regardless of whatever you're playing outside of the backbeats.

EXAMPLE 1

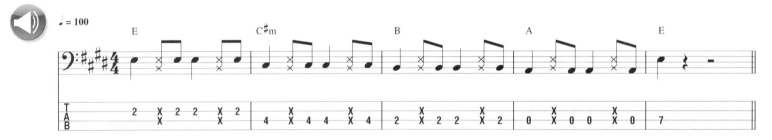

EXAMPLE 2

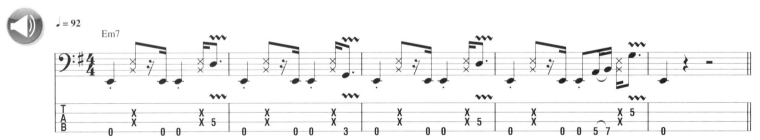

In addition to the muted-string backbeats on beats 2 and 4, we'll now incorporate single dead notes into the grooves, as well as more chord changes. Remember to keep the backbeats going!

EXAMPLE 3

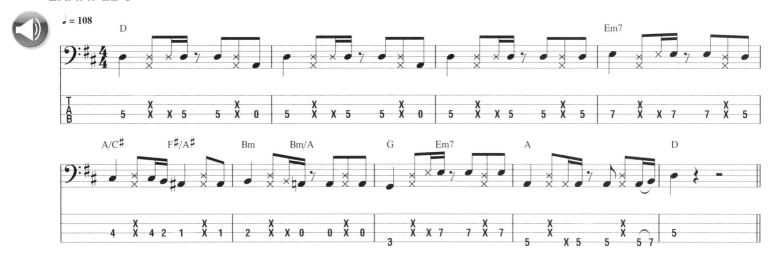

EXAMPLE 4

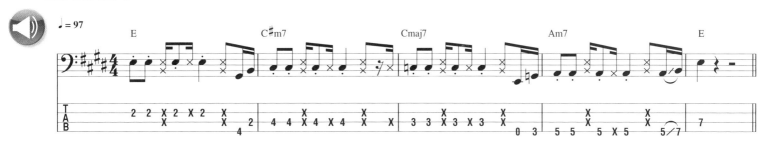

Years ago when I was studying music in school, I had another jazz instructor who told us not to just count in 4/4, but also *feel* in 8/8, especially when playing ballads, because the potential to rush is greater at slow tempos. In these situations, I listen to the high hat, not just the kick and snare, to help me land on the beat more precisely. Or if I'm in an ensemble in which there are no drums present at a particular time, such as when I'm accompanying a vocalist and the only other instrument is piano, I'll listen for the piano rhythm to help me arrive right on the downbeat.

These last two examples are slow grooves—where there may be a tendency to rush the tempo. For the first one, as you play along with the accompanying track, listen to how the hi-hat is playing 16th notes and try to concentrate on playing along to that, as opposed to just the kick and snare drums.

EXAMPLE 5

The accompanying track to our final example contains a keyboard and no drums, so you'll have to zone in on the rhythm of the keyboard part to ensure that you lock in accurately.

EXAMPLE 6

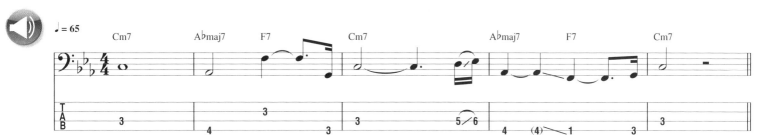

LESSON #58: BENDS

Although string bending is one of the most common and expressive of guitar techniques, it is certainly not solely the domain of guitarists. Let's take a look at how we can apply half- and whole-step bends to bass playing.

The first thing to keep in mind is that, due to the thicker strings, it's considerably more difficult to bend notes on a bass than on a guitar, so a good amount of finger strength is required to accomplish this successfully. Bends are usually executed with the ring or pinky finger, with the index and middle fingers right behind, reinforcing the bend.

As with the guitar, the higher up the neck you go, the easier bends are to accomplish. Generally speaking, bends on the higher two strings (D and G) are executed by pushing the strings in an upward direction, toward the ceiling, while bends on the lower strings (E and A) are pulled downward, toward the floor.

Our first example, inspired by Led Zeppelin's John Paul Jones, ends with a big, fat whole-step bend on the E string. Once you've got the note bent up to pitch, try adding a little vibrato for extra growl, but be sure to keep the bend in tune!

EXAMPLE 1

Half-step bends are featured prominently in this Jack Bruce-influenced repeating lick.

EXAMPLE 2

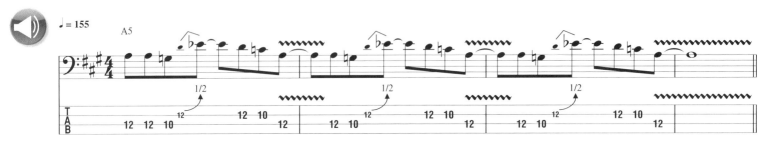

This old-school hard-rock lick, inspired by Black Sabbath's Geezer Butler, features whole-step bends. Dig in hard to make sure they're in tune!

EXAMPLE 3

Here's a bluesy metal riff in the style of Pantera's Rex Brown, featuring whole-step bends on the G string.

EXAMPLE 4

This call-and-response lead bass riff, inspired by Metallica's late, great bassist Cliff Burton, includes half- and whole-step bends. Be sure to mute the open E string before wailing on the G string!

EXAMPLE 5

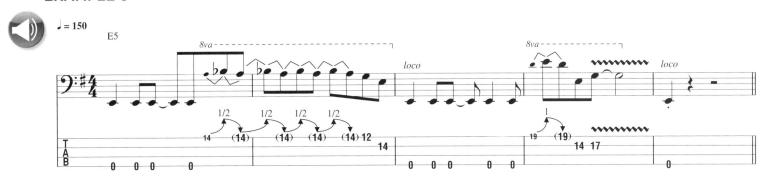

Here's another lead bass lick, but in a slow blues setting. Lay back on the rhythms and take your time with the bends.

EXAMPLE 6

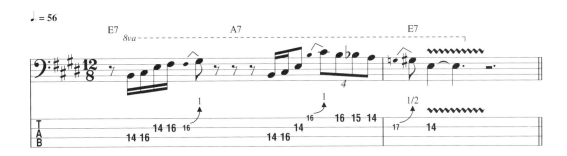

A pre-bend is a note that is bent to a certain interval *before* it's articulated. Since you can't hear the bend because it's not sounded until after the string is bent, it takes practice to ensure the note is in tune. Though not often associated with bass, the pre-bend is still a handy, soulful device to have in your musical toolbox. The example below, also in the style of Rex Brown, features half-step pre-bends on the E string.

EXAMPLE 7

LESSON #59: QUARTER-TONE BENDS

A quarter-tone bend is simply taking a note and bending it ever so slightly sharp, without going completely to the next pitch. For instance, if you were to bend the C note at the third fret of the A string by a quarter tone, you would pull the string just far enough to alter the pitch, without actually hitting the C♯ that would normally follow it. This is illustrated in the example below; listen for the difference in pitch as you play through each measure.

EXAMPLE 1

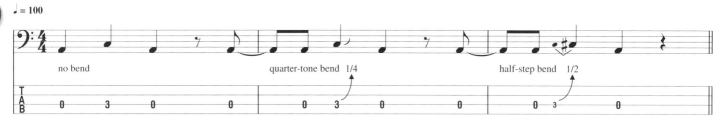

The quarter-tone bend is an easy and effective way to bring a touch of attitude to a note because there's an element of unresolved tension that comes from the anticipation of the bent note making it to the next pitch, but it never quite gets there. Guitarists have been using this idea in blues and rock for decades; we bassists can do it, too! Let's get familiar with it by playing through the blues scale below. Note the quarter-tone bends on the minor 3rds and minor 7th.

EXAMPLE 2

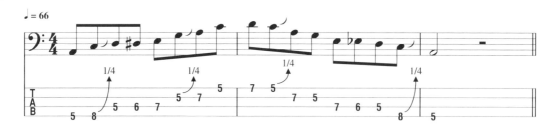

Now let's apply the quarter-tone bend to some grooves. In the lick below, we'll be bending the G note on the bottom string by subtly pulling it in, toward the palm. Sonically, it's almost like we're "curling" the G into the open A.

EXAMPLE 3

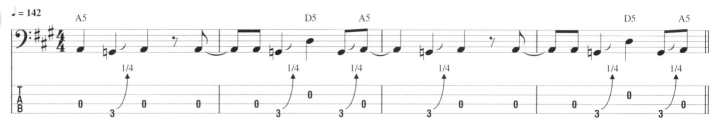

Here's another rock riff in the same vein, inspired by Led Zeppelin's John Paul Jones.

EXAMPLE 4

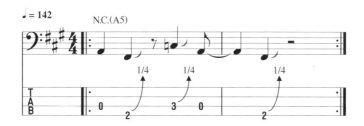

Now let's try stepping away from open strings with this closed-position, bluesy rock lick featuring quarter-tone bends on the high and low strings.

EXAMPLE 5

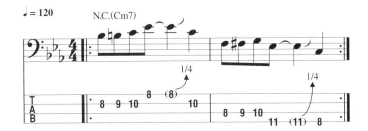

Quarter-tone bends are almost *made* for funk, as depicted in the next couple of examples.

EXAMPLE 6

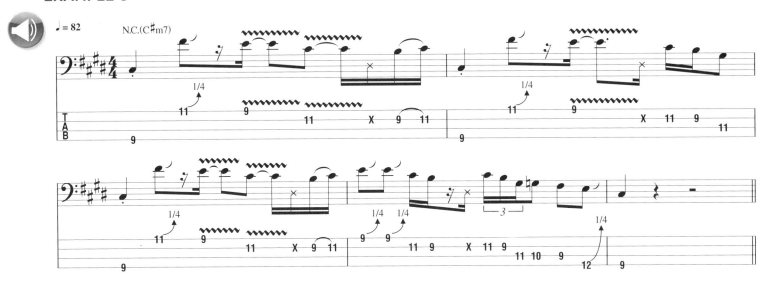

EXAMPLE 7

This last lick, inspired by Soundgarden, shows quarter-tone bends in a hard-rock context.

EXAMPLE 8

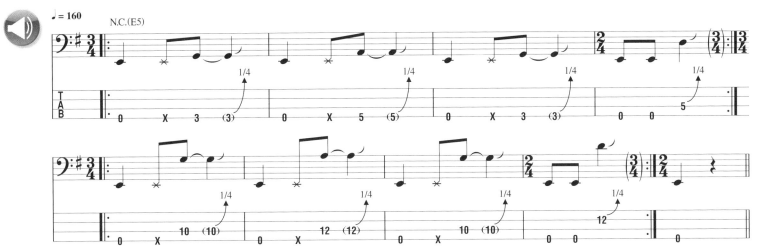

LESSON #60: COMBINING PICK-HAND TECHNIQUES

You can coax many different tones from your bass simply by the way you touch it—whether playing conventional fingerstyle, palm-muting with your thumb, slapping, or even just by how hard you hit the strings, as well as *where* you hit the strings. Mastering all of these techniques will make you a more well-rounded and versatile player, and employing more than one of them within the context of a single bass part is a highly musical and expressive way to enhance it and break monotony. Why use just one color when you have a whole palette available to you? For example, here's a slow, slinky fingerstyle groove with popped notes on the accents. One bass part, two different sounds.

EXAMPLE 1

In this next example, note how the mood changes once we switch from conventional fingerstyle to palm muting with the thumb.

EXAMPLE 2

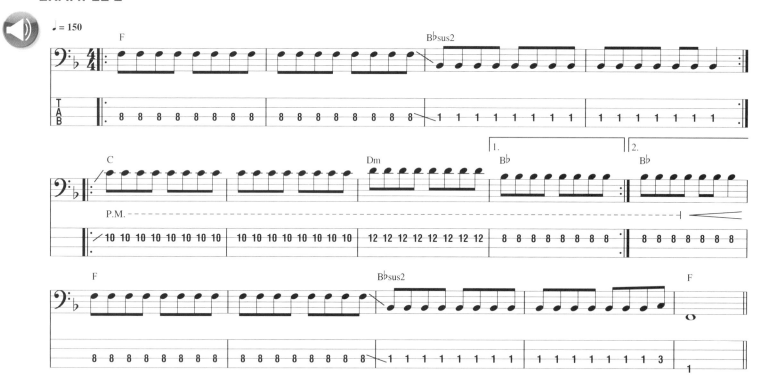

Similarly, this metal groove alternates a heavy, dark-sounding, aggressively fingerpicked riff with palm-muted hits.

EXAMPLE 3

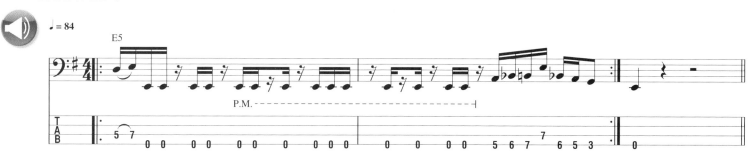

In this next bass line, we'll use a standard rock chord progression to demonstrate how we can achieve contrasting tones simply by adjusting where we hit the strings with the picking hand. Start in section A by playing near the bridge for a sharp, punchier tone; after the repeat, at section B, move your picking hand to the base of the fretboard, where it meets the body, for a fatter, duller timbre to better suit the feel of the music. At section C, we'll switch back to picking near the bridge to conclude the example.

EXAMPLE 4

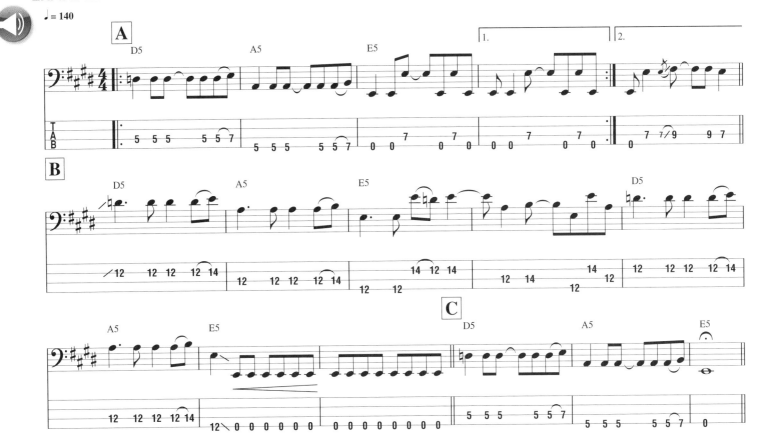

This last example is a repeated four-bar vamp over an implied A minor chord that covers three different pick-hand techniques.

EXAMPLE 5

Chances are pretty good that you've played a ton of pentatonic-based lines and riffs without even realizing it. Pentatonic scales, via the blues, are at the root of most rock music.

As you might surmise, the word "pentatonic" implies a scale of five notes. Consequently, there are five scale patterns—one that begins on each note of the scale. The music below illustrates how these patterns lay on the fretboard. For simplicity, we'll imagine them in the key of A (hollow notes denote the root).

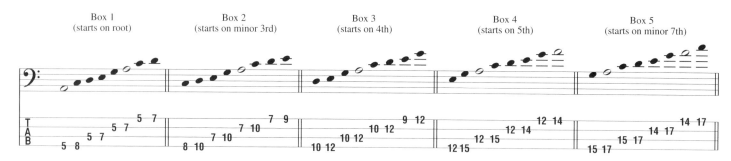

As bass players, we tend to think of everything from the bottom up, so you're probably already pretty familiar with box 1, since it starts on the root. If you're unfamiliar with any of the others, however, take a minute or two to play through them and get them under your fingers; doing so will open up the fretboard and allow you to seamlessly snake around from one pattern to the next.

For the sake of simplicity, all of the lines in this lesson are in A. Let's start snaking!

This slow metal riff is based on box 1, but starts in box 5. By sliding into beat 3 of each measure, we can seamlessly get into box 1.

EXAMPLE 1

Now we'll get box 2 in on the action, albeit briefly. We start firmly in box 1, moving to box 5 at the end of the first measure before sliding back into box 1. For a hot second, on beat 3 of the second measure, we slide into box 2 before settling once again back into box 1.

EXAMPLE 2

This next one is a quick, bluesy riff that connects boxes 2 and 3.

EXAMPLE 3

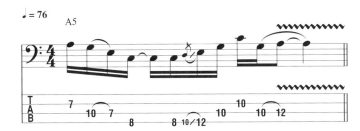

Now we'll step out of the background a bit with this soulful lead line, which starts in box 3 on the very first beat, shifting up to box 4 on the second beat.

EXAMPLE 4

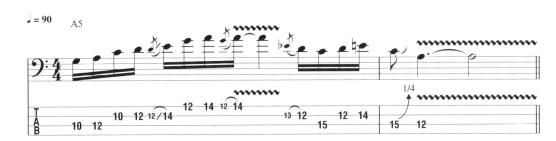

Our final lick is another solo line, inspired by legendary Stevie Wonder bassist Nathan Watts. Spanning box 5 in the lower register straight through to box 5 in the upper register, this riff features upright bass-style position shifts, facilitated by dead notes and hammer-ons. Note the suggested fret-hand fingerings and go for it!

EXAMPLE 5

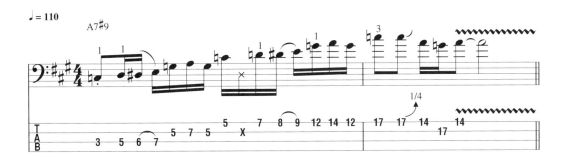

LESSON #62: DOUBLING THE GUITAR

Few things sound more badass than a guitar and bass attacking a riff together. In most cases, the bass naturally doubles the guitar part an octave lower (or perhaps it's the guitar doubling the bass part an octave higher, depending on your perspective), although sometimes the bass and guitar play in the same register. Countless rock classics—The Knack's "My Sharona"; Led Zeppelin's "Whole Lotta Love," "Moby Dick," and "Black Dog"; and of course, Black Sabbath's "Iron Man" immediately come to mind—were borne from this concept. In this lesson, we'll explore the joy of doubling.

This first series of examples features the bass doubling the guitar an octave lower. We'll start with a fast metal riff based on the descending blues scale.

EXAMPLE 1

The bass and guitar in this next example double each other in the first half and then the guitar breaks off into chords for the second half.

EXAMPLE 2

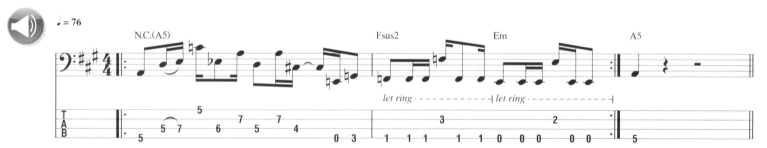

Here's a dirty, mid-tempo hard rock riff that finds the guitar playing fast-moving power chords while the bass doubles the roots an octave lower.

EXAMPLE 3

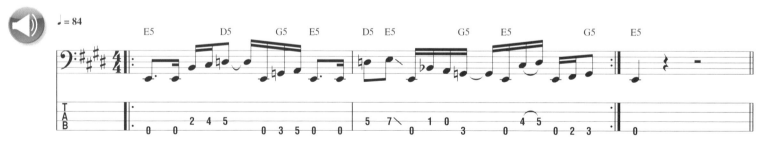

No one will argue that, when a guitar riff is reinforced by the bass an octave lower, the result is a sonic collage of awesome. But if you want to raise the danger level another notch, try playing in the same register (octave) as the guitar. One may ask, "What's the point of having the bass and guitar play precisely the same thing?" The answer: timbre. You may be playing the same exact notes, but you're doing so on two different instruments with two different sounds and characteristics. When you combine them, especially in a heavy rock context, the result is a thick wall of sound.

In the musical example below, the bass part starts low, in its traditional role of reinforcing the guitar part an octave lower, and then jumps up to join the guitar for quick accents.

EXAMPLE 4

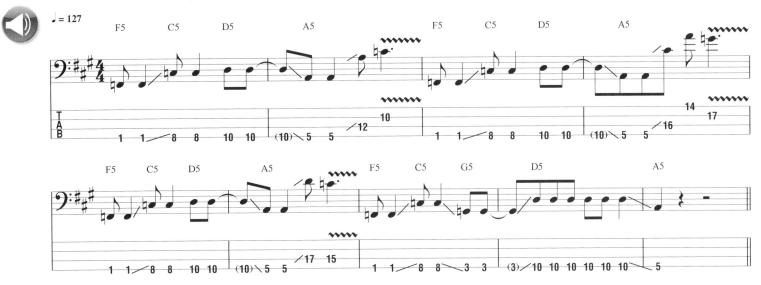

Similarly, in this next riff, the bass jumps up an octave to join the guitar in the last two measures.

EXAMPLE 5

This next lick is a grungy turnaround in which the bass and guitar play in unison at the beginning and then break off into separate registers when the chord progression resolves.

EXAMPLE 6

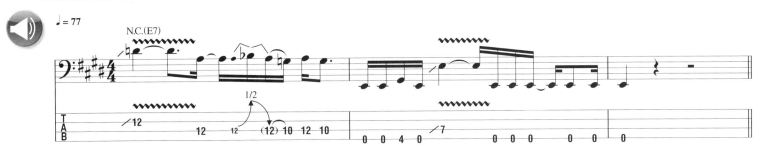

Last but not least, here's a fast bass and guitar unison riff that might occur if Rush and Motörhead were to procreate.

EXAMPLE 7

LESSON #63: DOWNTUNINGS

Downtunings on bass add heaviness in two ways: dropping the pitch automatically creates a darker mood, and the decreased string tension (or increased floppiness, depending on whether you're a "glass half empty" type) causes the strings to slap more frequently against the fretboard, making the tone more aggressive. So without further ado, let's jump in and explore the rumbling nether reaches of the bass!

(**Note:** all the musical examples in this lesson sound lower than the keys in which they are written. See the tuning legend with each figure.)

E♭ TUNING (DOWN ONE HALF STEP): E♭–A♭–D♭–G♭

OK, maybe it doesn't exactly rumble, but this common pop and rock tuning gives songs that would normally sound in conventional rock keys a bit of heaviness by bringing them down a half step. It is used by countless artists, including classic heavyweights such as Van Halen and Jimi Hendrix, and more modern bands such as Weezer, Guns N' Roses, and Smashing Pumpkins.

EXAMPLE 1

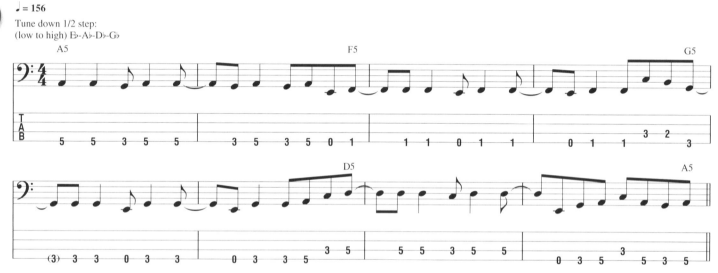

D TUNING (DOWN ONE WHOLE STEP): D–G–C–F

Used by bands as disparate as Mötley Crüe, Pantera, and Death.

EXAMPLE 2

C# TUNING (DOWN ONE-AND-A-HALF STEPS): C#–F#–B–E

Used by A Perfect Circle, Black Sabbath, and Killswitch Engage.

EXAMPLE 3

Tune down 1 1/2 steps:
(low to high) C#-F#-B-E

♩. = 60

C TUNING (DOWN TWO WHOLE STEPS): C–F–B♭–E♭

Used by Queens of the Stone Age and the Sword.

EXAMPLE 4

♩ = 136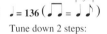

Tune down 2 steps:
(low to high) C-F-B♭-E♭

B TUNING (DOWN TWO-AND-A-HALF STEPS): B–E–A–D

Used perhaps most infamously by Type O Negative.

EXAMPLE 5

♩ = 100

Tune down 2 1/2 steps:
(low to high) B-E-A-D

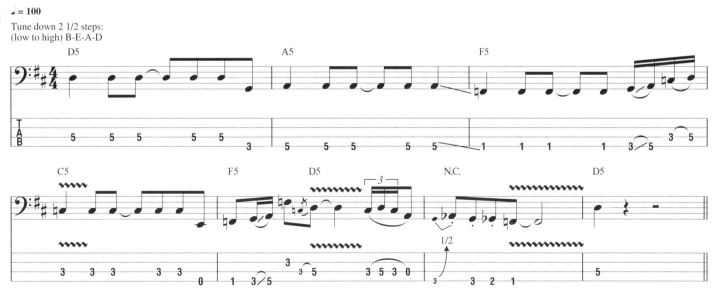

Obviously, we're only scratching the surface here; some bands go even lower! With any of these tunings, especially the lower ones, you may want to use thicker strings to avoid excessive floppiness and tuning issues. Also, any of the tunings in this lesson can be altered to a "drop tuning" by lowering the bottom string an additional whole step, as you would with conventional drop D tuning (D–A–D–G).

LESSON #64: GALLOP RHYTHM

In the early '80s, Iron Maiden bassist and mastermind Steve Harris popularized a rhythm that came to be known as the gallop—each beat consisting of an eighth note beamed to two 16th notes, usually played at faster tempos, somewhat evocative of the clomp of horses driven by surging heavy metal armies on their way to pillage your village. This rhythmic motif can also be heard outside of metal, in such songs as Muse's "Knights of Cydonia" and in Bachman Turner Overdrive's classic "Let It Ride" (are you sensing a theme here?).

Let's dive in and explore how this rhythm works in a musical context. This first example illustrates a basic mid-tempo gallop.

EXAMPLE 1

This next example demonstrates gallop rhythms set against a half-time feel while cycling through a classical-influenced chord progression and moving up the A string. With this one, you may want to experiment between using a pick and playing fingerstyle to achieve a smooth, consistent string attack.

EXAMPLE 2

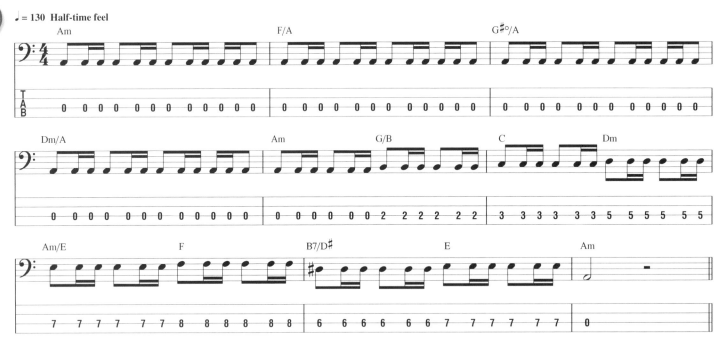

Now let's kick things up a notch. The following lick is a super-fast galloping line inspired by the aforementioned Steve Harris. We'll use a pedal tone for the first half and then follow the chord progression for the remainder of the figure. For the latter four measures, the trick is to navigate the string skips as seamlessly as possible. Also, for maximum speed, try to hit the strings with only the very tips of your fingers, using a light touch!

EXAMPLE 3

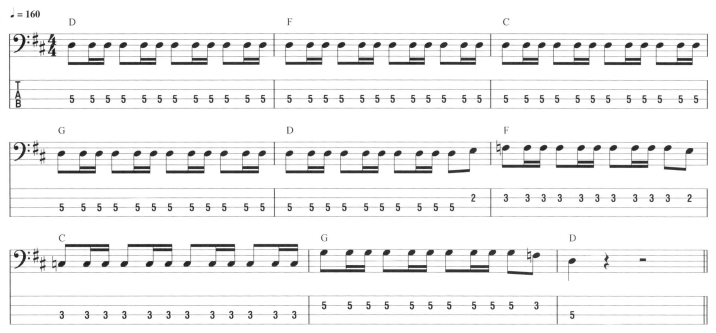

Gallops are also frequently heard in pop and dance music. The following chord progression combines gallops and arpeggios, which outline the notes in each chord.

EXAMPLE 4

In our last example, we'll play a dance groove consisting of gallops split into octaves. This is best played fingerstyle, though you may opt to pick the bottom notes with your thumb and the top notes with your index and middle fingers. Once again, pay careful attention to the string skips, especially since we're now skipping two strings instead of one. You'll also need a hefty amount of fret-hand strength in order to sustain those octave shapes for long periods of time!

EXAMPLE 5

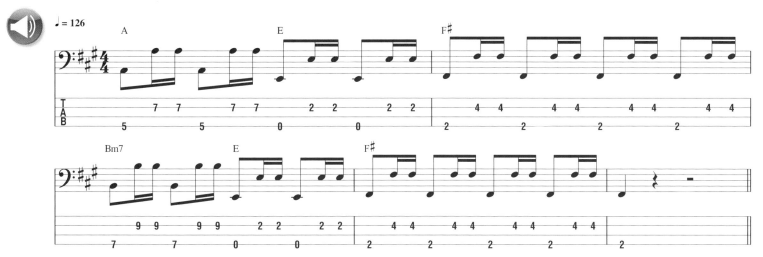

LESSON #65: GREASE

Ever hear a bass line described as "dirty"? We have what I call "grease"—that unquantifiable part of the bass line that oozes through the cracks between beats—to thank for that. Yes, the number-one rule of bass is "Thou Shalt Lock in with the Drums," but a little grit in the groove never hurt anyone. Precision is important, but rock music has also always been more about attitude and spirit. This isn't an excuse to be sloppy and unmusical, but more an exhortation to make low, rumbling noises and revel in it.

If you've ever listened to old-school R&B or Motown, you've heard grease. And it doesn't just occur in those genres; bassist John Paul Jones, himself a Motown disciple, gleefully rumbles his way through the "Hey baby, oh baby, pretty baby" section of Led Zeppelin's "Black Dog" with barely-there quarter-step bends and by irreverently lifting his finger off the low E string between licks, regardless of whatever noises may occur as a result—"controlled sloppiness," if you will.

Because bass grease is more of a feeling or vibe, it's difficult to capture it in music notation, so take a listen to the accompanying audio recordings as you play the licks in this lesson.

This first example demonstrates aggressive rock played "dirty"—wide vibrato for extra rumble, slide-outs so slow you can hear each fret on the way down, a soulful quarter-tone bend, and plenty of string noise.

EXAMPLE 1

Now we'll swing to the other extreme by going for subtlety and a light touch. This slow-burn funk groove, played behind the beat, makes use of extreme staccato, allowing the quick slides in the second and third measures to stand out.

EXAMPLE 2

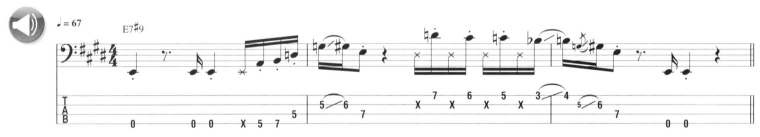

Here's another "chill" groove. It features just a hint of vibrato and a behind-the-beat grace note in the third measure.

EXAMPLE 3

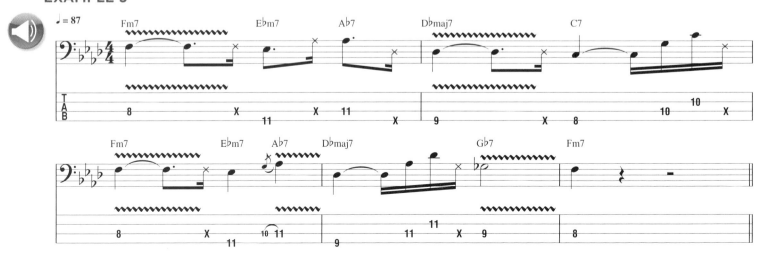

We'll stay with this "chill" theme for these last two examples. Both bass lines begin with an established two-bar groove, after which we'll sprinkle in subtle improvisations—slow grace notes, high-register double-stop stabs, a short trill, even dropping a note out or moving a phrase by a beat or two—all while maintaining the same basic groove throughout.

EXAMPLE 4

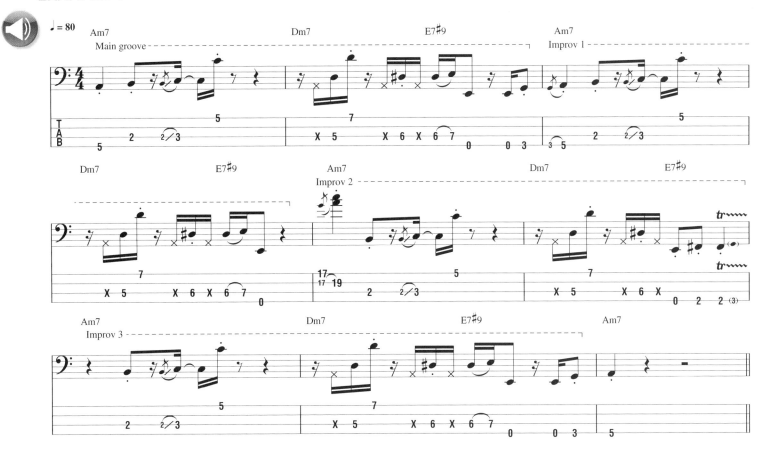

EXAMPLE 5

USING THE NATURAL MINOR SCALE

The natural minor scale, also known as the Aeolian mode, is at the root of innumerable classic hard rock tunes, among them Guns N' Roses' "Don't Cry," the conclusion of Led Zeppelin's "Stairway to Heaven," Lynyrd Skynyrd's "Simple Man," Mötley Crüe's "Live Wire," and Dio's "Rainbow in the Dark." With its dark mood and powerful harmonies, it's easy to see its appeal in heavy music. The Aeolian mode starts on the sixth degree of the major scale. So if we're in the key of C, the Aeolian mode begins on A. It's commonly referred to as "natural minor" because it contains all the same notes as its relative major scale.

What's cool about this type of minor scale is that you can take any major chord progression and completely change the color by simply dropping the bass line down a minor 3rd (one and a half steps), as illustrated in the following I–IV–V groove. As a result, C becomes Am7, F becomes Dm7, and G becomes Em7.

EXAMPLE 1

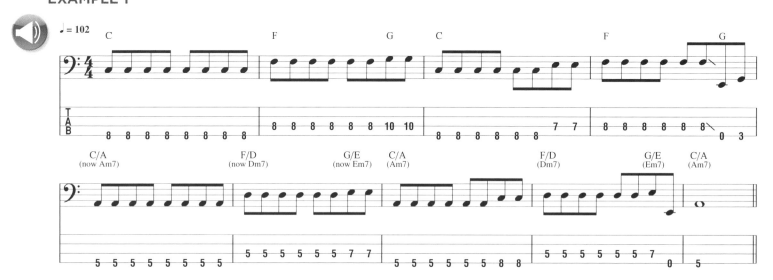

Of the three minor types—harmonic, melodic, and natural—only the natural minor scale has a minor v chord (the triad built on the fifth scale degree). To illustrate, the following three licks show the same bass line adapted to each type of minor scale. As you play through them, listen for how the harmonic and melodic types use major voice leading and harmony to resolve to the root chord, whereas the natural minor bass line stays strictly minor.

EXAMPLE 2A (HARMONIC MINOR)

EXAMPLE 2B (MELODIC MINOR)

EXAMPLE 2C (NATURAL MINOR)

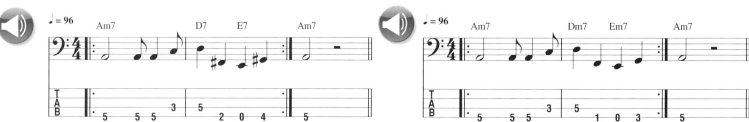

Now let's explore a few bass grooves grounded in the natural minor scale so you can hear it in context. This first one starts out with simple roots, becoming more melodic in the second half.

EXAMPLE 3

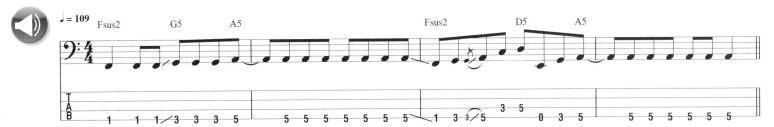

Here's a funky slap groove that partially outlines a descending B natural minor scale.

EXAMPLE 4

This next bass line illustrates a common natural minor pop/rock chord progression, with some slight improvisation sprinkled in.

EXAMPLE 5

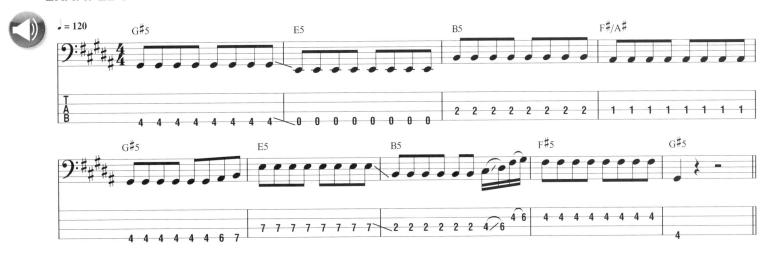

We'll conclude with a fast, Judas Priest-inspired metal groove in A minor.

EXAMPLE 6

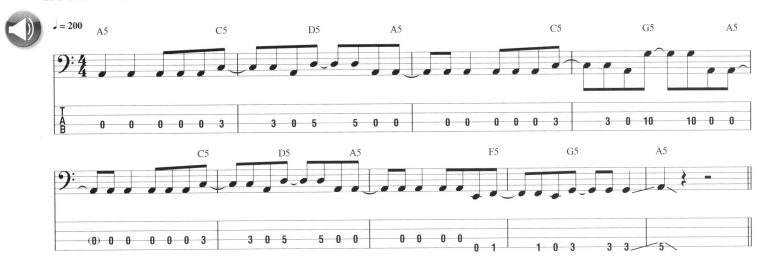

LESSON #67: HARMONIC MINOR SCALE

The harmonic minor scale is simply the natural minor scale with a raised (major) 7th. Its distinguishing characteristic is the dramatic change in pitch between the minor 6th and raised 7th, which is a more effective leading tone to the root than its minor 7th counterpart. By way of comparison, play through the natural minor and harmonic minor scales below so you can hear the difference.

Though Deep Purple flirted with harmonic minor in the '60s and '70s, guitarists such as Steve Vai and especially Yngwie Malmsteen helped to popularize it in the '80s, pairing it perfectly with rock. In this lesson, we'll explore how we can apply harmonic minor to bass lines in various musical styles and rhythmic feels.

We'll start with a basic eighth-note "pump" that outlines F# harmonic minor in a rock/pop context.

EXAMPLE 1

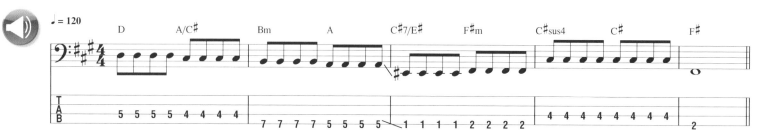

Here's another pop example, this time in the key of A minor. It fuses classical harmony with a funky James Jamerson/Motown feel.

EXAMPLE 2

This next one is a harder-edged rock bass line featuring a prominent 16th-note motif set against a half-time feel. Note the contour of the line, especially as it moves from B7/D# to Cadd2 in the second and third measures.

EXAMPLE 3

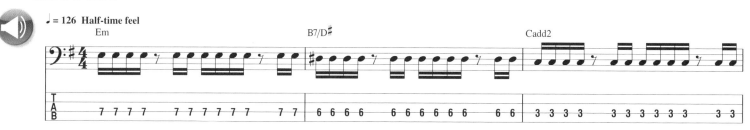

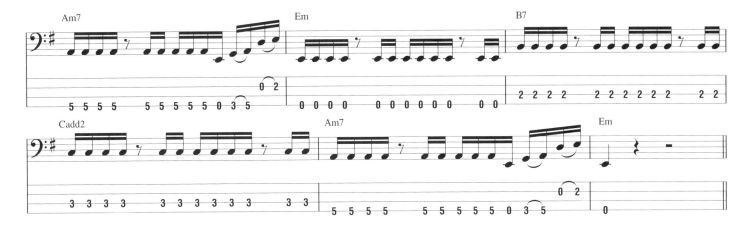

Harmonic minor can even be used in one-string up-tempo punk lines!

EXAMPLE 4

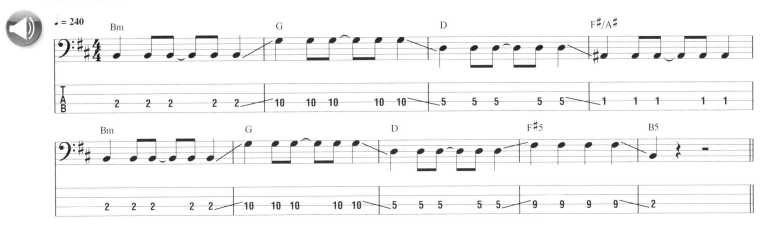

We'll close out this lesson with a fast metal song excerpt that makes use of D harmonic minor in both scalar and overall harmony contexts. Limber up those pick-hand fingers and go for it!

EXAMPLE 5

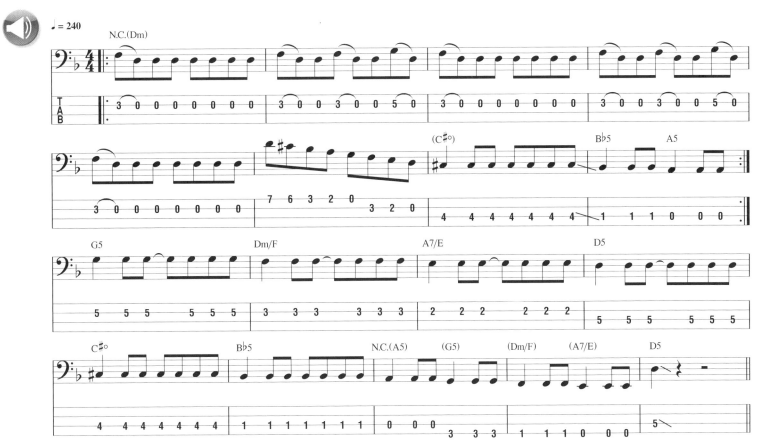

LESSON #68: MELODIC MINOR SCALE

The melodic minor scale is simply the natural minor scale with a raised (major) 6th and 7th. Or, you can just think of it as the major scale, but with a minor 3rd. The music examples below show the natural minor scale, followed by the melodic minor scale. Play through each of them so your ears can get a feel for the difference.

EXAMPLE 1 (A NATURAL MINOR SCALE)

EXAMPLE 2 (A MELODIC MINOR SCALE)

You may have noticed that the descending melodic minor scale is identical to the descending natural minor scale. The reason for this is that composers as far back as Mozart's time considered the raised (major) 6th and 7th to be harmonically awkward when writing descending melodies or bass parts, so it's generally accepted practice to descend in natural minor, though certainly not a hard and fast rule.

You've probably heard melodic minor at work in Bach's ubiquitous "Bourrée in E minor," as adapted for bass in the excerpt below. Note how the top voice ascends in melodic minor in the first half of the example, but descends in natural minor in the second half.

EXAMPLE 3

In the context of a bass line, we can see from the following pop ballad example how melodic minor helps us resolve naturally from a V chord to a i chord.

EXAMPLE 4

This next figure shows the bass using melodic minor voice leading in a descending/ascending Latin-inspired line.

EXAMPLE 5

Melodic minor can also be used in an up-tempo pop/rock context, as illustrated in the following bass line.

EXAMPLE 6

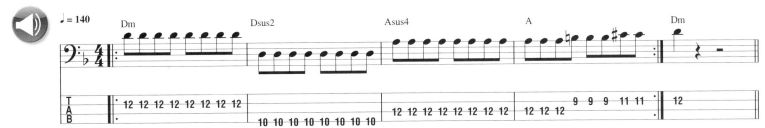

All of the examples in this lesson thus far have shown melodic minor set against minor keys. In this last bass line, we'll see how melodic minor can be useful in a *major* key. Starting on the root chord (G), we get to the relative minor (Em) in the third measure by cycling through the upper half of the E melodic minor scale in the second measure.

EXAMPLE 7

LESSON #69: PHRYGIAN MODE

The Phrygian mode is built upon the third degree of the major scale. So if we're in the key of F major, for example, the Phrygian mode would start on A, as illustrated below.

A PHRYGIAN MODE

You can also think of the Phrygian mode as simply the natural minor scale with a ♭2nd. When you add this characteristic to the natural minor's ♭3rd, ♭6th, and ♭7th, the result is a dark, exotic sound that works very well in hard rock and heavy metal, especially when the riffs are based on open strings.

Our first example, a mid-tempo groove in A Phrygian, uses the open A string as a springboard to get to the other notes.

EXAMPLE 1

Next up is this heavy riff in E Phrygian, which is rooted on the open E string; the other notes that outline the rest of the scale are fretted on the adjacent A string.

EXAMPLE 2

Here's another one, this time with the entire lick played on the D string. Even though the fretted pitches span the first fret through the 13th fret, you have plenty of time to shift fret-hand positions where needed because of the prominence of the open D string driving the riff, which frees up your fretting hand to move around.

EXAMPLE 3

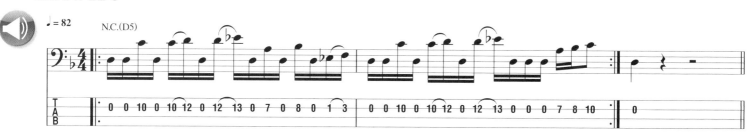

An altered version of the Phrygian mode, the Phrygian dominant scale is based on the fifth degree of the harmonic minor scale; if we're in the key of A, for instance, then the E Phrygian dominant scale would consist of (from low to high) E–F–G♯–A–B–C–D–E. Or, you could simply think of it as the Phrygian mode with a major (raised) 3rd.

E PHRYGIAN DOMINANT SCALE

The Phrygian dominant scale is common in Middle Eastern music, familiar examples being "Hava Nagila," the bridge of Led Zeppelin's "Kashmir," and "Misirlou" (made popular by surf-guitar icon Dick Dale). You've also heard it in Alice in Chains' "What the Hell Have I" and Tool's "Forty Six & 2." Like its unaltered counterpart, the Phrygian dominant scale has an exotic sound that lends itself quite well to metal, as the major 3rd, set against an otherwise decidedly minor scale, conjures an air of mystery.

As before, we're going to base the following licks on open strings to ground the riff, as well as to facilitate fret-hand position changes. This next example, in the style of Lamb of God, has us staying on the open E string while arpeggiating, in 3rds, E Phrygian dominant on the neighboring A string.

EXAMPLE 4

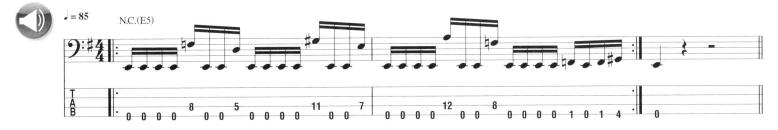

We'll slow the tempo down slightly for our final riff, a heavy four-bar phrase in A Phrygian dominant, which is outlined in a cool, descending 16th-note run at the end of the last bar. Though the lick is mainly based around the open A string, it's a bit trickier than the previous ones, as it also relies heavily on sustained, sliding octaves. Be sure to follow the "let ring" directions as much as possible in order to create a thick, aggressive wall of sound.

EXAMPLE 5

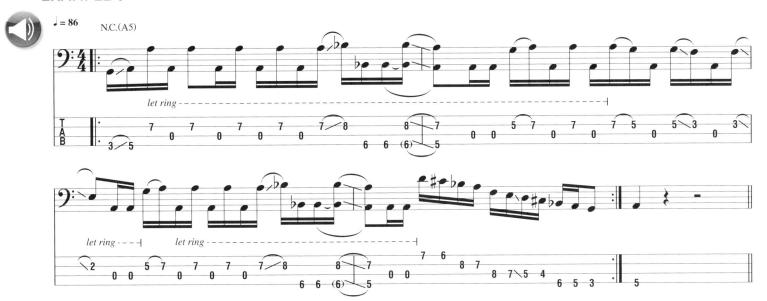

LESSON #70: LYDIAN MODE

The Lydian mode starts on the fourth note of the major scale. For example, if we're in the key of C, then the Lydian mode begins on F. You can also simply think of Lydian as the major scale with a raised 4th, as illustrated here:

F LYDIAN MODE

As you can hear, the raised 4th of the Lydian mode gives the scale a flowing, lyrical color.

When we speak of modes, many musicians tend to think of practicing scales and exercises in order to memorize what notes go where. That's all well and good, but perhaps a more hands-on way to explore an unusual mode (for rock, anyway) such as Lydian is by simply starting on one note and moving from there—just putting one foot in front of the other and seeing what happens, musically. We already know that Lydian is just the major scale with a raised 4th, but for improvisational purposes, you can also think of it as a regular major scale played a perfect 5th above the key you're in. Or to put it in English: let's say you're in C Lydian. The scale that's a 5th above C is G, so C Lydian can therefore be thought of as a G scale played over a C note, and you can therefore base your improvisation on any note in the G major scale.

Likewise, if we're in E Lydian, then you want to focus on the B major scale for improvising, as illustrated in Example 1. As we hold the open E in the bottom voice, we'll play a linear melody that outlines the regular B major scale in the upper voice. (You might want to use a pick to better allow the open low E to ring out.) After you play through this example, try moving some of the fretted notes around and see what you come up with. Then, try doing it in A Lydian, holding the open A while running through notes in the E major scale.

EXAMPLE 1

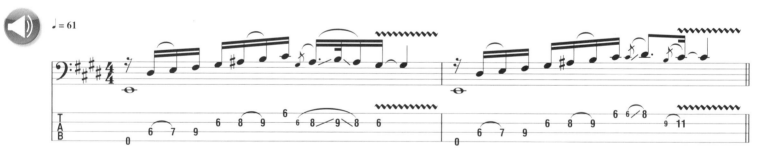

In modern music, the Lydian mode is often associated with guitar virtuosos such as Steve Vai and Joe Satriani, and of course, *The Simpsons* theme. This mode also figures prominently in a few signature hard rock riffs, among them Led Zeppelin's "Dancing Days" and, more recently, Stone Temple Pilots' "Sin." Now that we know how to construct lines from the Lydian mode, let's see how it applies to bass lines of varying stylistic contexts.

Example 2, inspired by Rush's "Freewill," applies the Lydian mode to a driving, straight-eighths rock rhythm. We're in the key of F but, again, we can think of it as using notes from the C major scale, only with F on the bottom.

EXAMPLE 2

Here's a dirty rock riff in C Lydian that resolves comfortably and diatonically to E minor. In this case, we're approaching it as a C chord with a raised 4th. Most of the notes are played on the same string for added slinkiness.

EXAMPLE 3

This last example shows the Lydian mode used at the conclusion of a blues turnaround.

EXAMPLE 4

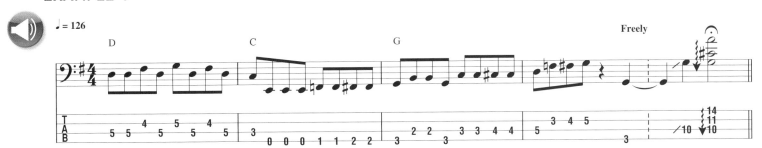

LESSON #71: MACHINE GUN 16TH NOTES

In the right hands, 16th-note grooves can be deadly. Three ingredients are needed for this to happen successfully: an unwavering pick-hand attack, smart note choices, and utter control over your instrument (instead of the other way around).

Hyperbole aside, a well-executed (sorry, couldn't resist referencing the "lethal" theme one last time) 16th-note groove can do everything from simply getting people to dance to raising the excitement level of a song. Further, mastery of this technique will do wonders for strengthening your time.

Ask most experienced bassists who comes to mind when this topic is mentioned, and they'll probably answer Jaco Pastorius or Tower of Power's Rocco Prestia. In this lesson, we'll not only learn a few lines inspired by their playing, we'll also examine what it is about the lines specifically that make them work.

Before we begin, a note about technique: when playing lines such as these, try to hit the strings with only the very tips of your pick-hand fingers, using a light touch. The former will cut down on the amount of fingertip surface area it takes to sound a note, while the latter will help you expend less effort—energy that will be needed to keep the groove going at the given tempo for as long as you wish, without your hand and forearm cramping up. These suggestions might sound "geeky," but observing them will enhance your speed and stamina.

To get our feet wet, let's start with a repeated 16th-note figure. Concentrate on keeping good time and pushing your pick hand to keep going for as long as you can. See if you can hear how the rigidity of the pitch builds intensity.

EXAMPLE 1

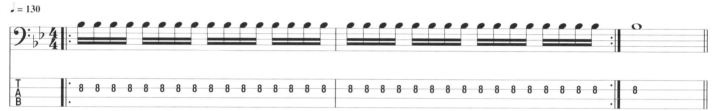

Now let's get into the nitty-gritty. This next lick, played in signature Jaco style, has four key components:

1. It outlines the chord by snaking around diatonic scale tones, including the 2nd and 6th (not just roots and 5ths), and using chromatic approach notes such as the raised 4th (♯4th) and lowered 2nd (♭2th), where necessary, to lead from one scale tone to another;

2. Percussive dead notes, muted with the fretting hand;

3. The use of rakes—picking two or more strings with a single downstroke, thus conserving energy;

4. Hammer-ons only *between* beats and in the *center* of a four-note series of 16th notes. Placing them in this manner helps the line swing more.

EXAMPLE 2

Let's try another example in the same vein but, instead of staying on one chord, we'll move from the I chord (E) to the IV chord (A) and insert a few rests. The same principles as the previous lick apply.

EXAMPLE 3

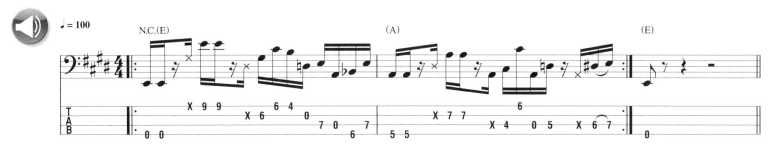

Here's another I–IV progression. This example has more of a Stax, old-school R&B feel, but with full-on 16ths throughout—almost as if we're applying Jaco's style to a Duck Dunn bass line. Note the contour of the line: although it has the same energy as the previous two examples, it's harmonically more static and not as frenetic.

EXAMPLE 4

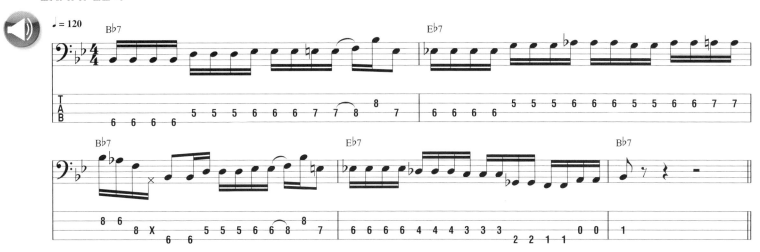

Up to this point, we've been dealing only with major keys, so for our last example, let's switch gears a bit with this minor key, Rocco Prestia-influenced groove. In the first three measures, we build tension by playing an unrelenting repeated figure; then, in the last measure, we'll play a quick octave run down the neck with the same intensity. As always, try to keep each note as short as possible so that they "pop."

EXAMPLE 5

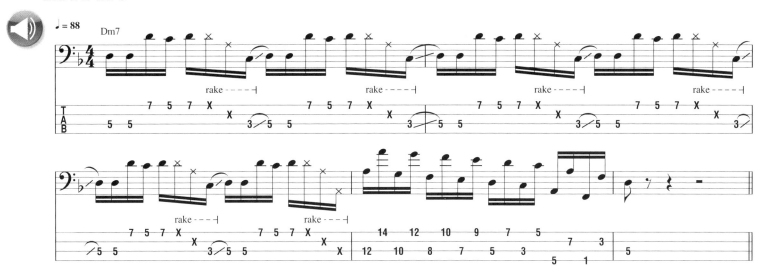

LESSON #72: MAJOR 7TH INTERVAL

The major 7th interval saw an uptick in popularity among songwriters in the '70s, especially among those in the pop and soft-rock genres due to its characteristically light sound. When composing grooves, incorporating major 7ths offers another tonal option, in addition to the usual 5th/octave paradigm.

Major 7ths are fretted in a similar way to octaves, but with the top note lowered by one fret, as illustrated below.

EXAMPLE 1

Let's jump right in. In this first example, we'll build a bass figure around a I–IV chord progression, specifically using major 7ths as the focal point.

EXAMPLE 2

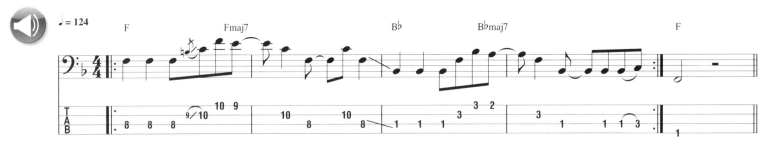

Major 7ths also sit very comfortably when combined with open strings, as illustrated in the following rock ballad groove.

EXAMPLE 3

Here's an example, in the style of Stone Temple Pilots' Robert DeLeo, showing another open-position major 7th, but fretted on adjacent strings.

EXAMPLE 4

This new wave-flavored bass riff, centered on upper-register major 7ths, also makes use of open strings played against melodic lines. As indicated in the music, be sure to let all the notes ring out.

EXAMPLE 5

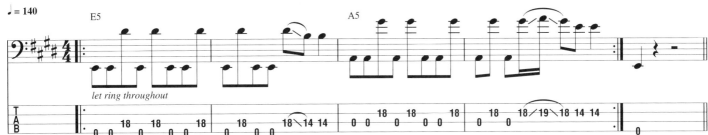

While the previous examples featured major 7ths mostly in the context of I–IV chord progressions, the following musical passage illustrates how a closed-position major 7th interval can be used as the foundation for a stand-alone bass riff. Fret the major 7th interval in the first measure with the ring and pinky fingers so you can make that fret-hand stretch in the second measure. And again, be sure to sustain all notes!

EXAMPLE 6

Let's conclude with one more stand-alone lick in this vein. The following riff starts with a power-chord fretboard shape, moves to a major 3rd shape in the second measure, and ends with a major 7th for the remainder of the figure. Fret the high E (played on the G string) with your ring finger.

EXAMPLE 7

LESSON #73: MINOR 7TH INTERVAL

In popular music, the minor 7th interval often reigns supreme due to its dark, forceful character, a fact not lost on bands as wildly disparate as AC/DC, the Red Hot Chili Peppers, Tool, Led Zeppelin, U2, Chic, and the Violent Femmes, to name just a handful.

In bass lines, it's pretty common to see this interval played with the root on an open string and the minor 7th fretted on the next higher string at the fifth fret, as illustrated here:

EXAMPLE 1

Let's see how this works in an applied musical context. In this mid-tempo rock groove, a minor 7th (G) is played against the open-string root (A) and then hammered onto the octave.

EXAMPLE 2

In this Tool-inspired heavy rock line, the bass and guitars join together to create a nasty, menacing wall of sound.

EXAMPLE 3

Here's a disco-tinged mashup of what the Rolling Stones might sound like if Chic's Bernard Edwards was their bass player.

EXAMPLE 4

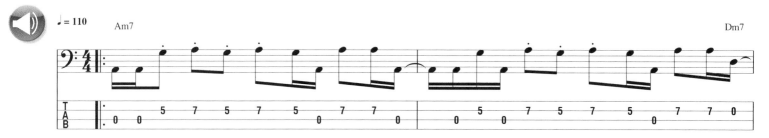

Tons upon tons of slap licks are established around the open-position Em7 interval because of its deep tone and easy accessibility on the fretboard.

EXAMPLE 5

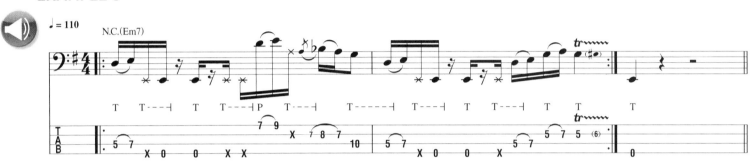

While open-string minor 7ths are easy to play and always sound good, it's useful to be familiar with closed-position minor 7ths as well. These are located on the same fret, two strings apart.

In this next lick, the minor 7th interval is fretted with the same finger on both notes by barring with the index finger across the third fret.

EXAMPLE 6

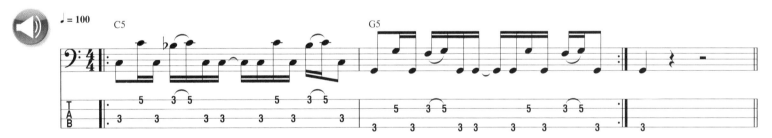

This last example shows closed-position minor 7ths resolving to major 3rds, descending chromatically. In this case, the minor 7ths are fretted with the middle and ring fingers.

EXAMPLE 7

LESSON #74: COOL BASS TRICKS

An oft-overlooked aspect of the playing of virtuoso guitarists and bassists such as Eddie Van Halen, Steve Vai, George Lynch, and Billy Sheehan is their use of noise to convey aggression, attitude, or even humor, as part of their expression. This lesson is devoted to a handful of little cool-sounding tricks, which, when used with discretion, can add another color to your playing.

QUARTER-STEP UNISON BENDS

A unison bend is when a guitarist frets a note with his index finger and then frets a note a whole step below on the adjacent, lower string, which is then bent up to the pitch of the first note. The resulting sound is huge and aggressive, and some guitarists even deliberately over-bend the bottom note slightly for a nastier, more dissonant effect.

Due to much thicker strings, unison bends are mostly impossible to execute on bass—or, at best, extremely difficult and impractical. However, we can still perform quarter-step bends and combine them with open strings, creating our own version of the unison bend.

The example below is a heavy lick inspired by Tool, featuring a quarter-step/open-string unison bend on a D note. To achieve the bend, push up (toward you) while avoiding choking out the open D string. Also, use a pick to add edge to your tone and to facilitate hitting both strings of the unison bend simultaneously. Grunge away!

EXAMPLE 1

SLIDING HARMONICS

Pearl Jam bassist Jeff Ament famously slides harmonics in his band's now-classic "Even Flow." To do this, simply strike a harmonic, keeping your finger on the string. Then push down onto the fretboard while the harmonic is still ringing and slide up the fretboard.

EXAMPLE 2

 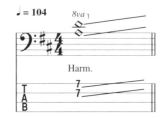

CASCADING HARMONICS

Long favored by guitarists such as Randy Rhoads and a host of '80s-era shredders, this little bit of ear candy is fairly easy to execute. While performing double pull-offs on the string of your choice, gently slide the edge of your pick hand, or perhaps the tip of your pick-hand index finger, down the string in the direction of the nut. This will produce a series of random harmonics that are constantly changing due to the combination of whatever note you happen to be on while performing the double pull-offs and the point on the string where your pick hand is sliding. You may want to add slight distortion or overdrive to help bring out the harmonics.

EXAMPLE 3

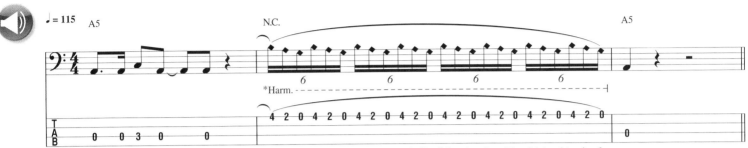

*Produce random harmonics by gradually sliding the edge of the pick hand (or tip of pick-hand index finger) along the length of the string while performing pull-offs.

This trick also works on trills.

EXAMPLE 4

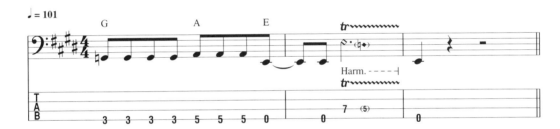

TAPPED OCTAVES

You can create a virtual octave pedal via artificial harmonics. Start by fretting a note, and then quickly tap onto the same string exactly one octave (12 frets) higher—without pressing the string onto the fretboard. Make sure you hit hard enough to get a good bounce off the string. Once you become accustomed to this technique, start changing pitches with your fretting hand, following along an octave higher with your tapping hand. Remember: you're not tapping the string conventionally; you're hitting it just hard enough to sound an octave harmonic.

EXAMPLE 5

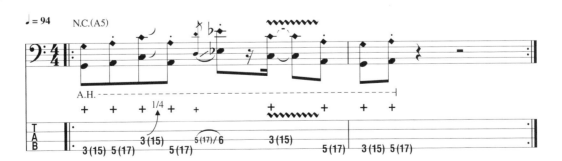

LESSON #75: NOTE SUBSTITUTIONS

One of the perks of being behind the instrument most often charged with the role of harmonic foundation is that we can completely change the overall harmony of the ensemble by moving one single note. In this lesson, we'll explore how cleverly placed note choices can breathe new life into a piece of music.

Before we get started, here's a quick theory roadmap on harmonic analysis. In the major scale below, you'll see triads—three-note chords—built upon each scale degree. Each one has a corresponding Roman numeral; major chords are in uppercase and minor chords are in lowercase. We will be using these Roman numerals to identify the common chord progressions shown throughout the rest of this lesson.

C MAJOR SCALE WITH TRIADS

Chord progressions are often described by numbers. For example, a "one-three-four-five," or "I–iii–IV–V," in the key of C (as shown here), would be C–Em–F–G.

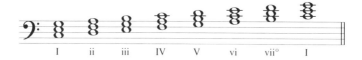

For our first example, we have a simple I–IV–I–IV progression in the key of G.

EXAMPLE 1

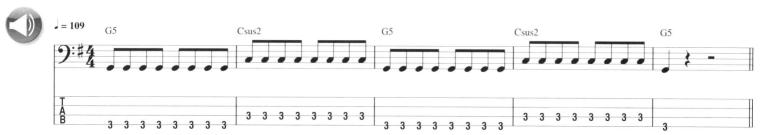

If we take the second G chord in the above example and replace the root with its relative minor, E, the resultant chord is Em7, effectively taking a major chord and making it minor, thus changing the flavor of the entire progression.

EXAMPLE 2

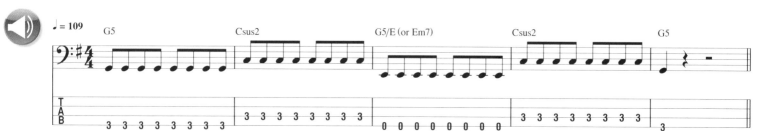

In this next example, we have a jazzy IV–iii–ii–V chord progression in the key of G, resolving to the I chord.

If we take the second chord—the Bm7—and replace the root (B) with an E, we end up with an E9sus4 chord—and a completely different tone color.

EXAMPLE 3

EXAMPLE 4

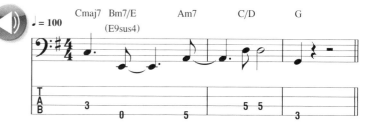

Let's try this chord progression again in a slightly different context.

We're going to replace the root of the Bm7 chord with an E again, only this time, instead of changing the whole chord, we're only going to move one note, creating a ii–v–i in A minor. This not only creates a nice tonal change as in Example 4, it's also good voice leading into the Am7 chord.

EXAMPLE 5

EXAMPLE 6

Let's try another. The following musical example shows a fairly standard IV–V–iii–vi chord progression in E♭.

Now run through it again, but after you play the first chord, stay on A♭ this time, instead of moving with the rest of the ensemble to B♭. Doing so raises tension and builds anticipation for the impending Gm7 chord.

EXAMPLE 7

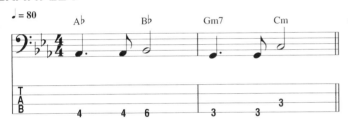

EXAMPLE 8

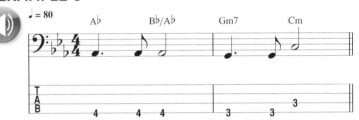

Here's a stock pop/rock chord progression in D minor:

EXAMPLE 9

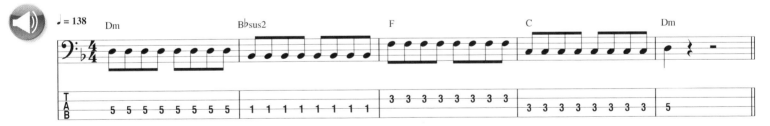

Now let's stay on the note D for the second chord, B♭, and replace the root of the subsequent F chord with its 5th, C. Doing so effectively turns the D in the first measure and the C in the third measure into pedal tones, or notes that remain stationary while other notes or chords are played above them.

EXAMPLE 10

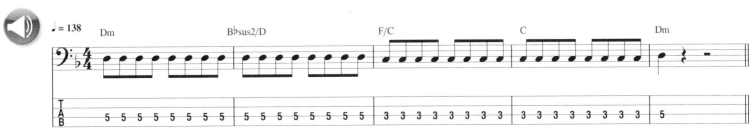

Octave intervals are great for when you want to make a bass line pop or to simply add another layer of beef to the low end. You can play them on their own, insert them into licks, slide into them, or even slide *with* them. In this lesson, we'll explore several ways that we can incorporate octaves into our playing. Let's get started with a very basic but funky i–iv chord progression.

EXAMPLE 1

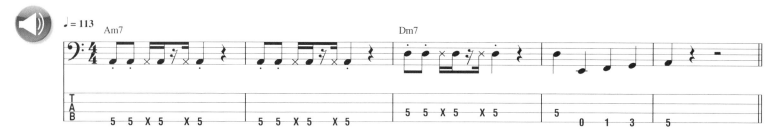

Now let's see what happens when we add octaves.

EXAMPLE 2

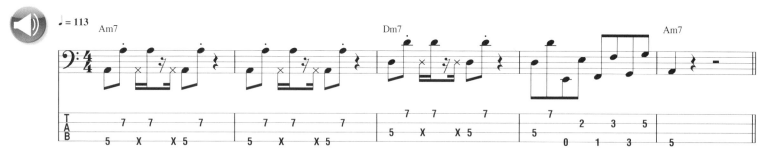

Now we'll take the same line and make it rumble and sound funkier by adding quick grace-note slides here and there.

EXAMPLE 3

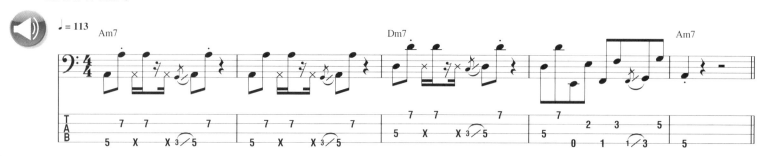

Speaking of slides, here's a lick where, in the fourth measure, the slides are actually part of the rhythm.

EXAMPLE 4

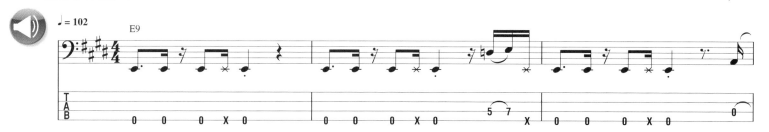

We can also use octaves to help drive the overall rhythm. In the example below, notice how something as simple as quarter notes and the octaves landing on the backbeats can evoke movement.

EXAMPLE 5

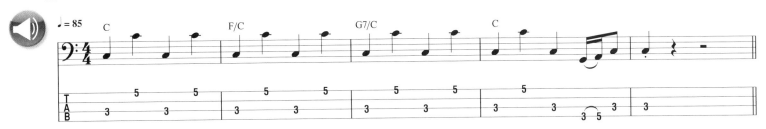

Now let's take a look at the mellow mid-tempo rock groove below. Example 6—the "before" version, if you will—shows a basic modal groove. We can make it pop by throwing in quick octaves, as illustrated in Example 7 (the "after" version). Incidentally, this particular move was one of the calling cards of the late, great Chic bassist Bernard Edwards.

EXAMPLE 6

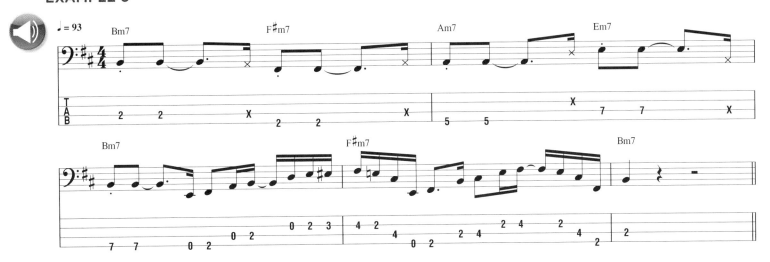

EXAMPLE 7

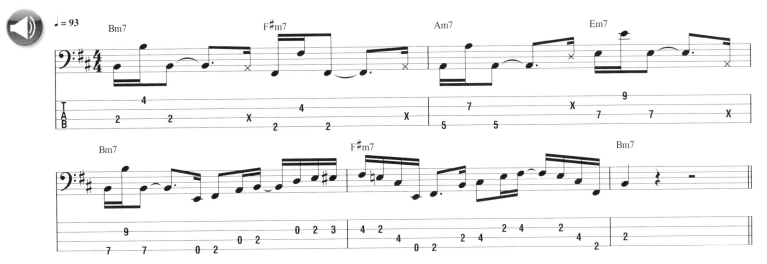

LESSON #77: OCTAVE CHOICE

As a bassist, you have the power to alter the mood of the music simply by your choice of register—the octave range in which you play your lines. For example, you can go heavy by staying on the lower strings and not venturing much past the third or fourth frets, or you can evoke a more tender vibe or raise the drama by going higher on the fretboard. Ultimately, musical context should dictate your octave selection. Let's explore this idea further with the following musical examples.

Traditionally, we bassists tend to stick to the low and middle registers, rarely venturing past a high C or D just above the musical staff. Indeed, this works in most musical situations; after all, our role is to anchor the rest of the band and provide "bottom" while the guitars, keyboards, and vocals handle the higher pitches.

Below is a typical low to middle pitched bass line that you might hear in a common pop/rock chord progression.

EXAMPLE 1

Certain styles of music, such as metal, often require a deliberately low center in the bass, either to reinforce a guitar riff or simply to provide power, as illustrated in the following drop D lick.

EXAMPLE 2

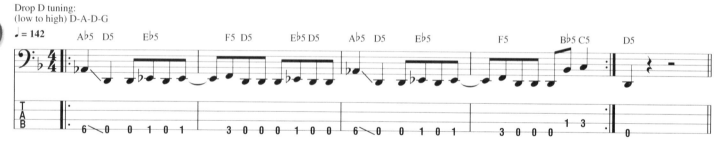

Other genres of music—for example, lighter, "jangly" styles of rock and pop—frequently call for the bass to stay closer to the middle register. In the examples below, note the difference in mood as the bass plays the progression in the lower octave (Example 3), and how it seems to sound lighter when the line is played an octave higher (Example 4).

EXAMPLE 3

EXAMPLE 4

There are times when it's totally appropriate to venture high up on the fretboard, such as when playing a delicate melodic line or when building tension. In this next example, the bass holds down a pedal tone for the first two bars and then jumps up an octave as the section builds.

EXAMPLE 5

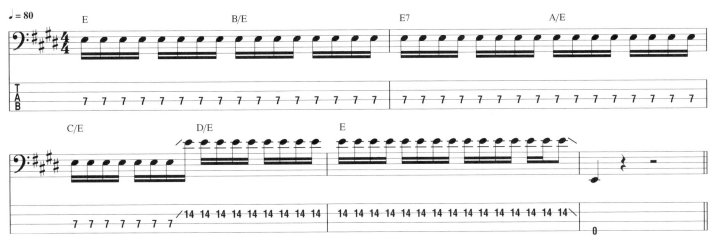

I took improvisation classes back in my college years. My instructor, saxophonist Joe Lovano, after listening to me solo in the upper register exclusively, pointed out that I was playing (at the time) a five-string bass with a 24-fret neck, and thus had an enormous range of notes at my disposal; so, why was I limiting myself to the relatively few notes at the top of the neck? His words left an impression, and I often heed them to this day when composing bass lines or interpreting arrangements.

In the example below, listen to the how the bass is low in the main section, jumps high toward the conclusion in order to raise anticipation, and then provides finality by resolving to the low open E.

EXAMPLE 6

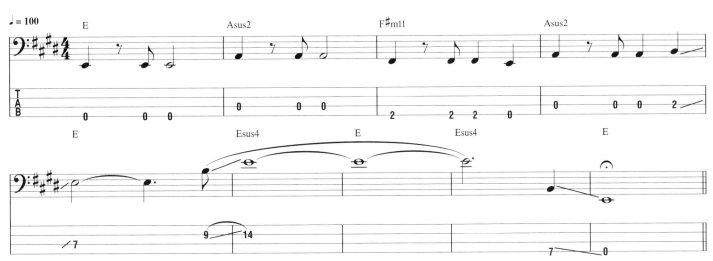

Other factors to consider are: where is the vocal sitting, and should you stay near it, or go well below it to provide contrast? Are you fighting the guitar for space? Developing an instinct for how octave choice affects overall mood is a key skill in providing support—or backbone—to a musical situation.

LESSON #78: THE OCTAVE JUMP

To keep a bass line from becoming too monotonous, it's sometimes musically beneficial to briefly jump up—or even down—an octave to help emphasize a musical passage or to build anticipation for an upcoming new section. In this lesson, we'll learn how to develop an instinct for when it's appropriate to do so.

For our first example, we'll play a straight groove that we'll think of as the end of a verse to an imaginary song. Notice that, at the end of the third measure, the bass line briefly jumps up an octave to highlight the transition into the next section, our virtual chorus.

EXAMPLE 1

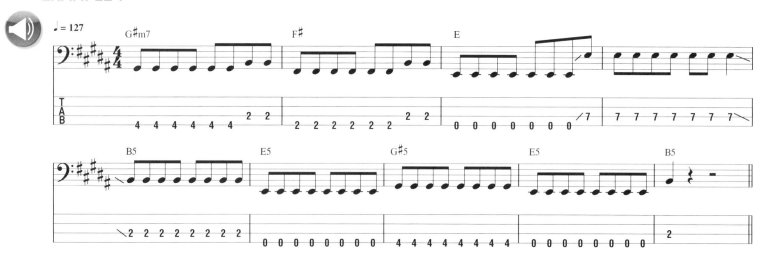

Octave jumps don't always have to be in an upward direction. In the following musical passage, we'll jump the octave in the same context, only we'll go down instead. It's the same level of anticipation, just expressed in a different way.

EXAMPLE 2

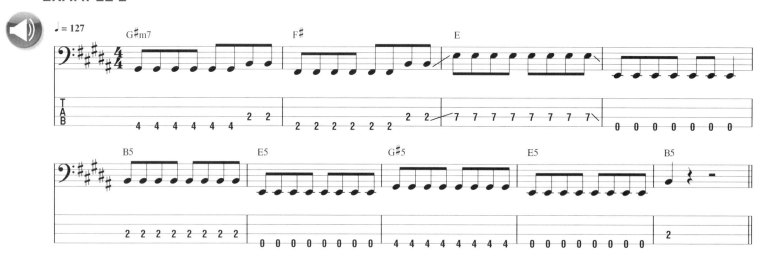

Jumping octaves was a signature move of the Who's John Entwistle. In the following example, inspired by his work in "Won't Get Fooled Again," note how the bass jumps up to emphasize the drum hits in measures 4 and 8.

EXAMPLE 3

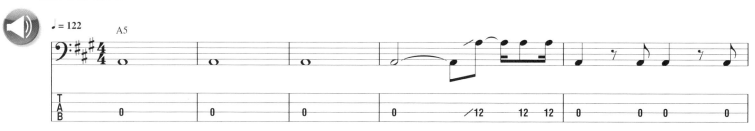

Similarly, Paul McCartney can be heard using this musical device in the Beatles' "Polythene Pam," which inspired the example below.

EXAMPLE 4

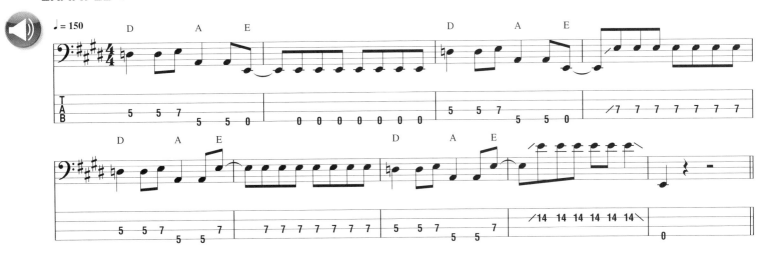

Octave jumps can add emphasis to a chord change without actually playing the root of the chord. This works particularly well in I–IV chord progressions, as shown in the following excerpt.

EXAMPLE 5

Sometimes octave jumps are simply used to raise tension, and don't necessarily have to coincide with drum hits or section changes. As we'll see in this last example, we can take a basic chord progression and increase the drama level by merely moving the bass part incrementally up the neck two octaves.

EXAMPLE 6

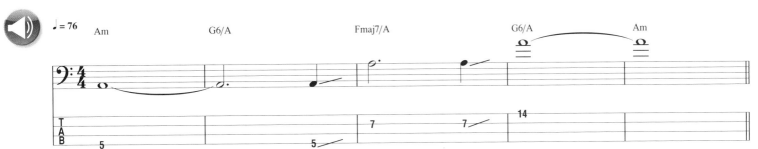

So you can slap and probably could hold your own through a few Red Hot Chili Peppers tunes. Nevertheless, sometimes more power is desired on the bottom end, and one way to accomplish this is by incorporating octaves, much like keyboardists playing octaves in the left hand. In this lesson, we'll explore the concept of slapping octave figures on two strings simultaneously.

The technique itself is pretty simple and self-explanatory: fret an octave shape as shown below and then pull the bottom string with the thumb while simultaneously snapping the top string with the index finger. However, for it to be effective, your pick-hand thumb and index finger must be completely in sync, attacking the strings at exactly the same time.

EXAMPLE 1

Slapped octaves work best when there's a lot of musical space between you and the guitarist or other instruments in the band, or it's just you and a drummer, or even just you. Let's get started with a few exercises. In Example 2, we'll stay on one octave group, moving it around in Example 3. Remember to ensure that your pick-hand thumb and index finger are perfectly synced up!

EXAMPLE 2

EXAMPLE 3

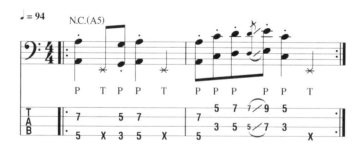

Now that we have the basics down, let's apply slapped octaves to some real-world grooves. In the following example, think like a drummer to help you feel where to slap with the thumb (kick drum) and snap or pull with the index finger (snare drum). If you like, add a little distortion for extra growl!

EXAMPLE 4

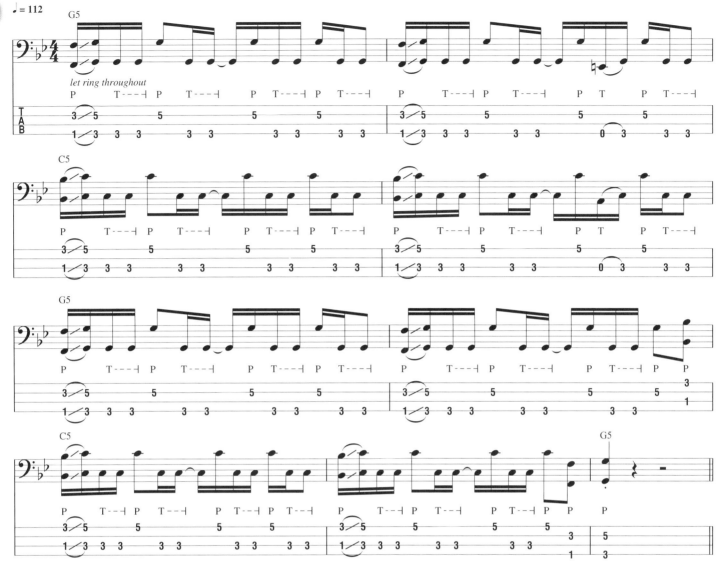

For our last two licks, we'll pick up the tempo and explore lines that combine muted notes, conventional single-note slap phrases, and slapped octaves.

EXAMPLE 5

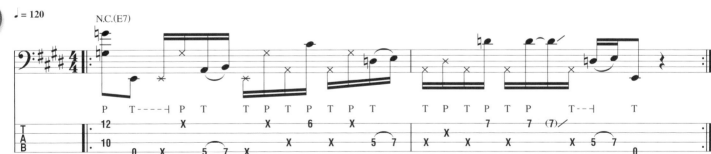

EXAMPLE 6

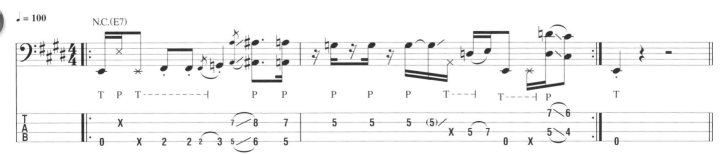

LESSON #80: ONE-STRING BASS LINES

Sometimes there's just nothing more glorious than picking up your bass, lowering the strap, dialing in a nice fat tone on your amp, assuming the rock stance, and snaking your way up and down one string while basking in the simplicity of it all.

As a kid who came of musical age in the shred-happy '80s, it was refreshing to see a small wave of musicians in the '90s, such as Presidents of the United States of America's Chris Ballew and Morphine's Mark Sandman, strip the bass down to its barest essentials. Ballew considers himself a "basitarist," having fashioned what is essentially a two-stringed bass on a guitar's body, while his friend and one-time bandmate Sandman's basses were modified, or sometimes built from scratch, into two-string instruments tuned to power chord-friendly 5ths, or even one-string instruments. Rather than limit their capabilities, these minimalistic basses helped Ballew and Sandman develop sounds unique and identifiable to them, as well as accomplish more with less in their songwriting.

Playing on one string is a good exercise in restraint, as it challenges you to come up with interesting lines without the assistance of the other strings. It also produces a slinkier sound due to having to slide from note to note, as well as a thicker tone resulting from fretting middle-range notes higher up on the neck.

Let's start by doing a comparison. Example 1 and Example 2 are comprised of the same notes, but the former is fretted across multiple strings, while the latter is played on only one string.

EXAMPLE 1

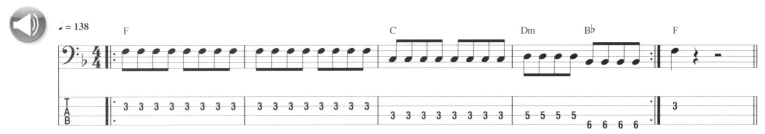

EXAMPLE 2

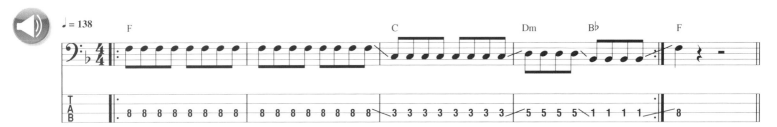

You probably noticed that this groove, as fretted in Example 2, has a slightly meatier tone, an edgier attitude due to the slides, and is just plain easier to play, at least as far as your picking hand is concerned, because you don't have to cross strings.

Let's explore more one-string bass lines. This next one is fast, performed exclusively on the A string, and should be played with a punk-rock sneer.

(Please don't rip any strings off your bass to get through the remainder of this lesson.)

EXAMPLE 3

The following hard rock lick shows how you can effectively imply harmony and rhythm by using only one string. Pick or pluck aggressively and pay attention to the accents on the muted notes. Also, to prevent extraneous noise and enhance the percussiveness of the muted notes, avoid muting the string at the major harmonic node points (generally, the fifth, seventh, ninth, and 12th frets). The idea is to keep the muted notes as dead and drum-like as possible.

EXAMPLE 4

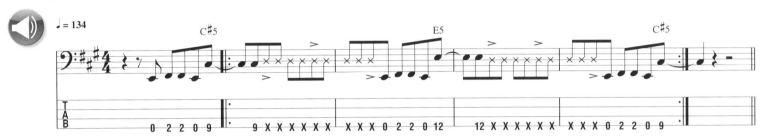

We'll conclude with a metal-inspired half-time groove that uses constant 16th notes up and down the E string. For an even attack, use a pick—and enjoy the slides!

EXAMPLE 5

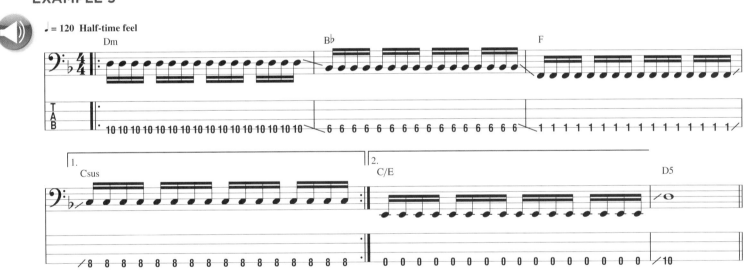

OPEN STRINGS:
FILLS AND GROOVES

In this lesson, we'll explore how to take advantage of open strings to create fills and grooves, or enhance them. Let's start with the most natural scenario, which is when the song you're playing is in any of the open keys—E, A, D, or G, or any of their parallel or relative minor keys. The following example shows a IV–V progression in the key of E. Note the fill on the last V (B) chord.

EXAMPLE 1

Now let's spice it up by re-fretting that same fill entirely on the D string and alternating each note against the open A string in a 16th-note pattern to match the drums, as well as add a little rumble (and a little flash too, if we're being honest).

EXAMPLE 2

This next one, inspired by Geddy Lee, follows the same idea.

EXAMPLE 3

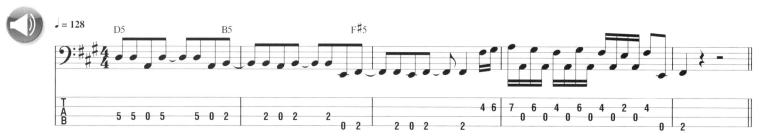

While the licks thus far are in keys in which the open strings are consonant, you don't necessarily have to be in a "cooperating" key to use this technique; you can utilize the open strings as a chromatic passing tone, an incidental "bridge" between diatonic or chromatic tones, or as a percussive lead-in to the next bar.

Example 4 is a repetitive ii–V chord progression in the style of Motown great James Jamerson, featuring the open A and E strings used in this fashion. Though the notes A and E don't "belong" in a Gm7 chord, they don't cause egregious dissonance in this bass line because they're not the focus of the phrase, the way they're placed puts them in more of a percussive function, and they simply just go by fast.

EXAMPLE 4

This next phrase, inspired by Led Zeppelin's John Paul Jones, follows the same principle. Notice how open strings are used as "skips" from one tone to the next, indicated by asterisks in the music.

EXAMPLE 5

And finally, here's a fingerstyle funk riff in D♭. Chances are very good that you will rarely encounter a groove in this style in such an unusual key, but I wrote it this way to demonstrate that, as long as the notes are placed correctly, even the most dissonant juxtaposition of open strings won't necessarily jar the listener.

EXAMPLE 6

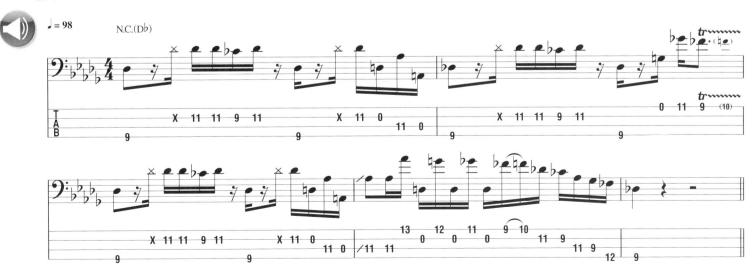

LESSON #82: OPEN-STRING DRONES

Guitarists have long achieved a full, rich, "jangly" sound by employing drones—open strings allowed to ring out over (or sometimes even under) fretted chords or single-note lines. Since the bass guitar is a multi-stringed instrument as well, why should we let the guitarists have all the fun? In this lesson, we'll explore ways to make use of open strings as part of creating an overall harmonic backdrop. (You may want to use a pick to play the examples in this lesson.)

Our first example demonstrates a simple but effective use of the open G string as a drone above power chords that move up and down the neck beneath it. Also, the D major dyad (major 3rd) against the open G in the first measure adds some nice shimmer.

EXAMPLE 1

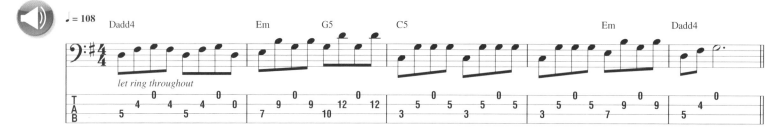

And now for something completely different, try out this fast banjo lick arranged for slap bass guitar! Again, the G string is used as a drone note, much like the five-string banjo's open-string drone.

EXAMPLE 2

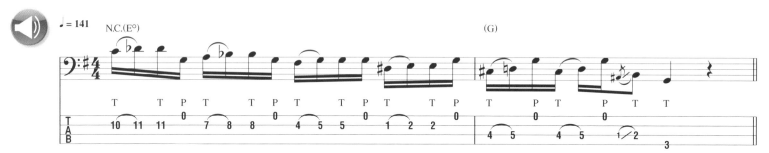

Droning on the D string enables us to accompany ourselves with a melody on the G string above it, and also allows us to fret moveable chords *around* it on the G and A strings.

EXAMPLE 3

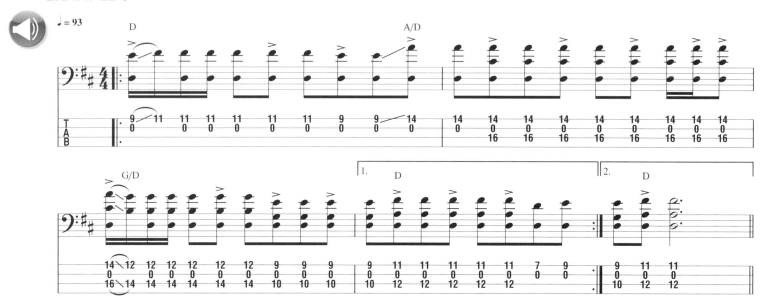

In this example, we'll move arpeggiated major triads up the fretboard against the open A string.

EXAMPLE 4

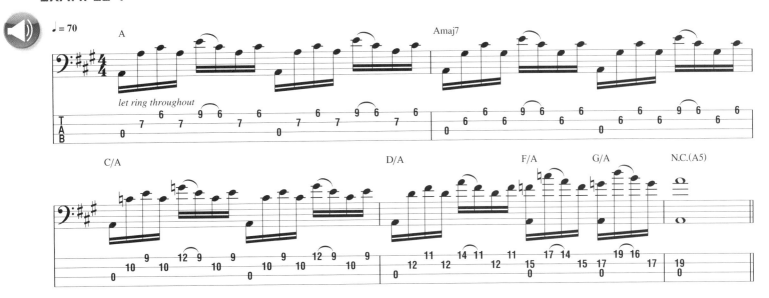

The open E string provides a powerful backdrop over which we can move chords.

EXAMPLE 5

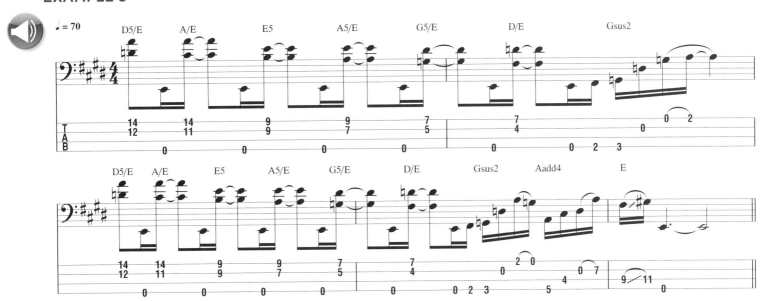

This lick, with its combination of melodies and strummed chords mixed in with various open strings, sums it all up pretty nicely!

EXAMPLE 6

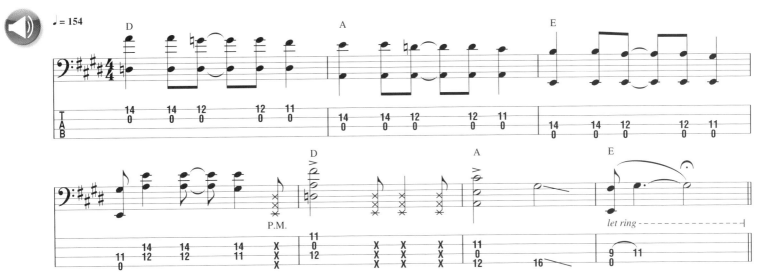

Muting the strings with the palm of the picking hand—well, technically, the heel of the hand—is most commonly associated with guitarists, especially those of the hard rock and metal species (see: Metallica's James Hetfield), but electric bass players have been doing it for decades, albeit in different musical contexts. Some are guitarists who transferred their natural technique to bass, while others, even those as disparate as Sting, Will Lee, and Geddy Lee, use it as another arrow in their musical quivers. In this lesson, we'll take a look at situations in bass lines where palm muting is advantageous.

R&B and funk music often contain bass parts that require quick staccato note passages, rests, and tone that emphasizes bottom end (or "booty," as my bass-playing friends in the genre call it). In these situations, strings that are overly bright can get in the way by causing too much noise or sustain, especially when the groove calls for something smoky and slinky. Palm muting is an effective way to rein it all in, so to speak. You can decide the degree to which the notes are clipped by adjusting the amount of pressure you place on the strings with the picking hand. This technique works equally well whether playing with your thumb or with a pick.

Let's apply palm muting to some stylistically diverse musical situations. We'll start with a simple, sparse, slow-burning A minor groove.

EXAMPLE 1

Now let's notch it up slightly with this Motown-inspired line. In this scenario, palm muting serves two purposes: 1) it allows us to emulate that vintage, dark, flatwound James Jamerson bass sound, and 2) the quick attack and decay caused by muting the strings emphasizes the rhythm. To navigate the quick 16th-note downstrokes with the thumb, don't pick too hard; instead, use a light touch.

EXAMPLE 2

Reggae music also traditionally calls for dull, low-end, heavy bass tones. Try playing the following groove with conventional fingerstyle and then try it with palm muting, preferably with the thumb, instead of a pick. Which technique sits in the pocket better?

EXAMPLE 3

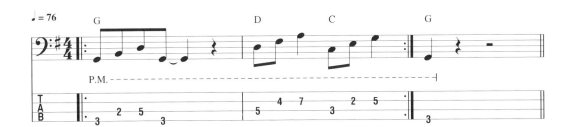

Sometimes palm mutes function as a way to vary the sound of your pick-hand articulation. For example, the following lick is picked with both the thumb and the index finger while palm muting, and the palm mute itself is tight at some points and more relaxed in others, especially on the accented notes, which should be picked aggressively with the index finger.

EXAMPLE 4

And finally, palm mutes can simply be used to emphasize crescendos in a musical passage. The following rock lick is best played with a pick. Start with a heavy palm mute, gradually relaxing it as the crescendo builds, eventually releasing it altogether.

EXAMPLE 5

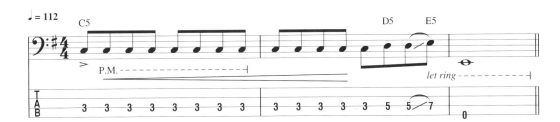

PEDAL TONES

A pedal tone is a sustained tone over which changing notes and chords are played. It can be used to add contrast to a chord progression in which the bass typically follows the chords or to increase tension, especially when the pedal tone in question is dissonant compared to the rest of the music. In this lesson, we'll explore how staying on one note can affect the overall sound in various musical situations.

Let's start with a IV–I–V–I progression in the key of D. We'll stay on the root, D, throughout. Because each chord in the progression is diatonic (belonging to the same key) to the sustained D note, this pedal tone is referred to as consonant.

EXAMPLE 1

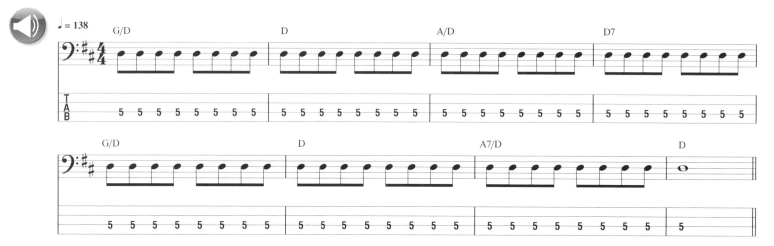

In our next example, we'll increase the drama by resolutely sticking to an open A as we cycle through a series of diatonic chords in A minor, slightly veering out of the box to a D *major* chord at the end.

EXAMPLE 2

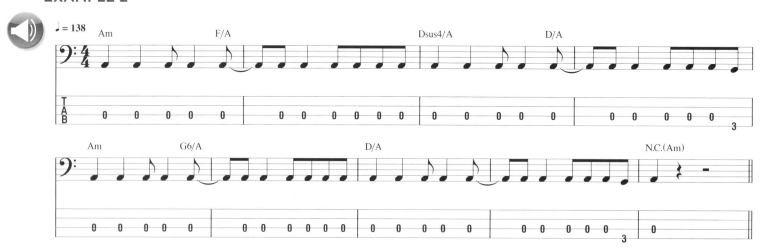

Sometimes staying on one note on the low end can create an intriguing major/minor dichotomy, as illustrated below. Here, the guitar starts on E major and then works its way to a G chord against the still-sounding E in the bass, creating an overall Em7 harmony.

EXAMPLE 3

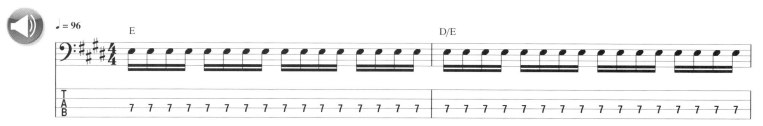

Pedal tones don't always have to be in the same key as the chords they're supporting; indeed, dissonant pedal tones are frequently used to raise tension, as demonstrated in the second half of the following example.

EXAMPLE 4

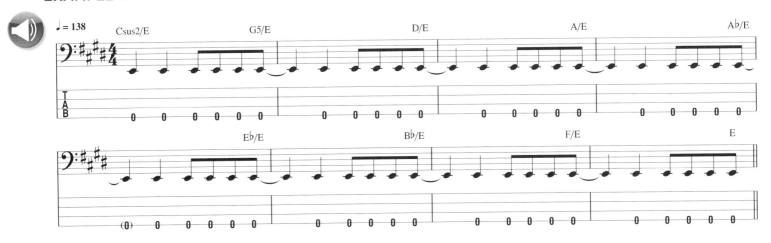

Pedal tones can also be a springboard for riffs and fills, rather than a harmonic device. In the example below, we'll use the open A string to facilitate the fast-moving, metal-tinged fill.

EXAMPLE 5

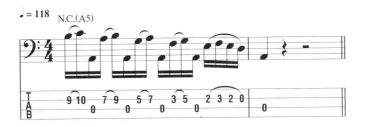

The following lick, inspired by bassist to the stars Pino Palladino, explores this same concept, but with a fretted pedal tone.

EXAMPLE 6

In this last example, we'll play a fully fleshed-out metal riff in which the guitar joins the bass to anchor the phrase with a pedal tone.

EXAMPLE 7

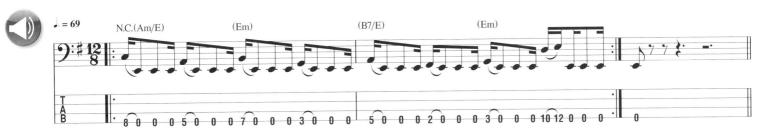

LESSON #85: INVERTED PEDAL TONE

A pedal tone is a sustained tone, usually in the bass or bottom voice, over which various notes and chords are played. An inverted pedal tone is one that occurs in parts other than the bottom voice. For example, you've probably heard inverted pedal tones in classical music, such as in the passage below, which features a moving bottom voice while the top note remains constant.

EXAMPLE 1

Let's explore how this musical device can be used in the context of a bass line. This next example is a moderately slow groove inspired by Paul McCartney's part in the Beatles' "Sun King." In this case, a high E is repeated throughout while the notes preceding it change.

EXAMPLE 2

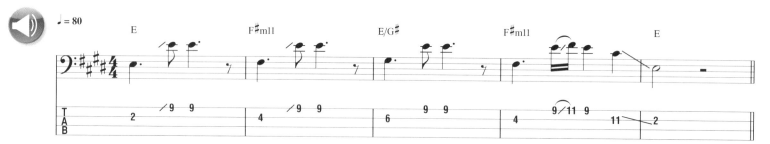

This next lick shows an inverted pedal tone (G) with slight embellishments, played over a similar groove.

EXAMPLE 3

Now we'll kick it up by playing a slightly up-tempo, four-on-the-floor rock groove.

EXAMPLE 4

Here's another mid-tempo rock groove utilizing an inverted pedal tone.

EXAMPLE 5

You can even use inverted pedal tones to create your own stand-alone bass riffs. As you play through the following lick, notice how the repeated high E implies other harmonies as you move the notes below it.

EXAMPLE 6

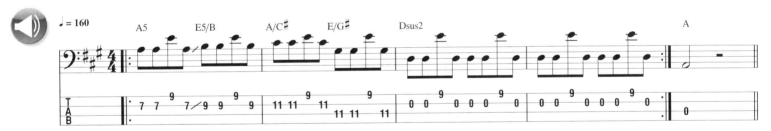

Inverted pedal tones aren't always in the top voice; they can occur in the middle voice as well. This is sometimes called an internal pedal tone. Though not commonly heard in rock bass lines, it's nevertheless good to be familiar with it, as understanding harmonies and voice leading can help inform your decisions when constructing your own bass lines.

EXAMPLE 7

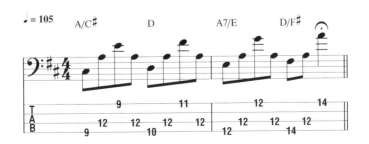

LESSON #86: PLAYING WITH A DRUMMER

Drums and bass—that musical bond so sacred, a musical genre was named after it. If the drums are the foundation, the bass is the glue that connects it to the rest of the band, and together they provide the band's harmonic and rhythmic backbone. Therefore, being in sync is a must.

You and I probably share the same drummer pet peeves—inability to keep good time, timidity with the kick drum, and similar annoyances. And we've probably snickered at the same vast catalog of drummer jokes. However, my drummer friends have generously shared their bass player pet peeves with me as well, and the ones I hear the most are: lack of listening (bass player is off in his own world) and showboating—the playing of gratuitous fills that show off the chops but, at best, distract from the song, and at worst, throw the band off completely.

You've probably heard that you should "lock in with the drums" hundreds of times, but what does this mean, exactly? Well, as this is more a philosophical topic and less an applied musical one, I'll put down my bass and humbly share some thoughts.

The first thing to remember is that the drummer is a fellow human, a sensitive being just like you, with an urge to create. Therefore, I can't stress how important communication is to a successful bassist-drummer interaction. Listen to each other, watch each either, and try to compromise if the groove is being pulled too much in one direction or another. I will even literally watch the drumstick hit the snare head or hi-hat and time my bass hits to it if I'm unsure of where the pocket is. Communicate, communicate, communicate!

Years ago, I was once told by a respected vocalist, "You are there to serve the music, not the other way around. The music will kick your ass." What is the song? What approach is most appropriate for the music? Don't come slamming right out of the gate with an overt technical display. Err on the side of keeping it simple and give yourself—and the drummer—time to feel out the situation and room to build.

Let's revisit the idea of how exactly bass and drums should "lock in" together. It's common knowledge that when the drums hit a downbeat, the bass should be right there. However, while some musicians are human metronomes, others prefer to sit back a hair behind the beat, especially when playing soul or blues. This is a subtle difference, but one that sometimes determines whether a piece of music has swagger. So listen closely to what's happening: is the drummer right on the beat, or does he lay back a bit? Do you prefer to lay back a bit yourself? Can you do so without dragging if the drummer is more of a "right on the click" guy? When you play syncopated lines and the drummer is playing straight, are you still in the pocket? And perhaps the most reliable litmus test of all: if the rest of the band were to suddenly be silenced by a giant mute button or gardening accident, would you and the drummer still sound good together?

There are other musical factors to consider as well. For example, let's say you're playing a basic rock tune with a common rhythm, like this one:

EXAMPLE 1

Is it better to fill the entire bar with sound, as in Example 1, or should you let up on the snare hits to allow them their own space, as shown in the following variation?

EXAMPLE 2

Decisions like these may seem minor, but they affect the overall feel in some way.

Let's go even beyond notes: are you paying attention to when to play loud versus soft, or big versus small, as a team? You'd be surprised how often dynamics go ignored; as the rhythm section, you and the drummer, collectively, have the ability to either light a fire under the band or pull things back, thus elevating even the most simple songs to another level.

Finally, let's talk about *time*. Yes, the drummer is the traditional timekeeper of the ensemble, but you should always be striving to have your own time together. It's indeed a pleasure to be able to lean on a great drummer, but it's not his job to keep time for everyone. What if he were to suddenly stop playing? Would you be able to hold the groove together by yourself? Or sometimes, even with the best of intentions, the vibe just isn't there; occasionally, it's the drummer who's off in his own world, negating any successful communication. So again, it's up to you to keep things on track.

All of this really just boils down to two things: being open and listening. If you and the drummer you're working with are on point, it won't take long before you're intuitively completing each other's thoughts and inspiring each other to play better.

LESSON #87: SHAKE IT

One of the funkiest moves that you can perform on a bass guitar is the fret-hand "shake"—literally shake your fret-hand finger along the string as you fret a note. To perform an effective shake, you have to employ proper fret-hand technique: grip the neck with the thumb firmly pinching the back of the neck, and avoid "clawing" the neck, both of which are shown.

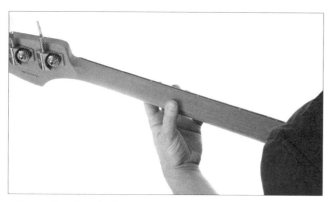

Proper fret-hand grip

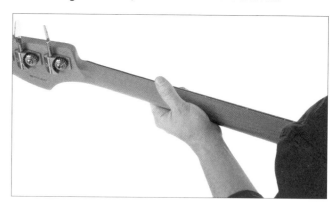

Improper fret-hand grip

With the thumb anchored to the back of the neck, fret the note and then quickly—and slightly—slide your finger back and forth. Be careful not to overdo it—just a little bit will do the trick. The key here is subtlety; it shouldn't take over the bass line, only enhance it.

This is similar to vibrato in that you're altering the pitch by causing it to waver, but shaking produces a deeper effect. To hear the difference, check out following lick, played with vibrato in the first measure and repeated with a shake in the second measure.

EXAMPLE 1

You can hear this technique performed to perfection by the legendary Verdine White all over the Earth Wind & Fire hit "Shining Star," but let's dive in and try it out ourselves. The following lick shows how a shake can add a little sass and punch.

EXAMPLE 2

In this next example, we'll use shakes to make certain notes in the bass line pop out.

EXAMPLE 3

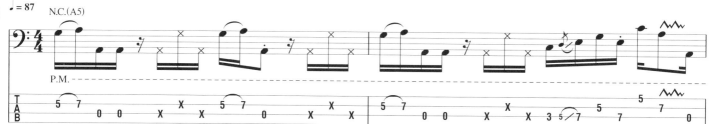

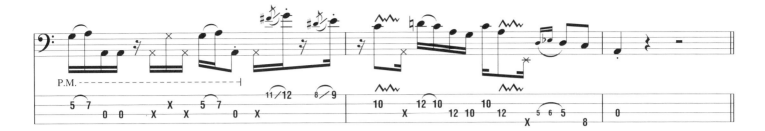

Now let's get nasty with this upper-register solo line.

EXAMPLE 4

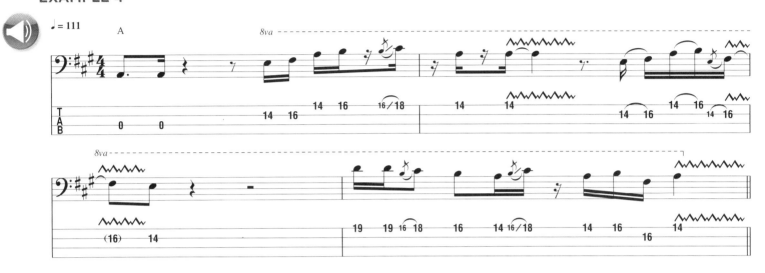

Shakes can also be performed on more than one string. In the next lick, inspired by session greats Pino Palladino and Nathan East, we'll explore how adding a shake to a double stop (two notes played simultaneously) can funk things up.

EXAMPLE 5

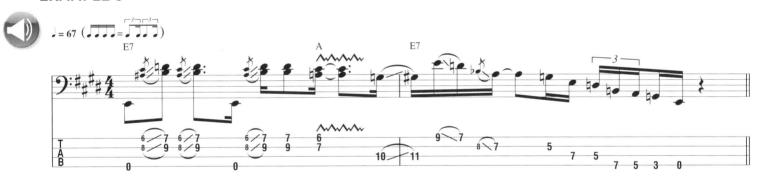

Double-stop shakes don't always have to be on adjacent strings; you can also shake octaves. In the following deep reggae groove, the lower note is picked with the thumb, and the higher note with the index finger. This one can be tricky because you have to keep the notes in tune with each other as you shake them, almost like a human octave pedal. Remember to anchor your thumb to the neck properly so the notes don't swerve out of control!

EXAMPLE 6

SOULFUL CHROMATICS

In the '60s, James Jamerson pioneered a style of bass playing that would go on to propel innumerable Motown hits to immortal status. The magic of his work is that it was colorful and funky, and while it indisputably drove the music, it bubbled just beneath the surface so as not to take attention away from the melody. The soulfulness of his approach appealed to rock players at the time, such as Paul McCartney, John Paul Jones, and John Entwistle, who themselves were forging ways to break the role of the bass out of the mundane root/5th paradigm. Indeed, one can hear Jamerson's influence in songs such as Led Zeppelin's "The Lemon Song" and "Ramble On," the Beatles' "Mean Mr. Mustard," and even in the work of current players such as Robert DeLeo, particularly Stone Temple Pilots' "Tripping on a Hole in a Paper Heart."

Jamerson's style was heavily characterized by chromatics and syncopation. In this lesson, we'll look at how to adapt these musical properties to your own bass lines.

First, let's discuss leading tones. These are notes that set you up for a target note; they are usually a half step lower (though sometimes they can be a half step higher, if approaching the target note from above) and played just before the target note. For example, if I'm aiming to hit a G on the downbeat of the next measure and I want to get there via a leading tone, I'll play an F♯ right before.

In the following musical example, we'll play a two-bar vamp over a G chord. Leading tones are indicated with an "L" between the notes and tablature.

EXAMPLE 1

When improvising bass lines in a funky, chromatic, Jamerson-like style, understanding the relationship between leading tones and target notes is half the battle.

Now let's get into some more complex lines. When there's a lot of space between a root note at the beginning of a measure and the next leading tone at the end of a measure, we can bridge the gaps between them by playing a combination of chord tones, such as 3rds and 5ths, percussive dead notes (muted with the fretting hand), and chromatic passing tones, as illustrated in this next example.

EXAMPLE 2

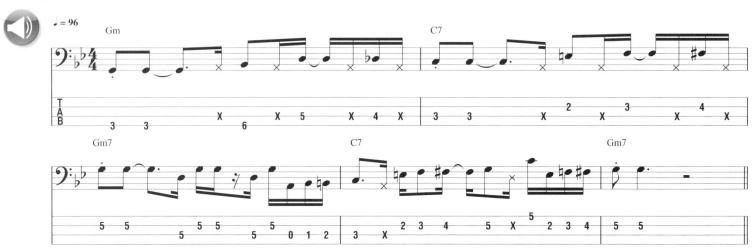

While the lines that we've been playing so far have been mostly linear, chromatics also sound cool when approached in an angular fashion, and it's good to try to incorporate both approaches when playing in this style.

This next example, inspired by John Paul Jones, features Jamerson-style phrasing and leading tones, but each bar is filled with wider intervals, such as tritones and 6ths.

EXAMPLE 3

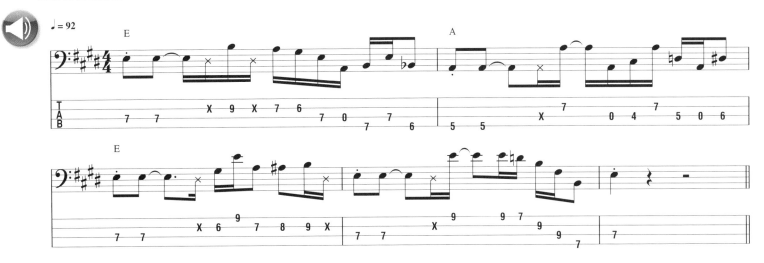

Let's conclude with an extended i–IV progression showing various ways, both linear and angular, to get from chord to chord using chromatics. This example is comprised of four four-bar phrases in which the first two measures stick mostly to the roots, and the second two measures add chromatic embellishments. After you get these licks under your fingers, try moving them up and down the fretboard in different keys. Give up the funk!

EXAMPLE 4

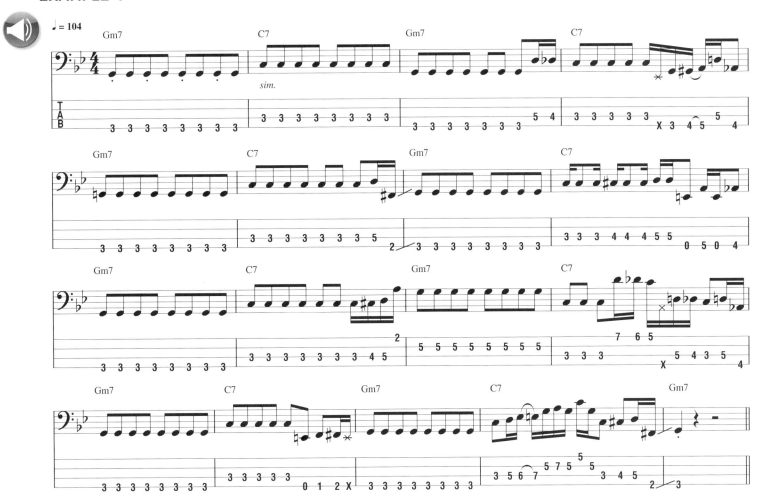

LESSON #89: SOULFUL EMBELLISHMENTS

Just because you're a rock player, it doesn't mean that you can't add soul. Indeed, rock's roots are in R&B, which itself is influenced by gospel, so it's not only perfectly appropriate to play like you're in a Harlem church on even the dirtiest rock tunes (see: Little Richard, the Rolling Stones), it's fundamental.

Much of rock music, especially classic rock, is based on improvisation. Sure, there's a template, such as a basic chord progression or blueprint for the song, but the rest is often left up to the players to interpret. I once asked a guitarist friend of mine, who happens to be a terrific improviser, how he never seems to get stuck for ideas. His advice? Sing while you play. If you can sing it, you can probably play it.

How does this apply to bass? Well most people, when they sing, use grace notes for ornamentation. This is a simple technique that, when employed judiciously, can add soul to an otherwise ordinary bass line. In this lesson, we'll explore a few ways to do just that.

This first example, inspired by Duff McKagan's solo intro to Guns N' Roses' "It's So Easy" and Flea's opening bass riff to the Red Hot Chili Peppers' "Around the World," shows how grace notes can be used to break up a series of repeated notes.

EXAMPLE 1

Classic rock bassists such as Aerosmith's Tom Hamilton and Black Sabbath's Geezer Butler have also been known to incorporate grace notes into their fills. The following licks are reminiscent of their respective styles.

EXAMPLE 2

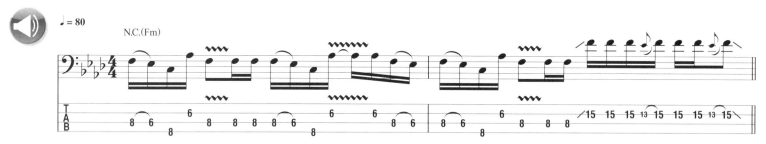

EXAMPLE 3

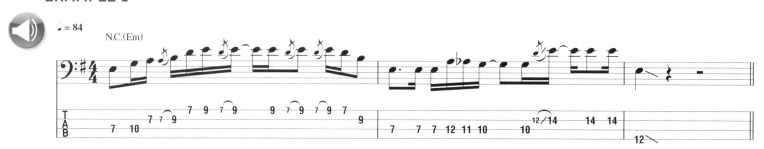

While our examples thus far have shown grace notes that are executed via hammer-ons, you probably noticed that the last one was performed as a slide. Indeed, sliding grace notes are also an effective way to make your lines sing.

This next example shows an ordinary descending A major scale ornamented with both hammered and slid grace notes, along with some subtle vibrato.

EXAMPLE 4

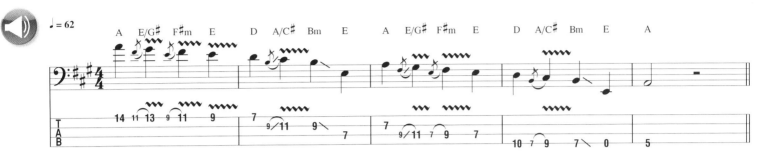

As you might imagine, grace notes work very well in ballad bass lines.

EXAMPLE 5

We can take this one step further by using a musical device known as melisma, which, in vocals, is the act of stretching a single syllable out over a few notes. This is a technique very commonly heard in soul and gospel music, popularized in the mainstream by singers such as Whitney Houston and Mariah Carey, and unfortunately, grotesquely overused on talent shows such as *American Idol*, which is why it must be used sparingly when applying it to bass!

My favorite way to use this technique is to hammer a grace note, quickly slide up to *another* grace note, and then slide back down to the target note. I came up with the lick below after listening to the Yellowjackets' Jimmy Haslip. Check out the melisma in the third measure.

EXAMPLE 6

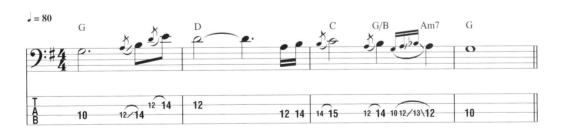

And finally, here's a melisma used in a hard rock fill:

EXAMPLE 7

LESSON #90: SPACE

There's an old adage, often attributed to musical giant Miles Davis, that goes something along the lines of: "It's not the notes you play; it's the notes you *don't* play." Sometimes playing nothing at all, especially where one might usually expect the bass to be present, can create a wonderfully stark effect. Other times, it's just simply necessary so that the music can breathe.

The best way to explore the value of space in music is to hear it, so let's just jump right in and play. In our first couple of musical examples, the bass plays the beginning of a phrase while letting the guitars take the remainder.

EXAMPLE 1

EXAMPLE 2

In other cases, it's sometimes beneficial to sprinkle spaces throughout a phrase, rather than dropping out altogether. This is especially effective, even essential, in funkier styles of music.

This next example is a funky rock lick featuring plenty of space between musical statements.

EXAMPLE 3

Sometimes all you need to create a danceable groove is a few well-selected notes—and space.

EXAMPLE 4

This slow-burn funk groove explores this idea further.

EXAMPLE 5

"Space" doesn't always have to mean silence; sometimes there's power in hitting one big, fat, glorious note and just letting it hang while the rest of the band does its thing.

EXAMPLE 6

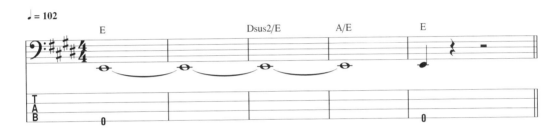

Yet another way that I like to use silence is when a verse or outro occurs after a particularly climactic moment in a song, such as a strong chorus or instrumental solo. To have the bass just drop out at these times brings stark contrast, both harmonically and in terms of volume. It also adds another dimension to the arrangement, which can help lift even the most minimal, repetitive songs to another level and, above all, allows the vocalist or lead instrument to shine. It also allows *you* to shine when you re-enter because the listener will have missed you.

This last example illustrates this idea in a pop ballad context: the bass plays a basic groove in the first four measures, drops out for the middle four, and comes back in strong for the final four.

EXAMPLE 7

Keeping your musical statements to the point, and giving your band mates plenty of room to lay down their own, will not go unappreciated.

LESSON #91: STACCATO AND LEGATO

Staccato and legato are two of the most commonly used musical articulations. Notes that are played staccato are short and detached, whereas legato notes are to be played long and connected. As the bass player, you can alter the overall feel of the music by the way you choose to articulate the notes. Staccato is often used to create a bouncing feel and is indicated in written music by a dot over or under a notehead. Legato is generally utilized for a more propulsive, driving mood and is denoted either with no symbol at all or with a line over or under a notehead when the composer or arranger wants the player to emphasize lengthening and connecting the notes. In this lesson, we'll explore when to best apply either of these articulations to a bass part.

Countless rock bass lines consist of legato eighth-note rhythms, such as in the musical example below.

EXAMPLE 1

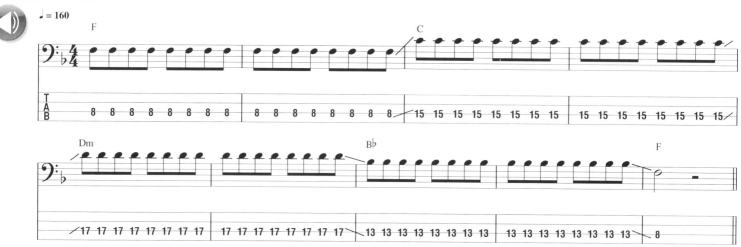

In this next bass line, we'll use detached, staccato notes to create a brisk, energetic feel, complemented by an accented, legato hit on the last beat of each two-bar phrase.

EXAMPLE 2

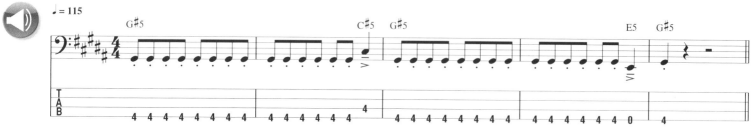

Now we'll take a rock shuffle and apply both staccato and legato articulations. See if you can hear how the staccato version (Example 3) bounces, while the legato version (Example 4) feels more open.

EXAMPLE 3

EXAMPLE 4

Legato/staccato combinations, such as Examples 5 and 6 below, frequently appear in slower rock bass lines.

EXAMPLE 5

EXAMPLE 6

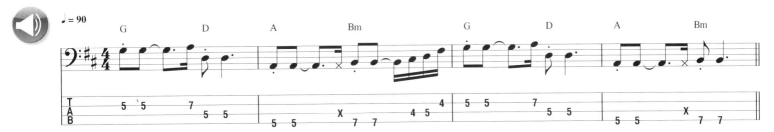

As illustrated in the next musical example, funk bass lines often require little more than a few well-placed staccato notes.

EXAMPLE 7

By contrast, the following funk line fills out the whole measure, but each note is played staccato to make the line bounce.

EXAMPLE 8

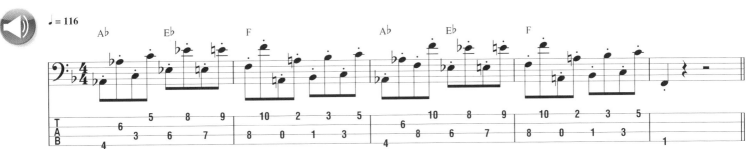

LESSON #92: STRAIGHT TIME, HALF TIME, AND DOUBLE TIME

Songwriters and composers will often add variety to a piece of music by changing up the rhythmic feel, either by doubling the pulse (double-time feel) or cutting it in half (half-time feel). This creates the illusion of a new piece of music, even though the melody and overall harmony may remain unchanged. As the bass player, your role is to keep it all steady while everything changes around you. In this lesson, we'll look at musical situations where changes in rhythmic feel may occur.

STRAIGHT TIME INTO HALF TIME

The passage below starts off in regular time (also referred to as "straight time"), at a tempo of 160 bpm. Eight bars in (after the second time through the four-bar repeat), we go into half-time feel. Notice how the actual part remains the same, but the *feel* is different. Because we've basically chopped the pulse in half, eighth notes now sound like 16th notes, though they remain eighth notes.

EXAMPLE 1

Now let's try one in which the musical content changes from one part to the next. The following example shows how a typical heavy rock song might sound when switching from one section in straight time to a completely different section in half-time feel. Again, even though the bass part has now changed, remember we've only altered the *feel*, not the tempo.

EXAMPLE 2

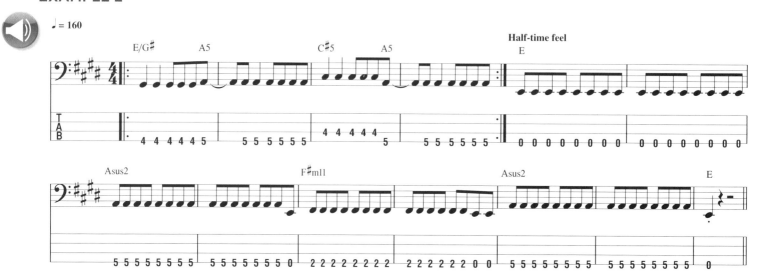

HALF-TIME SHUFFLE

Half-time feels can also be applied to shuffles. This is often known as the "Purdie Shuffle," so named because it was created by one of the most recorded session drummers in history, Bernard Purdie. Legendary rock drummers such as Toto's Jeff Porcaro and Led Zeppelin's John Bonham have also famously appropriated this drum groove. Additionally, in the following musical example, the tempo is four beats per measure, but it *feels* like two beats per measure. As you play along, note the juxtaposition of the bass part, as it gradually builds in 4/4 time, against the drums, which resolutely remain in half time.

EXAMPLE 3

STRAIGHT TIME INTO DOUBLE TIME

We can also turn the dial in the other direction and go from a straight-time groove into a double-time feel, as often occurs in metal, speed metal, and their associated genres.

In the example below, just as before, the music only *feels* twice as fast—in this instance, eighth notes will sound like fast quarter notes—but the tempo remains the same. Be careful not to rush!

EXAMPLE 4

LESSON #93: TWO-HANDED TAPPING

Musicians seem to be divided over the concept of two-handed fretboard tapping on bass. There's the traditional camp of groove and "feel" players who deem that tapping is merely about showboating and technical display, rather than about actual music. And then there are the shredders who feel that… well, what's wrong with showboating and technical display? This lesson asks: why can't it be a little of both? If used appropriately and sparingly, two-handed tapping can be another effective musical tool in the box. Tapping is a great way to fill out a harmony or extend a harmony that you otherwise might not be able to execute conventionally, such as anything with an obnoxious fret-hand stretch.

In this first example, we'll use two-handed tapping to achieve minor add2 and major add2 chords.

Now let's take the previous example and use tapping to create a flowing, arpeggiated line out of the same chord shapes.

EXAMPLE 1

EXAMPLE 2

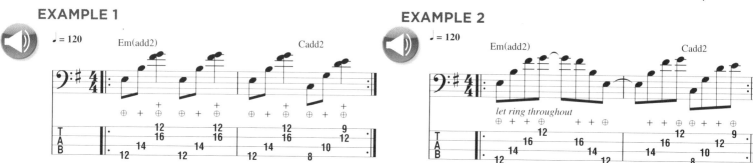

Though fretboard tapping on bass is usually associated with "shred" genres such as rock and metal, it lends itself surprisingly well to contrapuntal Latin grooves. In the next three examples, we'll explore the idea of voices moving independent of each other via the left and right hands. For each lick, the bottom voice is hammered with the fretting hand and the top voice is tapped with the picking hand. First, work on hammering the fret-hand part individually and then concentrate on tapping the higher part by itself. When you can do both confidently, put them together, starting as slowly as needed to get both hands/parts in sync. Example 3 is a basic samba. Once you've got this one down, try moving the pattern up and down the fretboard, and experiment with different tapped chord shapes.

EXAMPLE 3

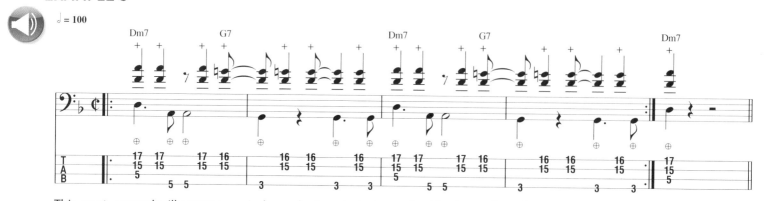

This next example illustrates an independent melody tapped with the picking hand against a basic half-note groove hammered with the fretting hand.

EXAMPLE 4

In the same vein, the following montuno (Cuban) groove features a syncopated bass line under percussive chord stabs. Again, the coordination between the two parts can be tricky, so take your time!

EXAMPLE 5

Although two-handed fretboard tapping has gone in and out of favor since the '80s—especially on bass—it can still be fun to whip out a flashy trick here and there when the mood strikes. There is much that can be written on the subject that goes beyond the scope of this lesson, but in the meantime, use these examples as a springboard to creating your own licks!

Here's an A minor pentatonic run that cycles through the scale by going up the G string in triplet patterns. Feel free to add a little distortion for extra shred!

EXAMPLE 6

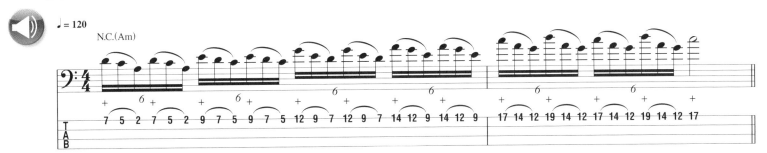

This last example starts out as a funky rock groove, leading to an obnoxious Eddie Van Halen-esque fill in the fourth measure. Note that the tapped fretboard pattern is mirrored on each string.

EXAMPLE 7

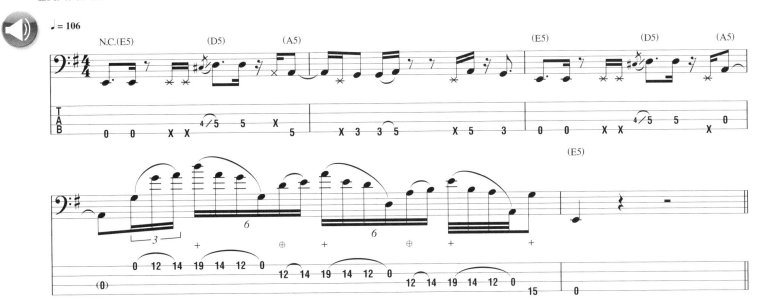

LESSON #94: TECHNO BASS

Bass brothers and sisters, let us not forget Larry Graham's call to arms: "I'm gonna add some bottom so that the dancers just won't hide." Music, and the technology used to create it, have both evolved greatly since those words were committed to vinyl in 1968, but the function of the bass as the impetus for people to get up and move hasn't changed.

In my travels as a bassist, I have to be adaptable in order to stay employed, which often means playing styles of music that are just on the fringes of rock, such as dance and techno. Though these styles are primarily synth- and computer-based, achieving a similar sound on a more organic instrument such as an electric bass is not that difficult. First of all, rhythmically speaking, rock and techno really aren't that far apart: in each, the kick drum hits on beats 1 and 3, or sometimes all four beats, and the snare lands on beats 2 on 4. Secondly, if we figure out what tonal and rhythmic characteristics are present in most electronic dance bass tracks, we can emulate them fairly convincingly with a simple bass/stomp box/amp setup. All you need after that is steady time and the ability to groove unrelentingly.

To start, you'll need a fat, bottom-heavy tone on your amp. To emulate a synth, you'll need a few effects; I always have a sub-octave divider and a distortion pedal (set to relatively light gain) at the ready, but you may also wish to add an envelope filter (sometimes also known as a "touch wah" effect). These effects can be achieved through common, individual stomp boxes such as the Boss OC-3 octave and ODB-3 bass overdrive pedals, or via higher-end multi-effect units.

Armed with these devices, let's take a look at some stylistic themes in dance music and adapt them to bass guitar. We'll start with a common rhythm figure that makes use of space between notes to establish a clear statement. On the accompanying recording, the bass is running through a sub-octave effect. Very simple, very effective.

EXAMPLE 1

By contrast, this next bass line fills in all the spaces, but uses octaves to create slinkiness. When playing this line, remember to think like a synth player: try to keep the transition between notes as smooth and seamless as possible, even when making wide fretboard jumps such as those in the first two measures. Suggested effect: mild overdrive.

EXAMPLE 2

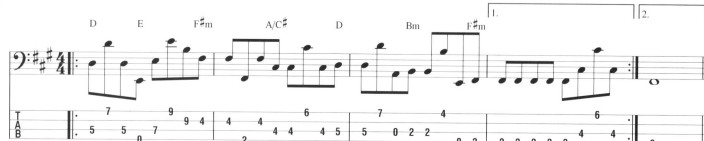

Getting back to basics for a moment, this next example shows a very simple eighth-note groove that follows a short-long-short-long articulation pattern, evoking a bounciness or pulse that lends itself to dancing. Try this one with a sub-octave effect and a little overdrive.

EXAMPLE 3

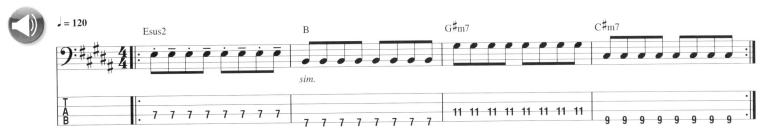

We can spice this up a bit by switching over to a gallop rhythm, as shown below.

EXAMPLE 4

Taking this idea even further, we can play the gallop in octaves.

EXAMPLE 5

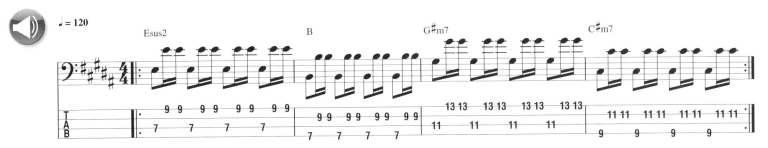

In addition to paying attention to the rhythm, we can make our faux-synth bass parts more convincing by using vibrato and quick grace-note slides. In our final example, the wide vibrato at the end of the phrase emulates the pitch wheel on a synth bass.

EXAMPLE 6

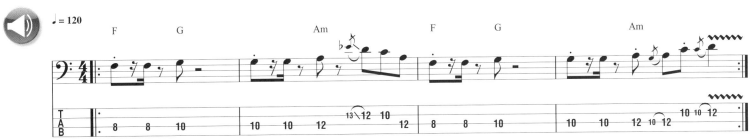

LESSON #95: TONE

One of the most important components of bass playing, besides technique and musicality, is tone. All the chops in the world won't amount to anything if the sound of your instrument is unpleasant.

I'm a firm believer in the adage "tone is in the hands," but of course, when you're playing electric bass, your amplifier dictates the rest of the equation. In some cases, what you hear coming out of the amp may even influence how you touch the strings.

As for what constitutes good bass tone, everyone's tastes are different. Some players prefer a flat, mellow tone; others blast the lower frequencies and turn down the highs; while others go for an aggressive midrange growl. You also have to consider what's appropriate for the style of music that you're playing. Progressive rock icons such as Rush's Geddy Lee and Yes's Chris Squire are known for their trademark growly, aggressive, slightly distorted bass sounds, which are great for cutting through layers of guitars and keyboards and emphasizing the prominence of the bass parts. On the other end of the spectrum, the late, great funk/R&B bassist Bernard Edwards created some of the most sampled and looped bass lines in modern music with his punchy tone, which was rich in low mids, with the highs rolled off. Aston "Family Man" Barrett's super-dull, heavy low end tone with Bob Marley helped to define the reggae genre. Led Zeppelin's John Paul Jones varied his tone according to the needs of the song, going from a lightly distorted growl in heavy riff-oriented rockers such as "Black Dog" and "Immigrant Song" to a thick, mellow, Motown-like sound for funkier tunes such as "Ramble On" and "The Lemon Song."

The musical examples below show two disparate styles: Example 1 is heavy rock, while Example 2 has a funky, R&B feel to it. For Example 1, you might gravitate toward a more aggressive, rich-midrange sound to be heard through the guitars and to enhance the intensity of the music. For the R&B line in Example 2, this tone may be too noisy and harsh, and you might find that dialing in a more mellow tone with the highs rolled off is better suited to the music and may even affect the way you touch the strings. Try playing each bass line with the "appropriate" tones and then switch it up and see how it feels.

EXAMPLE 1

EXAMPLE 2

DIALING IN YOUR SOUND

Tone controls on bass amps run the gamut from simple bass, midrange, and treble knobs to 10-band EQ sliders, whereby you can sculpt your tone with painstaking precision. I'm of the school that less is more—the simpler amps let the true tone of your instrument come out, and being limited in terms of how much you can mess with the amp conserves mental energy that can be devoted to concentrating on playing. That said, here's a rough guide to bass EQ. Keep in mind that these are approximate frequency ranges and this is not an exact science; both your instrument and your technique impact your sound. Finding the sweet spot on your amp's EQ is cause for celebration, but please remember that sometimes too much of a good thing can be toxic. Too much low end will render you muddy, too much midrange can rip your sinuses out, and too much high end can cause unnecessary noise. Let your ears be your guide, and EQ safely!

40–60Hz: SUB-BASS

Adds rumble. Too much can make your speakers distort, even at low volumes.

60–120Hz: LOW END

Adds bottom, power, and depth. Too much can make your tone muddy and notes indiscernible; avoid the temptation to overdo it, especially if you have a large amp. Cutting these frequencies excessively can cause your sound to thin out, but can also give you headroom to turn up the volume if needed.

120–700Hz: LOW MIDS

Adds boom, punch, and fullness. Again, too much can make you sound muddy or boxy, but too little might make your tone brittle.

800Hz–2K: MIDS

Adds growl, definition, and cut. Too much may sound harsh. Some players cut these frequencies to mellow out their tone.

2–6K: UPPER MIDS

Emphasizes string noise, adds snap, and opens up the tone. Good for slapping but too much can clutter up your sound with a lot of noise.

6K+: HIGH END

Boost for presence and "air." You most likely won't be able to hear these frequencies in any case. Many players even dial back the high end altogether to reduce clutter and fretboard clicking.

FINAL TIPS

If you have an amp with separate gain and master volume controls, turn the gain up just to the point where the sound is ever so slightly distorted and then control your overall volume with the master volume control. This will give you just enough fullness and presence, without going over the top. Also, if you play with a pick rather than fingerstyle, adjust your highs and mids accordingly, as the tone will be brighter and the string attack sharper.

LESSON #96: VIBRATO

Vibrato is an excellent way to add expression to a musical phrase. Though some guitarists are revered for it—Eric Clapton, B.B. King, and Leslie West among them—you don't often hear about vibrato in the context of bass playing, so we will remedy that in this lesson!

The first thing to remember is that your bass is an extension of you, and that it's your voice coming through it. When you use vibrato, you're essentially emulating your voice. And depending on the mood of the music, you can make the vibrato slow, fast, understated, or wide. Let's go over two common types of vibrato and explore the subtle differences between them.

WRIST VIBRATO

Probably the most common type of rock vibrato is wrist vibrato. As the name implies, the motion comes from rotating the wrist back and forth, similar to the way you'd turn a door knob. Focus on keeping the motion smooth and fluid.

Wrist vibrato is most commonly executed by pulling the string down (toward the floor), though when performed on the G string, you'll have to push up (toward the ceiling).

Here's a soulful lick that employs wrist vibrato on the D and A strings. Be sure to keep the motion steady.

EXAMPLE 1

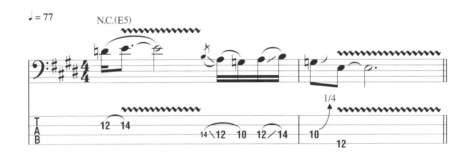

VIOLIN VIBRATO

The great fretless bassist Jaco Pastorius employed a vibrato not unlike that used by orchestral string players. The motion comes from keeping the fret-hand finger firmly planted on the note while moving the wrist from side to side. Unlike wrist vibrato, the string is never bent; all pitch wavering comes from a combination of wrist motion and rolling—not sliding—the fretting finger. This is a subtle vibrato that is suitable for delicate passages or for trying to achieve a cello or double bass-like vibe.

The following example shows violin vibrato being applied to long tones.

EXAMPLE 2

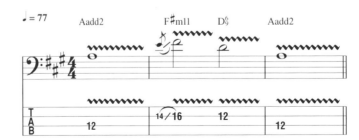

For the remainder of this lesson, we'll take a look at a few fairly common musical situations and see how we can apply different types of vibrato to them. We'll start with a dirty rock riff that employs a fast, wide vibrato on the last note for extra oomph.

EXAMPLE 3

In this next example, we'll emulate a soft, fretless vibe by employing violin vibrato with the pinky and index fingers. Pay extra attention to the "singing" quality at the end of the fourth measure.

EXAMPLE 4

By contrast, this next lick is a heavy, frantic metal riff with a wrist vibrato at the end to match.

EXAMPLE 5

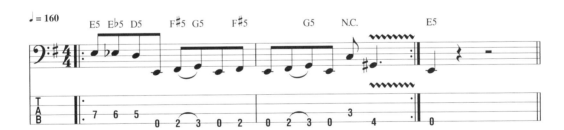

For this funk-flavored lick, we'll fret higher up on the neck in order to take advantage of the looser string tension, which will help you dig in and get a deep wrist vibrato on the final note.

EXAMPLE 6

LESSON #97: WALKING

The term "walking bass" refers to a bass line that is in perpetual motion—as opposed to staying on or reiterating one note—and "walks" up or down from one chord's root note to the next, mostly in a quarter-note rhythm with the occasional embellishment, using transition notes to smoothly connect different root notes as the chords change. The transition notes can be any combination of chord tones, scale tones that relate to the chords, or chromatic passing tones. Although usually associated with jazz or blues, this approach to composing bass lines has been adapted to rock music as far back as the early days of rock 'n' roll in the '50s through to the present day via artists as disparate as the Beatles, Led Zeppelin, Stevie Wonder, the Clash, and Green Day, just to name a few.

Walking bass lines in rock originated in rhythm & blues, which, in turn, was developed from blues and gospel. So we can arguably point to this simple, repeated I–IV chord progression, heard in churches all over the South in the early 20th century, as the first rock 'n' roll bass line:

EXAMPLE 1

Fast-forward to 1976 and we have Stevie Wonder's adaptation of this time-honored musical theme for his own enduring hit "I Wish." The beauty of this appropriation is that he showed that rock and funk don't need to be rhythmically or harmonically complicated.

The bass line below, in Wonder's style, shows the quarter notes in Example 1 changed to eighth notes, played short and clipped to add swagger.

EXAMPLE 2

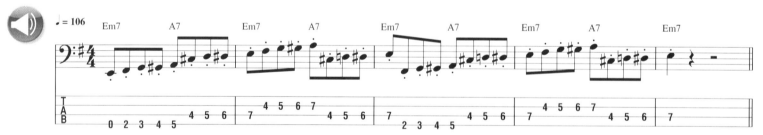

Our next example shows simple quarter notes mostly outlining chord tones. It's based on John Paul Jones' work in the outro of Led Zeppelin's "The Ocean."

EXAMPLE 3

The following line is inspired by Herbie Flowers' work in David Bowie's 1974 hit "Rebel Rebel." It's a fairly straightforward example of how to use scalar passing tones and fills to spice up a bass line over a repetitive two-chord progression.

EXAMPLE 4

This next figure is a nod to Paul McCartney, who made ample use of walking bass in such Beatles classics as "Penny Lane" and "All My Loving." This example is a good study in using basic scale tones, with the occasional chromatic leading tone (see measure 3), to connect one chord to the next.

EXAMPLE 5

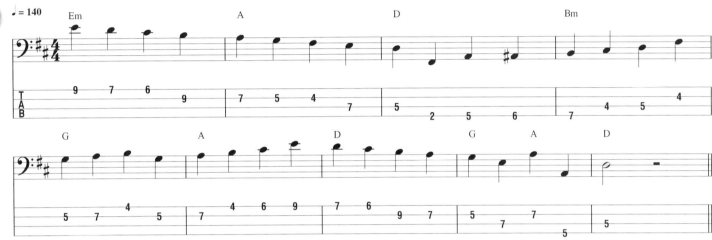

The Clash's Paul Simonon showed that walking lines can even be used in a punk rock setting.

EXAMPLE 6

Let's not forget minor key walking lines! This last example is in the style of classics such as Van Morrison's "Moondance" and the Doors' "Love Her Madly," and demonstrates how to navigate minor chord changes.

EXAMPLE 7

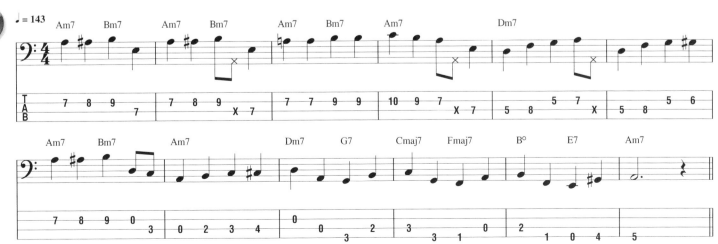

LESSON #98: WALL OF SOUND

Sometimes when the instrumentation is sparse—as is the case in a power trio, for example—you might feel a need to fill out the sound, especially when the guitarist is taking a solo and there's nothing in the middle to handle chords or the range of notes between the bottom end (you) and the guitar. A neat little trick that I like to pull out, when there's room in the music for it, is to play lots of sustained octaves. One of the most famous recorded examples of this in practice is Rob Grange's legendary bass riff upon which Ted Nugent's "Stranglehold" is based. Billy Sheehan, himself a veteran of the power-trio format, is also a frequent practitioner of this technique, as was the late, great John Entwistle of the Who.

Start by playing a root note and then play its corresponding octave, letting the top note ring out as you rearticulate the root note. This adds another layer to the bottom end that fills in the gap between you and the guitar while adding power to the bass part.

EXAMPLE 1

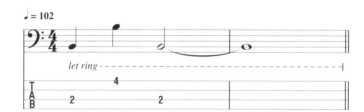

Now let's try this in a real-world musical context by sustaining octaves over a basic rock chord progression.

EXAMPLE 2

Holding out octaves is an effective yet simple tool when open strings are involved. Try playing this next example with a pick.

EXAMPLE 3

"Wall of Sound" octaves can also be used to great effect when moving notes up the fretboard. This not only gives the aural impression of filling in sonic space on the bottom end, but also raises tension and adds a nice, beefy rumble. In the following example, be sure to hold all notes out so that the wall may remain unbroken!

EXAMPLE 4

The "Wall of Sound" octave principle is also quite effective when going *down* the fretboard, as illustrated in this Flea-inspired slap example.

EXAMPLE 5

Here's a fingerstyle, disco-influenced lick featuring ascending and descending sustained octaves.

EXAMPLE 6

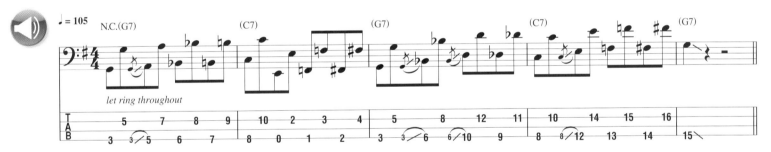

Sustained octaves can also add a sense of restrained power when used subtly in ballads and more delicate types of music.

EXAMPLE 7

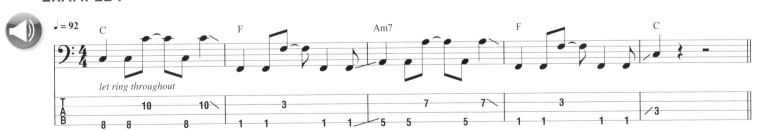

LESSON #99: WHERE TO PLUCK

A large component of your sound and technique comes from where you hit the string, be it with your fingers or a pick. Where you put your picking hand is a matter of personal comfort, as all basses—and their players—are different and come in varying sizes. It's also a matter of personal taste, as each player prefers his or her own type of tone. In this lesson, we'll explore the different ways that you can attack the strings and how they affect your playing.

TONE

Along different points of a string, you will encounter different timbres. If you pluck near the bridge, the sound is sharp, tight, and punchy due to increased tension near the point where the strings are anchored to the bass body. As you pluck more toward the neck, the string tension is gradually relaxed, resulting in a sound that is progressively rounder and deeper.

TECHNIQUE

Where you attack the string also affects your technique. Much of this is dictated by the style of music that you're playing; for example, if you're going for fast, sharp, precise fingerstyle funk lines, playing closer to the bridge will enhance your speed because the strings are more taut and won't "give" as much, helping you to re-attack the string more quickly. Conversely, if you're playing a slow or mid-tempo heavy rock groove in which speed is not as much of a factor, you may opt to pick closer to the neck for more resonance. Some bassists who play harder styles of rock even pluck the strings closer to the neck in an aggressive fashion to make them slap against the fingerboard.

As you play through this lesson, keep your amp settings the same for each musical example; we're going to vary the tone simply by altering our picking-hand approach. We'll begin with a simple mid-tempo Latin groove. For a deep, dull tone, try playing right at the base of the neck, where it meets the body, with the side of your thumb and then try the phrase again, using your fingers by the bridge. Which pick-hand technique suits the music better?

EXAMPLE 1

Now let's step it up a bit with this hard rock lick, inspired by Black Sabbath's Geezer Butler. Again, try fingerpicking close to the neck and then experiment by plucking near the bridge. Listen for the difference in sound, but also see how the disparity in technique *feels* in your hands.

EXAMPLE 2

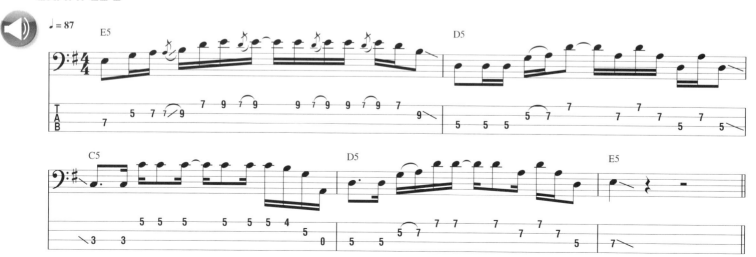

Now we'll start from the end of the string, near the bridge, with a pair of 16th-note funk riffs inspired by funk-jazz bass masters Jaco Pastorius and Rocco Prestia. To aid your speed and precision, try to use only the very tips of your fingers.

EXAMPLE 3

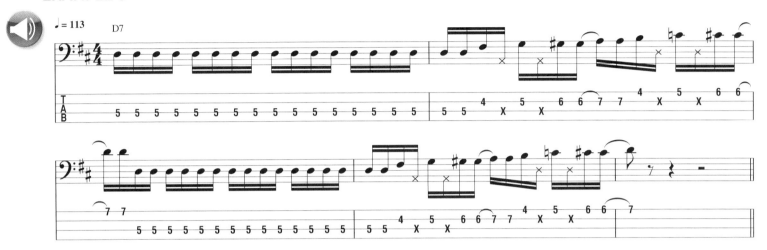

EXAMPLE 4

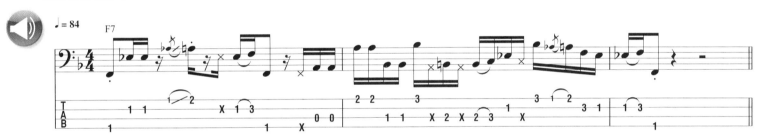

And finally, this mellow lick, inspired by Sting, uses the thumb right in between the bridge and neck pickups (assuming your bass has two pickups; if not, just thumbpick the string at the midpoint between the bridge and neck).

EXAMPLE 5

There's a saying among string players that "tone is in the hands." Clearly, there are many different sounds that you can get out of your instrument without even turning a single knob on your amp. Experiment and find the pick-hand approach that's best for you and your individual style.

This lesson is entitled "Workingman's Slapping" because covering everything that's been developed in the world of slap and pop would go far beyond the scope of a two-page lesson. Therefore, I'm going to focus on meaty, aggressive, absurdly funky licks that, while inspired by the bass greats, are still technically accessible and musically practical without going too far over the top for most situations. These will serve you well as a gigging musician, and most importantly, will hopefully be of use to you as a starting point for creating your own licks.

Let's begin with a basic climb using slapped and popped octave patterns. Nothing too flashy here—the emphasis is mostly on laying down a heavy groove and backbeat.

EXAMPLE 1

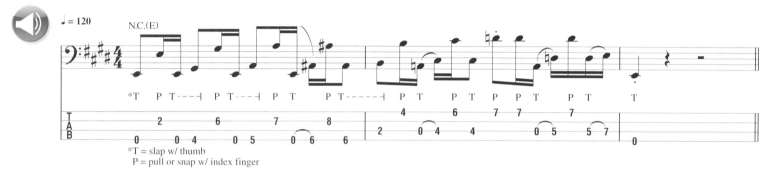

Now we'll bring the tempo up and incorporate dead notes. Though this lick is decidedly aggressive, the trick here is to actually slap and pop with a lighter touch to conserve pick-hand energy and quickly "reset" for the next slap or pop, especially in the eighth measure.

EXAMPLE 2

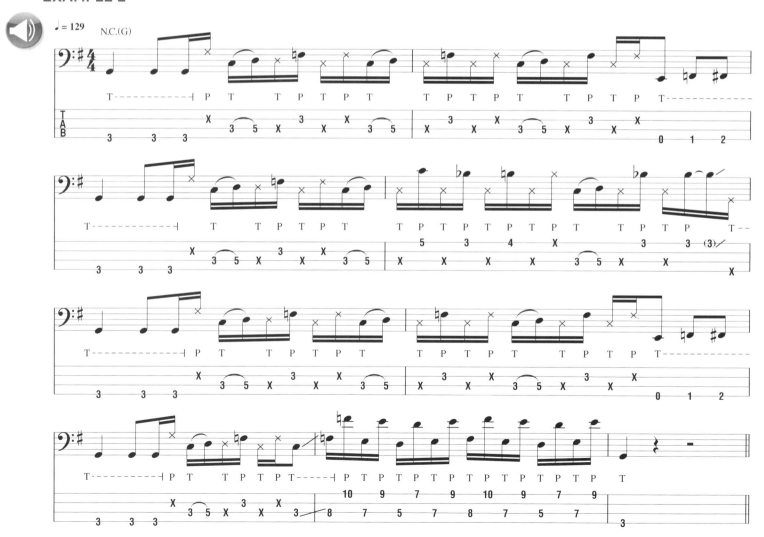

This next lick features 16th-note triplets executed via hammer-ons, as shown on the first beat of measures 1 and 3.

EXAMPLE 3

Example 4 finds us further exploring the hammered 16th-note triplet motif. Again, as with Example 2, use a light touch when launching into rapid-fire slap/pop figures such as those shown in measure 4.

EXAMPLE 4

Now let's bring your other hand into the action. This next example takes the natural act of muting open strings with your fretting hand and uses it as a percussive thump, making your fretting hand as much a part of the rhythm as your picking hand. As you look at the music below, notice that there's a very specific two-beat pattern between the pick-hand slap/pop and the fret-hand mute. Getting the coordination down may be difficult at first, so start slowly, using a metronome to ensure good time, and gradually work up to speed as you get more comfortable with this technique. The music for Example 5 is presented two ways: with the pick hand and fret hand in different voices so you can zone in on what each hand is doing and then a condensed version so you can see the overall line.

EXAMPLE 5

BASS RECORDED VERSIONS

Bass Recorded Versions feature authentic transcriptions written in standard notation and tablature for bass guitar. This series features complete bass lines from the classics to contemporary superstars.

25 All-Time Rock Bass Classics
00690445 / $14.95

25 Essential Rock Bass Classics
00690210 / $15.95

Avenged Sevenfold – Nightmare
00691054 / $19.99

Best of Victor Bailey
00690718 / $19.95

Bass Tab 1990-1999
00690400 / $16.95

Bass Tab 1999-2000
00690404 / $14.95

Bass Tab 2013
00121899 / $19.99

Bass Tab White Pages
00690508 / $29.99

The Beatles Bass Lines
00690170 / $14.95

The Beatles 1962-1966
00690556 / $18.99

The Beatles 1967-1970
00690557 / $19.99

The Best of Blink 182
00690549 / $18.95

Blues Bass Classics
00690291 / $14.95

Boston Bass Collection
00690935 / $19.95

The Best of Eric Clapton
00660187 / $19.95

Stanley Clarke Collection
00672307 / $19.95

Funk Bass Bible
00690744 / $19.95

Hard Rock Bass Bible
00690746 / $17.95

Jimi Hendrix – Are You Experienced?
00690371 / $17.95

Incubus – Morning View
00690639 / $17.95

Iron Maiden Bass Anthology
00690867 / $22.99

Jazz Bass Classics
00102070 / $17.99

Best of Kiss for Bass
00690080 / $19.95

Lynyrd Skynyrd – All-Time Greatest Hits
00690956 / $19.99

Bob Marley Bass Collection
00690568 / $19.95

Mastodon – Crack the Skye
00691007 / $19.99

Megadeth Bass Anthology
00691191 / $19.99

Metal Bass Tabs
00103358 / $19.99

Best of Marcus Miller
00690811 / $24.99

Motown Bass Classics
00690253 / $14.95

Muse Bass Tab Collection
00123275 / $19.99

Nirvana Bass Collection
00690066 / $19.95

No Doubt – Tragic Kingdom
00120112 / $22.95

The Offspring – Greatest Hits
00690809 / $17.95

Jaco Pastorius – Greatest Jazz Fusion Bass Player
00690421 / $19.99

The Essential Jaco Pastorius
00690420 / $19.99

Pearl Jam – Ten
00694882 / $16.99

Pink Floyd – Dark Side of the Moon
00660172 / $14.95

The Best of Police
00660207 / $14.95

Pop/Rock Bass Bible
00690747 / $17.95

Queen – The Bass Collection
00690065 / $19.99

R&B Bass Bible
00690745 / $17.95

Rage Against the Machine
00690248 / $17.99

The Best of Red Hot Chili Peppers
00695285 / $24.95

Red Hot Chili Peppers – Blood Sugar Sex Magik
00690064 / $19.95

Red Hot Chili Peppers – By the Way
00690585 / $19.95

Red Hot Chili Peppers – Californication
00690390 / $19.95

Red Hot Chili Peppers – Greatest Hits
00690675 / $18.95

Red Hot Chili Peppers – I'm with You
00691167 / $22.99

Red Hot Chili Peppers – One Hot Minute
00690091 / $18.95

Red Hot Chili Peppers – Stadium Arcadium
00690853 / $24.95

Red Hot Chili Peppers – Stadium Arcadium: Deluxe Edition
Book/2-CD Pack
00690863 / $39.95

Rock Bass Bible
00690446 / $19.95

Rolling Stones
00690256 / $16.95

Stevie Ray Vaughan – Lightnin' Blues 1983-1987
00694778 / $19.95

Best of Yes
00103044 / $19.99

Best of ZZ Top for Bass
00691069 / $22.99

HAL•LEONARD® CORPORATION
7777 W. BLUEMOUND RD. P.O. BOX 13819
MILWAUKEE, WISCONSIN 53213

Visit Hal Leonard Online at
www.halleonard.com

Prices, contents & availability subject to change without notice.
Some products may not be available outside the U.S.A.

0214

HAL·LEONARD BASS PLAY-ALONG

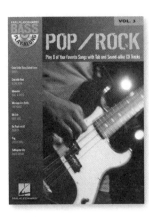
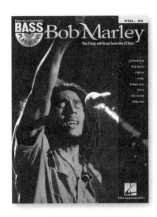

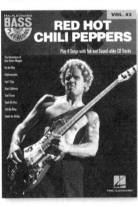

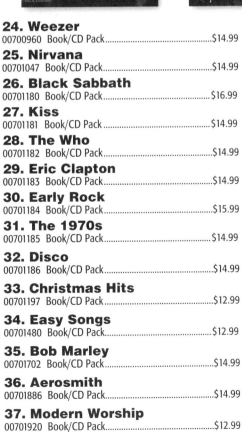

The Bass Play-Along™ Series will help you play your favorite songs quickly and easily! Just follow the tab, listen to the CD or online audio to hear how the bass should sound, and then play along using the separate backing tracks. The melody and lyrics are also included in the book in case you want to sing, or to simply help you follow along. The audio files are enhanced so you can adjust the recording to any tempo without changing pitch!

1. Rock
00699674 Book/CD Pack.........................$12.95

2. R&B
00699675 Book/CD Pack.........................$14.99

3. Pop/Rock
00699677 Book/CD Pack.........................$12.95

4. '90s Rock
00699679 Book/CD Pack.........................$12.95

5. Funk
00699680 Book/CD Pack.........................$12.95

6. Classic Rock
00699678 Book/CD Pack.........................$12.95

7. Hard Rock
00699676 Book/CD Pack.........................$14.95

9. Blues
00699817 Book/CD Pack.........................$14.99

10. Jimi Hendrix Smash Hits
00699815 Book/CD Pack.........................$17.99

11. Country
00699818 Book/CD Pack.........................$12.95

12. Punk Classics
00699814 Book/CD Pack.........................$12.99

13. Lennon & McCartney
00699816 Book/CD Pack.........................$14.99

14. Modern Rock
00699821 Book/CD Pack.........................$14.99

15. Mainstream Rock
00699822 Book/CD Pack.........................$14.99

16. '80s Metal
00699825 Book/CD Pack.........................$16.99

17. Pop Metal
00699826 Book/CD Pack.........................$14.99

18. Blues Rock
00699828 Book/CD Pack.........................$14.99

19. Steely Dan
00700203 Book/CD Pack.........................$16.99

20. The Police
00700270 Book/CD Pack.........................$14.99

21. Rock Band – Modern Rock
00700705 Book/CD Pack.........................$14.95

22. Rock Band – Classic Rock
00700706 Book/CD Pack.........................$14.95

**23. Pink Floyd –
Dark Side of The Moon**
00700847 Book/CD Pack.........................$14.99

24. Weezer
00700960 Book/CD Pack.........................$14.99

25. Nirvana
00701047 Book/CD Pack.........................$14.99

26. Black Sabbath
00701180 Book/CD Pack.........................$16.99

27. Kiss
00701181 Book/CD Pack.........................$14.99

28. The Who
00701182 Book/CD Pack.........................$14.99

29. Eric Clapton
00701183 Book/CD Pack.........................$14.99

30. Early Rock
00701184 Book/CD Pack.........................$15.99

31. The 1970s
00701185 Book/CD Pack.........................$14.99

32. Disco
00701186 Book/CD Pack.........................$14.99

33. Christmas Hits
00701197 Book/CD Pack.........................$12.99

34. Easy Songs
00701480 Book/CD Pack.........................$12.99

35. Bob Marley
00701702 Book/CD Pack.........................$14.99

36. Aerosmith
00701886 Book/CD Pack.........................$14.99

37. Modern Worship
00701920 Book/CD Pack.........................$12.99

38. Avenged Sevenfold
00702386 Book/CD Pack.........................$16.99

40. AC/DC
14041594 Book/CD Pack.........................$16.99

41. U2
00702582 Book/CD Pack.........................$16.99

42. Red Hot Chili Peppers
00702991 Book/CD Pack.........................$19.99

43. Paul McCartney
00703079 Book/CD Pack.........................$17.99

44. Megadeth
00703080 Book/CD Pack.........................$16.99

45. Slipknot
00703201 Book/CD Pack.........................$16.99

46. Best Bass Lines Ever
00103359 Book/Online Audio..................$17.99

48. James Brown
00117421 Book/CD Pack.........................$16.99

49. Eagles
00119936 Book/CD Pack.........................$17.99

FOR MORE INFORMATION, SEE YOUR LOCAL MUSIC DEALER,
OR WRITE TO:

HAL·LEONARD® CORPORATION
7777 W. BLUEMOUND RD. P.O. BOX 13819 Milwaukee, WI 53213

Prices, contents, and availability subject to change without notice.

Visit Hal Leonard Online at **www.halleonard.com**

BASS BUILDERS

A series of technique book/CD packages created for the purposeful building and development of your chops. Each volume is written by an expert in that particular technique. And with the inclusion of audio, the added dimension of hearing exactly how to play particular grooves and techniques make these truly like private lessons.

BASS AEROBICS
by Jon Liebman
00696437 Book/CD Pack.......................... $19.99

BASS FITNESS – AN EXERCISING HANDBOOK
by Josquin des Prés
00660177 .... $10.99

BASS FOR BEGINNERS
by Glenn Letsch
00695099 Book/CD Pack.......................... $19.95

BASS GROOVES
by Jon Liebman
00696028 Book/CD Pack.......................... $19.99

BASS IMPROVISATION
by Ed Friedland
00695164 Book/CD Pack.......................... $17.95

BLUES BASS
by Jon Liebman
00695235 Book/CD Pack.......................... $19.95

BUILDING ROCK BASS LINES
by Ed Friedland
00695692 Book/CD Pack.......................... $17.95

BUILDING WALKING BASS LINES
by Ed Friedland
00695008 Book/CD Pack.......................... $19.99

RON CARTER – BUILDING JAZZ BASS LINES
00841240 Book/CD Pack.......................... $19.95

DICTIONARY OF BASS GROOVES
by Sean Malone
00695266 Book/CD Pack.......................... $14.95

EXPANDING WALKING BASS LINES
by Ed Friedland
00695026 Book/CD Pack.......................... $19.95

FINGERBOARD HARMONY FOR BASS
by Gary Willis
00695043 Book/CD Pack.......................... $17.95

FUNK BASS
by Jon Liebman
00699348 Book/CD Pack.......................... $19.99

FUNK/FUSION BASS
by Jon Liebman
00696553 Book/CD Pack.......................... $19.95

HIP-HOP BASS
by Josquin des Prés
00695589 Book/CD Pack.......................... $14.95

JAZZ BASS
by Ed Friedland
00695084 Book/CD Pack.......................... $17.95

JERRY JEMMOTT – BLUES AND RHYTHM & BLUES BASS TECHNIQUE
00695176 Book/CD Pack.......................... $17.95

JUMP 'N' BLUES BASS
by Keith Rosier
00695292 Book/CD Pack.......................... $16.95

THE LOST ART OF COUNTRY BASS
by Keith Rosier
00695107 Book/CD Pack.......................... $19.95

PENTATONIC SCALES FOR BASS
by Ed Friedland
00696224 Book/CD Pack.......................... $19.99

REGGAE BASS
by Ed Friedland
00695163 Book/CD Pack.......................... $16.95

'70S FUNK & DISCO BASS
by Josquin des Prés
00695614 Book/CD Pack.......................... $15.99

SIMPLIFIED SIGHT-READING FOR BASS
by Josquin des Prés
00695085 Book/CD Pack.......................... $17.95

6-STRING BASSICS
by David Gross
00695221 Book/CD Pack.......................... $12.95

WORLD BEAT GROOVES FOR BASS
by Tony Cimorosi
00695335 Book/CD Pack.......................... $14.95

HAL•LEONARD® CORPORATION
7777 W. BLUEMOUND RD. P.O. BOX 13819 MILWAUKEE, WI 53213

Visit Hal Leonard Online at **www.halleonard.com**

Prices, contents and availability subject to change without notice; All prices are listed in U.S. funds

0514